Great Leaders Equal Great Schools

Alliances and Discourse for Educational Reform

A Volume in
Leaders, Schools, and Change

Series Editor
Autumn Cyprès
The University of Tennessee

Leaders, Schools, and Change
Autumn Cyprès, Series Editor

Great Leaders Equal Great Schools:
Alliances and Discourse for Educational Reform (2012)
edited by Autumn Cyprès and John Breckner

Great Leaders
Equal Great Schools

Alliances and Discourse
for Educational Reform

Edited by

Autumn Cyprès and John Breckner
University of Tennessee

Information Age Publishing, Inc.
Charlotte, North Carolina • www.infoagepub.com

Library of Congress Cataloging-in-Publication Data

Great leaders equal great schools : alliances and discourse for educational
reform.
    p. cm. — (Leaders, schools, and change)
  Includes bibliographical references.
  ISBN 978-1-62396-013-1 (paperback) — ISBN 978-1-62396-014-8 (hardcover) —
ISBN 978-1-62396-015-5 (e-book) 1. School improvement
programs—Tennessee—Case studies. 2. Educational
leadership—Tennessee—Case studies.
  LB2822.83.T2G74 2012
  371.2'0709768—dc23

                                                        2012027936

Printed in the United States of America

CONTENTS

PART III: LEADERSHIP DISCOURSES

FOREWORD

Jamie Woodson

In the last few years, Tennessee has transformed into a national leader in K-12 public education reform. The Volunteer State has demonstrated its commitment to improving outcomes for students and has dramatically increased its academic standards, passed the largest piece of education reform legislation since 1992, and won the inaugural Race to the Top competition, resulting in significant funding for innovative reform efforts. Tennessee's actions to establish itself as a leader in education reform have put the state in a unique position to start realizing significant gains in student achievement and, ultimately, prepare more of its students for college and the workforce.

In August 2011, United States Secretary of Education Arne Duncan visited Tennessee to highlight and celebrate our state's reform efforts. During a panel discussion, Secretary Duncan challenged Tennessee to become the fastest improving state in the nation in education. Secretary Duncan made another remark that highlighted the importance of his challenge. He said, "There are basically no jobs out there in today's economy for high school dropouts." If there ever was a rationale for the work that is being done in our state to improve public education, this is it. The purpose of school reform goes beyond simply improving test scores or rising in state rankings. The purpose of school reform is centered squarely on supporting the potential for better-paying jobs, improving our citizens' quality of life, and creating a foundation for personal and professional success that is made possible by a quality education.

Great Leaders Equal Great Schools:
Alliances and Discourse for Educational Reform, pp. vii–viii
Copyright © 2012 by Information Age Publishing

Policymakers, educators, and parents in our state are focused on ensuring students are prepared for the global economy. We are now engaging in critical conversations about what works in terms of engaging students, instead of continuing to do what is comfortable. There is an urgent need to scale up effective programs and practices in meaningful ways. Research tells us that the most important school-based factor to improve student achievement is effective teaching. Research also tells us that in order to support excellent teachers and ensure that they stay in schools that need them the most, having an effective school leader is paramount. When it comes to setting a culture of high expectations, providing teachers with the instructional supports they need to improve their practice, and engaging the broader community in school reform efforts, effective leaders are key. Indeed, the improvement of schools rests on the quality preparation of school leaders that is centered on strong research and best practices in the field. If we want to ensure that all of our schools have a quality leader at the helm, we will need to ensure that research and policies around effective practice are not disconnected from what's happening in our schools on a daily basis.

New Leaders Equal New Schools is testament to the view that research, practice, and policy can be meaningfully integrated to impact the daily work of a school. The ideas outlined in each chapter demonstrate that practitioners can produce authentic, relevant, cutting-edge research and use it as a basis for school reform, not only in the State of Tennessee, but across the nation. We no longer have to think of academics and practitioners as living in separate worlds with different purposes and functions. The authors make a compelling case that school reform depends on the concerted effort of education leaders themselves, and that the art of school leadership is fluid and requires a reflective collaboration between among education stakeholders.

If we are to reach out goals as a state, we will need to train school leaders who think differently about their roles and the work they must do to prepare our students for a changing world. *New Leaders Equal New Schools* presents serious points of consideration for those who are truly interested in taking the road less traveled when it comes to facilitating school reform on a consistent, systemic level.

ACKNOWLEDGMENTS

As with any effort of this kind, the contributions of many people beyond the authors and coeditors were critical to the development of this project. In particular we wish to acknowledge the fierce dedication of our esteemed colleague Christine Riggs. Her security clearance along with her technological skills proved to be invaluable. Autumn would like to thank her husband, Jean-Philippe, the only person able to teach her "tout autre chose n'estque pure distraction." John would like to thank his parents for their continual love and support as well as his beloved wife Brenda whose never-ending stream of patience and passion for research was a true source of inspiration.

INTRODUCTION

Leadership and The Winter Snowball Prom

Autumn Cyprès and Nicole Wilson

In December of 2011, our staff was deeply focused on the planning and execution of something we informally (and affectionately) called, "The Winter Snowball Prom." This formal and painstakingly detailed event was intended to accomplish three goals:

1. celebrate the partnership between the University of Tennessee and Knox County Schools;
2. honor the work of the fellows (graduate students who were in the leadership academy); and
3. acknowledge the hard work of stakeholders in the partnership including mentor principals and school administrators.

In short our staff had a love-hate relationship with the party planning aspect of this event that we all knew was important to build relationships and create a culture of collaboration. The event was held at Club LeConte; a venue in Knoxville with a serious swank factor. Located ten stories above the ground, the club boasts a 360-degree view of the Smoky Mountains. In the midst of a first-rate dinner and presentations, some-

Great Leaders Equal Great Schools:
Alliances and Discourse for Educational Reform, pp. xi–xv
Copyright © 2012 by Information Age Publishing

thing important and surprising happened. The Fellows assembled at the front of the dining room and asked the Principal in Residence, Mrs. Betty Sue Sparks, to join them. Much to her astonishment, the Fellows invited her to sit in a chair of honor in front of the audience and it was announced there would be a reading of the children's book *The Eagle and the Wren* by Jane Goodall. This book, based on a favorite childhood fable, tells of a variety of birds competing for the same goal—the honor to fly the highest. Each of the birds described in the book are special in their own way, which was elegantly stated by the ostrich, "You all have wings, but each of you flies to a different height for a different purpose" (Goodall, 2000, p. 8).

As the reading progressed, it became clear to those of us in the audience that the book was a metaphor between the Fellows and their mentors; most specifically Betty Sue. Goodall's tale explained that the strength of the eagle, allowed even the smallest and weakest of birds, the wren, to fly higher than if he had flown alone. By the end of the reading there was not a dry eye in the house because the Fellows explained that while Betty Sue was the focus of this reading the cohort members were aware of the many mentors and unsung heroes who had contributed to growth and development of these school leaders.

The "Winter Snowball Prom" has now become a touchstone allegory for those involved in the Leadership Academy because it reminds us that we often are so mired in the strife and conflict of the everydayness in contributions to leadership that we forget who we are helping to soar and whom is helping us. Every retelling of the "Winter Snowball Prom" brings smiles of humility and satisfaction rooted in the diligent work that brings change to both schools *and* school leaders.

We unrepentantly proclaim this is an important book because of the very important and brave people who have graciously contributed chapters. We know this book is important because it chronicles the real work of real school leaders who are vigilant in their commitment to embrace accountability and lift the schools they serve to a greater level of excellence. This book is organized into three parts, *The Model, New Leaders in Action,* and *Reflections from Allies. The Model* includes chapters written through the eyes of university professors who taught in the Leadership Academy. *New Leaders in Action* encompasses the research and school reform work of the Leadership Academy Fellows. The last part consists of a tapestry of reflective narratives from key stakeholders in Tennessee education and their interpretation of school leadership.

We visualize the organization of this book through the metaphor of seasons. Since their effort opens with the story of the "Winter Snowball Prom", it seemed to make sense. The three parts reflect the hallmarks of a season. For example, *The Model* speaks to the vernal conceptualization and birth of The Center for Educational Leadership and The Leadership Academy. *New Leaders in Action* showcases the summer winds of change in the form active leadership based on authentic research conducted by Leadership Academy Fellows. Prominent school issues discussed in the second part focus on three themes (1) Inspiring instruction across writing, mathematics, and reading, (2) The principals role in professional development, and (3) indicators influencing student achievement.

Finally the *Reflections From Allies* part offers the sagacious wisdom of people who are in the Autumn of their careers dedicated to school improvement. *Reflections From Allies* is a collection of narratives from seasoned educational leaders and policy makers at both the state and national level. This daisy chain of independent reflections serves a part history lesson on policy (see Lamar Alexander), tone poem for reform (see Buzz Thomas), and celebration of collaboration across the silos of education (see both Jimmy Cheek & Jim McIntyre). Each narrative that follows sought to answer the following questions:

(a) What is the purpose of school?
(b) How can we make schools better?
(c) Why should we change how school leaders are trained?
(d) What are some exciting changes happening in your work concerning schools and school leadership?

The voices in this part are more polished and more seasoned: Such is the gift of leadership experience. The stories in this part remind us of what a special phenomenon leadership preparation is because it requires attention to both person and skillset. Leadership preparation and authentic organizational reform is sticky, complex work. It is also noble and rife with moments of inspiration.

For example, Mrs. Betty Sue Sparks conducted an interview with Senator Lamar Alexander for this book. During the interview Senator Alexander was explaining that under his governorship, Tennessee was one of the first states in the country to implement a career ladder program for teachers. Mrs. Sparks gleefully interjected that she was one of the first career level three principals in his program. More than 20 years after Mrs. Sparks earned her level three certificate, she exclaimed after the Senator concluded the interview that she was inspired all over again. That is the kind of magic found within the engagement of new leadership to create new schools.

You will note that the voices of each chapter sound anything but homogenous. This was most intentional as the editors wanted this work to reflect authentic leaders talking about leadership theory, practice, and policy as if they were sitting across the table from you with a glass of Tennessee sweet tea and a plate of meat and three fresh from Sweet Ps Bar-beque and Soul House on Maryville Pike in South Knoxville. These chapters are authentic, individual reflections about real efforts to improve schools. The academics who contributed to this book sound like academics; the schools leaders sound like school leaders, and those who swim in the world of policy are authentic to their own voice as well.

HOW TO READ THIS BOOK

Because both editors (to some degree) are postmodernist researchers, we have organized this book so that one does not have to read it in any one particular order. Because we also are pragmatists we have also organized this book so it can be also be read front to back in the exact order of the chapters. We invite you walk through the seasons with us as you wish. You will note there are only three seasons in this effort. That is because the Center for Educational Leadership is still quite young and it will be a long time before a winter of discontent descends. This is the first of a series of books based on the different research and reform efforts of each cohort that graduates from the Leadership Academy. This book demonstrates the preliminary harvest of our first summer as a model for school reform through leadership preparation: We see the promise of a trajectory that remains upward and strong. Our hope is that you will read this book with a pen or pencil in hand because we feel that the core of a book is best digested and appreciated with scribbles in the margins and highlights in text.

The concepts illustrated throughout create a framework for everyday experiences and everyday accountability. Beyond the training expectations and assignments for Fellows, the Leadership Academy weaves a tapestry of fraternity, commitment, honor, and the zeitgeist of teamwork for change among school leaders. It is this teamwork that allows leaders to cross the boundaries of what is thinkable to change schools, one heart and one mind at a time.

Which brings us back to Club LaConte, the Winter Snowball Prom, and the reading of *The Eagle and the Wren*. The Fellows spontaneous recognition of Mrs. Sparks' leadership and contributions is symbolic of the cycle found within the Center for Educational Leadership. While there is no way that Senator Alexander could have known Mrs. Sparks was a level three certificate holder, he did foresee a legacy of leadership related to those outliers who dared to work a little harder to make schools better. And this lifelong commitment to elevating schools to the next level of greatness has shown itself again in a different generation of school leaders who are eager to think about how the gap between theory and practice, (as well as politics and education) can be traversed with both logic and heart. Such is the stuff of eagles and wrens, such is the stuff of great leaders committed to great schools. So get a plate of meat and three, grab an iced tea and get ready to dig in. There is lots of stuff to chew on in these pages.

REFERENCE

Goodall, J. (2000). *The eagle and the wren.* New York, NY: North South Books.

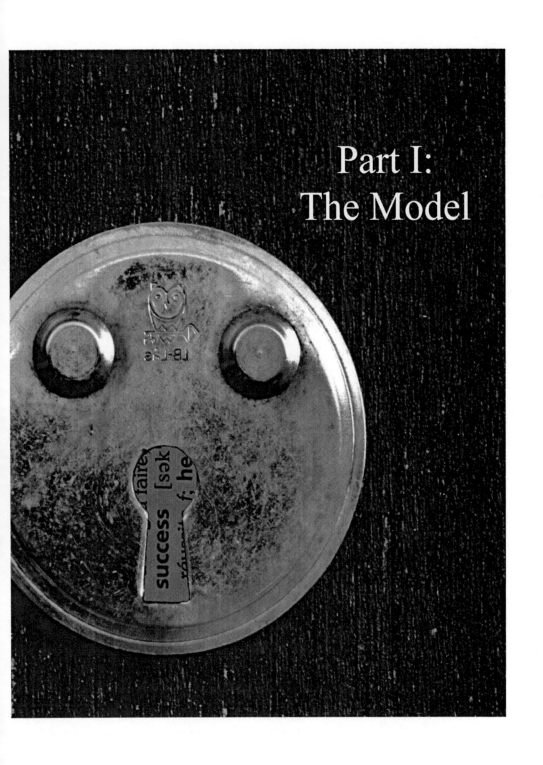

Part I:
The Model

CHAPTER 1

A NEW PARADIGM FOR LEADERSHIP PREPARATION

The Center for Educational Leadership

Pamela S. Angelle and Vincent A. Anfara, Jr.

THE IMPORTANCE OF LEADERSHIP PREPARATION

The importance of leadership to organizational success is well established (Bass, 1990; Bass & Avolio, 1994; Blake & Mouton, 1989; Selznick, 1957), and schools are no exception (Hallinger & Heck, 1996). Strong leadership is one of the distinguishing attributes that effective schools research consistently identifies as characteristic of schools in which students are successful (Edmonds, 1979; Hallinger & Murphy, 1986). Principals no longer serve as just supervisors or managers but are being called upon to redesign their schools. "They must be educational visionaries and change agents, instructional leaders, curriculum and assessment experts, budget analysts, facility managers, special program administrators, and community builders" (Darling-Hammond, LaPointe, Meyerson, Orr, & Cohen, 2007, p. 1). Every social institution has been challenged by the global

Great Leaders Equal Great Schools:
Alliances and Discourse for Educational Reform, pp. 3–20
Copyright © 2012 by Information Age Publishing
All rights of reproduction in any form reserved.

information economy and schools are looked upon as the "most powerful engine driving our economy" (Levine, 2005, p. 11).

With the 2001 legislation *No Child Left Behind*, the number of schools "in need of improvement" has reached into the thousands and is expected to grow as standards for making Adequate Yearly Progress (AYP) become more and more stringent. There is no question that expectations are high for schools and school leaders. School leaders must recognize that they can no longer rely on intuition, tradition, or convenience in making decisions about the best practices and strategies to improve student academic performance.

With the heightened emphasis on school leadership and the need for greater accountability for student academic performance comes the recognition that we can no longer continue to prepare school leaders as we have in the past. Numerous indictments against school leadership preparation programs have surfaced over the past decade (see Levine, 2005) requiring a significant shift in the way we "do the business" of equipping school leaders with the knowledge, skills, and dispositions to effectively and efficiently run America's schools. Critics have charged that leadership preparation programs lack quality, are not effective, are disconnected from the work of schools, and offer internships that lack depth and the opportunity for leadership practice (Davis, Darling-Hammond, LaPointe, & Meyerson, 2005).

Following years of education reform, improving student achievement has remained an elusive goal for school districts throughout the United States. A critical ingredient—second only to what occurs in the classroom—is high quality leadership. The relationship between leadership excellence and school excellence was the impetus to The University of Tennessee's *Center for Educational Leadership*.

The center is innovative in its approach to leadership preparation and professional development. Problems in school leadership have long been identified and studied, yet there are few examples of an interdisciplinary approach to developing leaders. Moreover, of those universities advocating an interdisciplinary approach, most begin and end with university coursework. *The Center for Educational Leadership* provides a preparation experience that will encompass components not found in traditional leadership preparation programs, as well as components to support practicing school and district leaders. This chapter first documents historical indictments of educational administration programs followed by a review of research targeting exemplary leadership preparation programs. An overview of the vision for the Center for Educational Leadership will include a discussion of the four pillars upon which the Center is based. The chapter will then conclude with a more detailed focus on The Leadership Academy, the leadership preparation program housed in the center.

INDICTMENTS AGAINST EDUCATIONAL
ADMINISTRATION PROGRAMS

Levine (2005) posits that educational programs have long been uncertain about their mission, purpose, and goals. In 1987, *Leaders for America's Schools* was issued and its conclusion noted that fewer than 200 of the country's 505 graduate programs in educational administration were capable of meeting necessary standards of excellence. According to the National Commission on Excellence in Educational Administration (1987), the remainder of the programs should be closed. Twenty-five years after the Commission issued its report, the "reputation of school leadership programs has declined sufficiently that critics could credibly suggest scrapping those programs altogether and replacing them with a variety of alternatives, developed and managed not by universities but by schools, districts, and states" (Levine, 2005, p. 18). Most recently, private enterprises have gotten into the business of educating school leaders.

The indictments have come from both outside and inside the field of educational administration. Insiders worried that criticism would provide fodder for their opponents and outsiders feared any praise would protect the status quo. Levine (2005) noted that the educational administration programs: (a) are not engaged in systematic self-assessment, (b) set low admission standards, (c) are characterized by faculty ill-equipped to educate school leaders, (d) do not pay sufficient attention to clinical faculty and mentorship by successful practitioners, and (e) are detached from practice. Additionally, there is an increase in the number of institutions offering educational administration programs often staffed with adjunct faculty.

Darling-Hammond and colleagues (2007) offer concerns that today's educational administration programs do not offer: (a) a comprehensive and coherent curriculum, (b) a philosophy and curriculum focused on instructional leadership. (c) active student-centered instruction which integrates theory and practice, (d) faculty who are knowledgeable of their subject area, (e) cohort structures, (f) vigorous recruitment and selection, and (g) well designed and supervised administrative internships. From within the field of educational administration, Murphy (1999) claimed that teaching and school administration need to be reconnected. The profession has become divided with school principals who clearly lack sufficient skills to lead schools. He noted that this separation began back in the early 1900s and has widened with each passing decade. With the rise of industrial capitalism, bureaucratic tenets required the separation of workers into distinct groups—those who did the work (teachers) and those who supervised the labor (principals). In short, "educational administration has remarkably little to do with education" (p. 2).

English (2002) noted that the "theory-practice gap stands as the Gordian Knot of educational administration" (p. 1). Because of this, the theory to practice connection is lacking in many current preparation programs. English tells us that "our influence will continue to diminish as we are incapable of producing research that predicts, let alone explains, leadership" (p. 1). Woolfolk Hoy (2001) acknowledged that administrators must have a "clear and deep understanding of teaching, learning, students, motivation, and assessment" (p. 1). Kochan and Twale (2000) focused their indictment of educational administration on our inability to collaborate with schools and school districts. This is echoed by Norton (1999) who claimed that we need to collaborate with "various individuals and groups interested in preparing quality administrators" (p. 11). Curricular change should also involve principal/teacher collaboration to insure effective knowledge about classroom needs (Kochan & Sabo, 1995; Lopez, 1996). Indictments have also centered on the use of data and technology (Murphy, 2006) and attempts to teach broad social science theories of organizations (Lakomski, 1998).

COMPONENTS OF EXEMPLAR PROGRAMS

Studies of exemplary leadership preparation programs (Darling-Hammond et al., 2007; Devita, Colvin, Darling-Hammond, & Haycock, 2007; Dilworth & Thomas, 2001) have consistently found similar components. These components, if implemented with fidelity, led to outcomes which included principals who felt better prepared to lead instruction and garner support from all stakeholderss, were more positive about the work of a principal, had a greater intent to stay in the field of administration, and were better able to develop a school vision. Moreover, schools with principals who focused on instructional leadership found increased student achievement and greater job satisfaction in their teachers (Darling-Hammond et al., 2007).

Components of exemplary leadership programs found throughout the literature included: (1) standards based curriculum; (2) focused recruitment and selection; (3) university-school district partnership, including instruction from both university professors and school practitioners; (4) formal mentoring; (5) emphasis on instructional leadership; (6) cohort model; (7) dynamic internship experience; and (8) financial support.

Standards-Based Curriculum

State and professional standards are the foundation of the leadership preparation program curriculum. Standards clearly indicate what principals should know and be able to do. In exemplary preparation programs, aspiring leaders understood expectations of the profession and their role in accountability for practicing these standards (Darling-Hammond et al., 2007; Devita et al., 2007).

The work of the National Policy Board to Develop Curriculum Guidelines established accreditation standards for the National Council for Accreditation of Teacher Education. These guidelines included the requirement that leadership preparation programs must include coursework, as well as internship experiences, which address organizational leadership, instructional leadership, strategic leadership, political leadership, and an internship (Jackson, 2001; National Policy Board for Educational Administration, 1989). In the early 1990s the Interstate School Leader Licensure Consortium added a set of standards to guide preparation programs in the outcomes and behaviors necessary for school principals (Jackson, 2001). Leadership preparation programs which hope to graduate students prepared to enter schools and successfully lead build the entirety of their programs around these standards as well as any state mandated instructional leader standards.

Focused Recruitment and Selection

University programs which are not proactive in recruiting talented aspiring leaders remain uncertain about the quality of candidates who enter the graduate school classroom each year. In the exemplary programs found in the literature, both universities and school districts worked to target outstanding teachers for leadership training (Darling-Hammond et al., 2007; Devita et al., 2007; Schmidt-Davis, Bottoms, & O'Neill, 2009). "Tapping" potential leaders required an investment on the part of both those preparing the leaders and those for whom the new leaders will work. Though the "up front" work of recruitment is time intensive, the end benefits are great.

Outstanding preparation programs also have rigorous selection processes (Schmidt-Davis et al., 2009). Evidence of exemplary success in the classroom may portend evidence of leadership which will transfer to the principalship. Thus, application packets which include previous evaluations, professional development plans, and evidence of collaborative experiences as a teacher will be useful. Including school district personnel in the selection process may also demonstrate the inclusive nature of the university-district partnership.

University-School District Partnerships

Strong partnerships between the university and the school districts increase the likelihood of quality candidates for the university, opportunities for valuable internship experiences, and active, on-going conversations on the best way to marry research and practice (Darling-Hammond et al., 2007; Devita et al., 2007; Dilworth & Thomas, 2001; Schmidt-Davis et al., 2009). Darling-Hammond and colleagues (2007) found that university-school district collaboration at the beginning of leadership preparation ensured that support would continue to be provided once graduates became principals.

Williamson and Hudson (2001) remarked on the essential nature of school-university partnerships by noting that school districts must come to value the partnerships as necessary. These researchers stated that the

> value must be grounded in school and district belief that university personnel appreciate the realities and complexities of the principal's job. Schools and districts must share commitments to the dispositions, knowledge, and skills that will enable future principals to accept those complexities and stay focused on successful teaching and learning for all students. (p. 18)

In exemplary programs, instruction from both university faculty and practicing school and district level administrators provided aspiring leaders the theory-to-practice connection so critical to understanding (Darling-Hammond et al., 2007; Devita et al., 2007). The big picture of theory with application to schools provided students of leadership with real world problem solving skills. As these students become practicing principals, this ability to problem solve will be essential to success.

Formal Mentoring

Mentoring of principal interns has long been held as significant to the success of a profession. This is particularly true for principal interns. Darling-Hammond and colleagues (2007) noted the social and professional support provided by quality mentors was essential to the persistence and level of satisfaction with the leadership program. Mentors acted as a "critical safeguard" (Schmidt-Davis et al., 2009, p. 9) during the internship, providing expertise and invaluable transfer of knowledge to the aspiring leader.

Browne-Ferrigno and Muth (2004) posit that the mentoring process is a form of role socialization for aspiring leaders. The essential nature of this process is one of "learning and reflection that requires working closely with leadership mentors in authentic field-based experiences" (p. 471). These researchers call for "transformative field experiences ... that facilitate in-depth and authentic, hands-on practice" (p. 483). The importance of the mentor in the preparation of aspiring leaders cannot be understated. Mentors serve as models for not only the behaviors of an ethical, instructional leader but also, through critical conversations, can convey the mechanisms of deliberative decision making in ways that course textbooks cannot.

Emphasis on Instructional Leadership

Planning coursework which emphasizes curriculum, leadership, teaching and learning, and organizational change, while deemphasizing the management aspects of the principalship, better prepares aspiring leaders for the world of accountability (Schmidt-Davis et al., 2009). Instructional strategies most often used in exemplary programs included portfolios, reflective practice, action research, experiential learning, application, and problems based learning (Darling-Hammond et al., 2007; Davis et al., 2005).

The work of the principal today extends far beyond the management of a school campus. The core work of the principal in this era of accountability is student learning for all subgroups of students, including students of poverty, students of color, students with disabilities, and students whose first language is other than English (U.S. Department of Education, 2004). Principals are expected to promote a culture of instructional leadership by

- articulating and modeling core values that support a challenging and successful education for all;
- establishing a persistent, public focus on learning at the school, classroom, community, and individual levels;
- working with others to set ambitious standards for learning; and
- demonstrating and inspiring shared responsibility and accountability for student outcomes. (U.S. Department of Education, 2004, p. 3)

Cohort Model

Preparation programs may group students into unique clusters whose membership remains set throughout the program of study. The cohort model affords participants the opportunity for collaboration and team work in a socially cohesive structure (Barnett, Basom, Yerkes, & Norris, 2000; Devita et al., 2007; Schmidt-Davis, 2009). Barnett and colleagues (2000) noted that over half of all leadership preparation programs utilize the cohort model. These researchers reported that this approach to program design influences not only group learning but also their persistence.

Thus, students in a cohort may be more likely to complete the program of study. Moreover, Davis and colleagues (2005) found that cohorts offer "enhanced feelings of group affiliation and acceptance, social and emotional support, motivation, persistence, group learning, and mutual assistance" (p. 10), as well as multiple perspectives on problem solving. While benefits to the cohort model are many, Barnett and colleagues (2000) also report some faculty have expressed concerns with inflexible program structure and increased program costs which resulted from the use of cohorts.

Dynamic Internship Experience

The ideal internship experience found in the research allowed aspiring leaders extended time to practice the art of leadership in a real world setting under the guidance of an experienced principal or district level leader. In-depth, comprehensive internships prepared students for the skills needed to take on the role of the principal fully prepared (Darling-Hammond et al., 2007; Davis et al., 2005; Devita et al., 2007; Hale & Moorman, 2003; Hess, 2006; Schmidt-Davis et al., 2009).

The internship experience should be one that not only provides aspiring leaders with experience in the day to day management of a school but should also be one that provides opportunities for students to reflect upon their own leadership practice (Daresh, 1988). Williamson and Hudson (2001) found that a weekly seminar which supports the internship provides a forum for students to reflect, challenge, question, and process their intern experiences.

Dynamic intern experiences provide students with opportunities to practice tasks under all standards. This ensures that students are not relegated to the management tasks of the organization such as bus duty, paperwork, and tracking absences. Important as these tasks are, the essential nature of instructional leadership, political leadership, and ethical leadership are critical to the preparation of school leaders.

Financial Support

Darling-Hammond and colleagues (2007) called financial support the "important enabling condition of strong programs" (p. 16). Moreover, in their study of exemplary programs, they found that "the most powerful effect of financing occurred through its impact on the design of internships and the ability of candidates in some programs to undertake full-time study" (p. 17).

One key to the success of the North Carolina Principal Fellows Program was the scholarship provided to the aspiring leaders so that full time internships and coursework could be undertaken. Moreover, the financial support allowed students to intern at sites other than their own school building and to receive mentoring from administrators, other than those for whom they worked. Students also had the opportunity to work in a variety of school sites, which would not have been possible without the financial support that allowed for full time internships (Williamson & Hudson, 2001).

THE CENTER FOR EDUCATIONAL LEADERSHIP

Affirming this commitment to a multidisciplinary approach to leadership preparation and continual development, The Center for Educational Leadership at The University of Tennessee is based on four pillars of leadership preparation and continuous development, including:

- Pillar I: Developing essential skill sets for practicing leaders;
- Pillar II: Increasing leadership capacity of an organization;
- Pillar III: Recruiting potential school leaders; and
- Pillar IV: Preparing aspiring leaders.

To accomplish this task The Center for Educational Leadership includes the following components:

- The Leadership Resource Center
- Job-embedded Leadership Support
- The Educational Leadership Institute
- The Executive Leadership Institute
- The Leadership Academy

The Leadership Resource Center and Job-embedded Leadership Support are directed at both the first and second pillars of skill development and building leadership capacity. The Educational Leadership Institute and the Executive Leadership Institute also target pillar one: developing the necessary skill sets for effectively leading schools and improving student academic performance. Finally, The Leadership Academy focuses on the last two pillars—recruitment and preparation of aspiring school leaders.

Through its commitment to lifelong leadership support, The Center for Educational Leadership works to sustain exemplary leadership by providing practicing leaders in skill development and support for organizational capacity building. This is accomplished through The Educational Leadership Institute, The Executive Leadership Institute, job-embedded support through the Principal-in-Residence, and the Leadership Resource Center.

The Educational Leadership Institute is a week long summer seminar for practicing school leaders which would combine faculty expertise from the College of Education, Health, and Human Sciences and the College of Business Administration, as well as from the larger university community, to offer professional development and skill building in areas such as financial leadership, ethical leadership, data-driven leadership, innovative leadership, and curricular leadership.

The Executive Leadership Institute is also a week long summer seminar offering the same content as the Educational Leadership Institute. However, the Executive Leadership Institute targets skill development to those leaders who oversee school systems from a district level, such as superintendents, directors, coordinators, and supervisors.

The Leadership Resource Center offers support to leaders in several ways. These resources may include:

- roundtable sessions with community experts in the fields of personnel management, budgeting, policy implementation, employee motivation, educational law, collaboration, reform and change, and efficient constituent communications;
- technology resources including web discussions, list serves, training sessions, and databases;
- library resources including journals, books, DVDs, and other relevant materials;
- problem solving and collaboration sessions with practicing principals and district level administrators; and
- horizontal and vertical articulation sessions between elementary, middle, and high school leaders.

A unique feature of The Center for Educational Leadership is the Principal-in-Residence. The Principal-in-Residence will provide ongoing professional development that includes, but is not limited to, the following:

- serves as a mentor who models professional, moral, and ethical standards as well as personal integrity in all interactions;
- provides assistance to principal candidates in the analysis, interpretation and utilization of data to make curricular and school-based decisions;

- offers in-school support to assist leaders with embedding learning as a part of their professional day;
- provides consultation as to the most effective methods to manage assigned human, material, and financial resources necessary for school operation;
- recommends strategies to connect leadership to instruction;
- recommends strategies and techniques to improve the performance of marginal teachers;
- collaborates in developing effective discipline methods and in fostering a safe and positive environment for students and staff;
- consults on the development and implementation of school improvement plans;
- recommends techniques and practices to select, support, evaluate, and retain, and quality instructional and support personnel.
- Recommends effective problem solving techniques; and
- Promotes effective communication and interpersonal relations strategies with students, staff, parents, and other community members.

The Leadership Academy Components

The Leadership Academy is the preparation program for aspiring leaders. The program is being supported with funding from an anonymous donor and includes, but is not limited to:

- partnering with a local school district to tap aspiring leaders;
- coursework (leading to a masters or education specialist degree) taught by university professors in partnership with practicing professionals from surrounding school districts;
- innovative scheduling which allows for an immersed, extended internship experience;
- additional instruction from university professors outside of the Department of Educational Leadership and Policy Studies; and
- The Capstone Project which includes presentation to university faculty and members of the school system central office.

Partnership With Local School Districts

The University of Tennessee entered into a partnership with a local school district, formalized through a memorandum of understanding, signed by both the dean of the College of Education, Health, and Human Sciences at the University of Tennessee as well as the superintendent of schools in Knox County. This memorandum of understanding spells out the responsibilities of the university and the school district. As part of the agreement, the school district will initiate a process of tapping 10-15 aspiring leaders through a rigorous and comprehensive process. Upon selection of these aspiring leaders, university faculty will interview the candidates for prospective entry into the program.

This pathway, leading to administrative licensure, will be a full-time cohort program designed to provide a deep and intensive 18-month principal preparation experience. The program will be designed with and primarily for the Knox County Schools, but other interested school districts may participate on a more limited basis. The program will combine graduate-level coursework (taught jointly by university faculty and practicing education professionals) with a full-time 4-day per week leadership residency in a public school, working with an outstanding mentor principal. Candidates selected for the program will be removed from the classroom to work full time as a principal-in-training and are paid their regular teacher salary while working as an administrative intern. This commitment from the Knox County School System is an integral component to the success of the program. The Tennessee State Board of Education is implementing an aspiring leader's license in support of universities and school districts that are able to fund such an internship. This is a temporary principal's license issued to graduate students in a leadership preparation program who are under the guidance and mentorship of a practicing licensed principal. The Knox County Schools and other participating school districts will provide the opportunity for the interns to hold these administrative positions in schools, and will identify and support the sites where a proven, excellent instructional leader can provide supervision, support and mentorship to the candidates.

Coursework

The Leadership Academy offers a 33 hour program taught in a continuous 18-month program. Students will participate in their administrative internship experience Monday-Thursday and will attend class on Fridays. Courses are taught in a module format with some modules taught by university faculty from the Colleges of Arts and Sciences, Business Administration, Communication, Law, Social Work, and Teacher Education (see Table 1.1).

In addition to faculty from colleges beyond the College of Education, Health, and Human Sciences, Educational Leadership faculty will be

Table 1.1. Coursework for The University of Tennessee Leadership Academy

Coursework for The Leadership Academy	Course Taken	Course Instructors
School/Community Relations	Summer 1	Educational leadership faculty/ College of Communication faculty
Best Practices for School Leaders	Summer 1	Educational leadership faculty
Leaders as Change Agents	Summer 1	Educational leadership faculty/College of Social Work faculty
Data Driven Decision Making	Fall	Educational leadership faculty/College of Business Administration faculty
Supervision & Personnel Administration	Fall	Educational leadership faculty/Retail & Hospitality Education faculty
Organizational Leadership	Winter	ELPS educational leadership faculty/College of Social Work faculty
Instructional Leadership	Winter	ELPS educational leadership faculty/Theory and Practice in Teacher Education faculty
School Finance	Spring	Educational leadership faculty/College of Business Administration faculty
Policy	Spring	Educational leadership faculty/College of Arts and Sciences faculty
Law	Summer 2	Educational leadership faculty/College of Law faculty
Capstone Project	Summer 2	Educational leadership faculty/Knox County District office personnel
Aspiring Leader Seminar	Throughout the program	Educational leadership faculty

assisted by practitioner partners. A primary focus of the principal preparation program in the Department of Educational Leadership and Policy Studies involves strong collaborative relationships with school-based personnel. A cornerstone of this collaboration is the integration of practitioners who will function as coinstructors with university-based professors.

These partners are district level administrators or building level principals who hold an expertise in the major content area of the course. The essential elements of this practitioner partnership include the following:

1. The school-based practitioner will clearly be considered an "expert" in the content of the course in which he/she coteaches. Experiential knowledge is to be primarily considered when establishing someone as an "expert."

2. The school-based practitioner will work with the university professor in ongoing syllabus development and revision. This involves, among other activities, a careful review of the course syllabus focusing especially on content being taught, assignments being required, and evaluations be made of student performance.

3. The school-based practitioner functions in the role of a coteacher, not a guest lecturer. The expectation is that this practitioner will coteach three to four classes during a given semester. It is likely that this practitioner will also meet with the faculty member on a regular basis to plan classes and review syllabi, assignments, etcetera.

4. The school-based practitioner will work on the development of meaningful course assignments that are based in real-world school contexts.

Instructional strategies for The Leadership Academy will be founded on collaborative learning, interdisciplinary teaching, problem based learning, integration of theory and practice, and teaming with practitioner partners for instruction.

Scheduling

The 4-day administrative internship is a key element in The Leadership Academy. Thus, coursework is built to ensure that graduate students in the program will be able to fully immerse in the life of the school, both during the day and in after school and night activities. School leaders are also often called upon to attend Saturday activities, such as athletic events, speech and debate tournaments, and parent/family activities.

In consideration of this, courses are offered only on Fridays throughout the 18-month program. Remaining cognizant of university requirements for contact time, each course offered during the academic year meets for 12 3-hour sessions, rotating every 3 months to a new course. Two courses are offered every Friday. Every other Friday, faculty meet with the Leadership Academy students for an additional hour in the Aspiring Leaders Seminar. Course content in the seminar will work toward the final Capstone Project and will include the online portfolio, an action research project to be completed by each graduate student, and preparation for the School Leader Licensure Assessment, a requirement for completion of the program.

Summer sessions include 18 three-hour sessions during June and July during the first summer for three courses and 12 four-hour sessions during June of the second summer for one course. A culminating meeting during the second summer will find the participants presenting their Capstone Project, reporting on the findings from their action research and the online portfolio.

MEASURES OF SUCCESS

The success of The Center for Educational Leadership will be measured by the work of school principals who possess the knowledge, skills, and dispositions to effectively lead schools facing the challenge of improving student academic performance. In order to measure this success, data related to student academic performance and overall school performance will be examined. This analysis will be shared with in-service school leaders who have participated in activities to further self-reflection and continued improvement of their schools. Employee perceptions regarding teacher job satisfaction, teacher efficacy, school climate and culture, parental involvement, and the effectiveness of the principal will be collected and analyzed. Data on the effectiveness of the interdisciplinary approach to leadership preparation and development will be gathered in order to establish the efficacy of this new model for leadership preparation.

Elements of the program, such as practitioner partnering, and negotiating memorandum of understanding were piloted to refine and improve the components. Other elements of The Leadership Academy such as the cohort model, the electronic portfolio, and quality training for mentoring have been ongoing components of the University of Tennessee leadership preparation program for some time. The Leadership Academy as outlined in this paper began full implementation with tapping of new leaders in spring 2010 and program implementation in summer 2010. Longitudinal data collection began with the cohort of summer 2010 through their program completion and the first 3 years of their principalship experience. School level data will be used by *The Center for Educational Leadership* to continually refine the Center's mission to enhance the knowledge and skills of school leaders which will lead to improving achievement for the children of Tennessee.

THE FUTURE

Creating The Center for Educational Leadership will enrich the student and faculty experience in the College of Education, Health, and Human Sciences. Through its various initiatives and programs, The Center for Educational Leadership will:

- provide training for current and future principals focused on yielding heightened student learning and success as well as recruitment, development, and retention of outstanding administrators in an era of accountability and school diversity;
- raise individual school performance levels through leadership training and collaborative programming aimed at enhancing partnerships among stakeholders—including teachers, parents, board of education members, and school and district administrators;
- improve student achievement as well as principal and teacher effectiveness;
- approach the preparation of aspiring leaders from an innovative and hands-on approach. Immersion in the daily work, challenges, and problem solving of building level leaders will provide aspiring leaders with a real world experiences, prior to their own appointment to an administrator position; and
- build bridges between schools and the larger community, bringing both into a partnership for the effective education of students and the development of a more highly skilled workforce.

We were given the charge to dream. The Center for Educational Leadership has allowed us to see that dream become a reality. The University of Tennessee is committed to the preparation of future instructional leaders in an exemplary model of leadership preparation. Faculty are willing to think beyond traditional leadership preparation to offer students expertise from across the university, experiences beyond the classroom, and practitioner oriented opportunities so that University of Tennessee will graduate students prepared to enter the principal's office and succeed.

REFERENCES

Barnett, B. G., Basom, M. R., Yerkes, D. M., & Norris, C. J. (2000). Cohorts in educational leadership programs: Benefits, difficulties, and the potential for developing school leaders. *Educational Administration Quarterly, 36*(2), 255-282.

Bass, B. M. (Ed.). (1990). Consideration, initiating structure, and related factors for describing the behavior of leaders. In *Bass & Stogdill's handbook of leadership: Theory, research, and managerial applications* (3rd ed., pp. 511-543). New York, NY: Free Press.

Bass, B. M., & Avolio, B. J. (Eds.). (1994). *Improving organizational effectiveness though transformational leadership.* Thousand Oaks, CA: SAGE.

Blake, R. R., & Mouton, J. S. (1989). Grid organization development. In W. E. Natemayer & J. T. McMahon (Eds.), *Classics of organizational behavior* (2nd ed., pp. 436-445). Prospect Heights, IL: Waveland.

Browne-Ferrigno, T., & Muth, R. (2004). Leadership mentoring in clinical practice: Role socialization, professional development, and capacity building. *Educational Administration Quarterly, 40*(4), 468-494.

Daresh, J. (1988). "Learning at Nellie's elbow:" Will it truly improve the preparation of educational administrators? *Planning and Change, 19*(3), 178-187.

Darling-Hammond, L., LaPointe, M., Meyerson, D., Orr, M., & Cohen, C. (2007). *Preparing school leaders for a changing world: Lessons from exemplary leadership development programs.* Stanford, CA: Stanford University, Stanford Educational Leadership Institute.

Davis, S., Darling-Hammond, L., LaPointe, M., & Meyerson, D. (2005). *School leadership study: Developing successful principals (Review of research).* Stanford, CA: Stanford University, Standford Educational Leadership Institute.

Devita, M. C., Colvin, R. L., Darling-Hammond, L., & Haycock, K. (2007, October). *A bridge to school reform.* Paper presented at The Wallace Foundations National Conference, New York, NY.

Dilworth, M. D., & Thomas, I. K. (2001). *PK-12 Educational leadership and administration.* Washington, DC: American Association of Colleges for Teacher Education.

Edmonds, R. R. (1979). Effective schools for the urban poor. *Educational Leadership, 37*(10), 15-24.

English, F. (2002). Cutting the Gordian Knot of educational administration: The theory-practice gap. *UCEA The Review, XLIV*(1), 1-3.

Hale, E. L., & Moorman, H. N. (2003). *Preparing school principals: A national perspective on policy and program innovations.* Washington, DC: Institute for Education Leadership.

Hallinger, P., & Heck, R. H. (1996). Reassessing the principal's role in school effectiveness: A review of empirical research, 1980-1995. *Educational Administration Quarterly, 32*, 5-44.

Hallinger, P., & Murphy, J. (1986). The social context of effective schools. *American Journal of Education, 94*, 328-55.

Hess, F. M. (2006). Looking beyond the schoolhouse door. *Phi Delta Kappan, 87*(7), 513-515.

Jackson, B. L. (2001, September). *Exceptional and innovative programs in educational leadership*. Paper commissioned for the meeting of the National Commission for the Advancement of Educational Leadership Preparation, Racine, WI.

Kochan, F. K., & Sabo, D. J. (1995). Transforming educational leadership programs through collaboration: Practicing what we preach. *Planning and Change, 26*(3-4), 168-178.

Kochan, F. K., & Twale, D. J. (2000). Advisory groups in educational leadership programs: Whose voice counts? *UCEA Review, XLI*(2), 1-3.

Lakomski, G. (1998). Training administrators in the wild: A naturalistic perspective. *UCEA Review, XXXIX*(3), 1, 5, 10-11.

Levine, A. (2005). *Educating school leaders*. Washington, DC: The Education Schools Project.

Lopez, V. M. (1996). *People, programs, and partnerships: ABCs of advisory committee technical programs in community colleges*. Parma Heights, CA: Cuyahoga Community College. (ERIC Document Reproduction Services No. ED 392 478)

Murphy, J. (1999). Reconnecting teaching and school administration: A call for a unified profession. *UCEA Review, XL*(2), 1-1-3, 6-7.

Murphy, J. T. (2006). Dancing lessons for elephants: Reforming ed school leadership programs. *Phi Delta Kappan, 87*(7), 488-491.

National Commission on Excellence in Educational Administration. (1987). *Leaders for America's schools: The report of the National Commission on Excellence in Educational Administration*. Temple, AZ: University Council for Educational Administration.

National Policy Board for Educational Administration. (1989). *Improving the preparation of school administrators: An agenda for reform*. Charlottesville, VA: Author.

Norton, M. S. (1999). The status of collaboration in the preparation of school leaders. *UCEA Review, XL*(3), 11-18.

Schmidt-Davis, J., Bottoms, G., & O'Neill, K. (2009). *Preparing a new breed of principals in Tennessee: Instructional leadership redesign in action*. Atlanta, GA: Southern Regional Education Board.

Selznick, P. (1957). *Leadership in administration: A sociological interpretation*. Berkley, CA: University of California Press.

U.S. Department of Education, Office of Innovation and Improvement. (2004). *Innovations in education: Innovative pathways to school leadership*, Washington, DC: Author.

Williamson, R., & Hudson, M. (2001, August). *The good, the bad, and the ugly: Internships in principal preparation*. Paper presented at the annual meeting of the National Council of Professors of Educational Administration, Houston, TX.

Woolfolk Hoy, A. (2001). Leading for learning: An education psychologist's perspective. *UCEA The Review, XLIII*(3), 1-1-4.

CHAPTER 2

TEACHING NEW LEADERS

A View From the Academy

Jason Huff

INTRODUCTION

Traditional principal training programs have been the subject of criticism from a number of directions, with practitioners, policymakers, and academics raising questions about their curricula (Hess & Kelly, 2007; Levin, 2005), and connections of pedagogy to practical issues that these leaders face and a lack of rigorous evaluation (Hale & Moorman, 2003; Jackson & Kelly, 2002). Actors in and outside the academy have responded to these concerns in multiple ways, from establishing nontraditional routes to the principalship (such as New Leaders for New Schools) to analyzing innovative leadership preparation programs in an effort to identify the best policies and strategies for training new and existing principals (Davis, Darling-Hammond, Meyerson & LaPointe, 2005; Orr & Barber, 2007; Orr & Orphanos, 2011; Talbert & Scharff, 2008; Talbert et al., 2009). While this research has detailed a common set of features that serve as a guide for program faculty and/or trainers to use, few faculty have written

Great Leaders Equal Great Schools:
Alliances and Discourse for Educational Reform, pp. 21–36
Copyright © 2012 by Information Age Publishing
All rights of reproduction in any form reserved.

extensively about their efforts and reflections on implementing these specific components.

Such writing is vital to changes in leadership training programs as faculty and other instructors reflect on and refine their strategies to prepare school leaders for the increasingly complex work they face. Scholars in the field of educational administration have long supported the use of reflective practice and authentic communication of ideas and findings (Andrews & Grogan, 2001; Schön, 1983, 1987; Short & Rinehart, 1993; Sirotnik & Kimball, 1996), and this need will continue as program faculty seek to connect leadership development theory and research with practical challenges for just how to design and teach these concepts to aspiring school leaders. The purpose of this chapter is to explore how other faculty members and I implemented a series of program features highlighted in the literature and to reflect on the practical details and challenges we faced. Because the chapter focuses on in-depth reflections on the program, I use a biographical methodological approach highlighted in other reflective studies (see for example Shields, LaRocque, & Oberg, 2002). This approach employs personal experience and narrative to highlight our strategies to design courses based on findings from the literature. In the chapter I summarize each key program feature with findings and recommendations from the literature; I then provide a series of reflections on our efforts to implement these features in the Leadership Academy, and I include comments on both the strengths and weaknesses of our efforts. I conclude with a discussion of how these reflections might inform other educational administration faculty and future research efforts.

An Emerging Consensus on Quality Program Components

Orr and Pounder (2011) describe how recent research of high quality principal training programs has identified similar attributes across them. These include the following:

- a use of adult learning theory, along with developmental learning principles, or active learning strategies to design learning experiences and connect coursework with participants' fieldwork;
- collaborative partnerships with local districts in program development and delivery;
- quality internships and other field-based experiences that provide intensive opportunities to apply leadership knowledge and skills while under the guidance of experience mentors or supervisors; and

- a cohort structure that enhances learning and promotes student-faculty connections (pp. 27-28).

Jackson and Kelly (2002) argue that at the core of quality programs is a "synergistic relationship" between students, faculty, and content. The more that faculty pay attention to the structures, processes, and strategies that facilitate these interactions, the more powerful students' learning will be. In the next sections I elaborate on each of the program features above and discuss how our faculty implemented these, and I reflect on how these fostered student learning by encouraging cohesive connections between faculty, students, and content. Where applicable, I also discuss challenges that we faced in implementing these.

Adult Learning Theory/Active Learning Strategies to Connect Coursework and Fieldwork

Various studies have cited how many professional development programs lack adult-specific theories of learning and do not provide adequate conceptual frameworks to facilitate participants' growth and development (Drago-Severson, 2007; Kegan & Lahey, 2001). These critiques have laid out various components to guide the design of adult programs; chief among them are active participation and group reflection on activities (Drago-Severson, 2007; Lawler, 2003; Lawler & King, 2000). We have woven both of these components through multiple Leadership Academy courses to first provide students with opportunities to engage in activities that mirror their practical work as leaders and then to discuss their experiences with faculty and fellow students. Following are examples of one class project along with my reflections of how participants responded to it and how it affected students' learning.

Realistic Role Plays

For one summer course entitled "Best Practices," students' final projects consisted of a set of role plays in which students prepared for and then participated in faculty meetings based on a series of case studies. I designed these projects to place students in hypothetical situations that were as close to leaders' actual experiences as possible; the case studies (a total of four) focused on different practical issues that school leaders might face in their work. They consisted of the following situations.

1. facilitating a meeting between parents and a teacher who has dismissed racist and bullying comments that other students have made toward their son;

2. leading a faculty meeting in which a new principal responds to teachers' and students' strident criticisms of his/her style of leadership that contrasts greatly with that of the previous principal;

3. running a faculty meeting in which a principal must decide to

    (a) support a reading curriculum voted for by the teachers or
    (b) return to a district curriculum the superintendent strongly encourages him/her to adopt; and

4. facilitating a meeting in which teachers strongly disagree over using curriculum that focused on standardized test content versus curriculum that includes discussion of social justice topics and issues.

For each of these cases a group of two to three students collectively played the role of the principal, working together to plan the meeting schedule and then leading the discussion. Other students (seven to eight total) played specified roles of parents or other faculty members attending the meeting. These projects were the culmination of a class based in part on Mezirow's (2000) emphasis that professional development focus on informing students' "frame of reference" for understanding the world (p. 7) and that had used organizational frames (with Bolman & Deal's 2008 book *Reframing Organizations*) to discuss different leadership practices for analyzing and responding to various issues in schools. The role plays required the students to actively use these different practices in leading and participating in the meetings.

Students' demeanors changed as they became both leaders and characters in the meetings. Gone were the casual comments and questions used in class discussions: the leading groups of two to three students took on serious tones to direct meeting agendas and discussions, and the other characters ranged from supportive to critical comments and personas, depending on their assigned roles. At times the tension in the room became real as leaders wrestled with how to address concerns voiced in the meetings. In the first role play meeting with a teacher and parents frustrated by her lack of concern for bullying of their son, one leader maintained a calm demeanor in listening to their palpable anger while her partner leader struggled to strike a balanced tone. In the second meeting both coleaders wrestled with listening to teachers' complaints while focusing on a discussion that would identify positive changes the two of them needed to make as the collective leadership of the school. Unlike traditional class conversations, these role plays provided no space in which to hide—everyone was required to engage in the discussions and apply the course content we had covered. Leadership teams were under extra pressure to guide and navigate the discussions toward productive ends instead of allowing the meetings to devolve into shouting matches (a very real possibility in each case given the roles students took on).

At the conclusion of each case, the group spent time reflecting on the meeting. We first asked the leaders about their decisions to structure and guide the discussions. They answered questions such as "what was your agenda or plan for the meeting," "what were your biggest concerns coming into the meeting," "what did you want to accomplish?" We also asked them to reflect on specific comments they made during the meeting— "why did you focus on this issue," "what was your purpose in making this comment?" These discussions allowed both the leaders to share their decisions and strategies and the participants to ask clarifying questions, provide different perspectives on the events, and propose alternative strategies to consider. Program faculty—three local district office supervisors who observed the role plays and myself—provided additional questions and suggestions.

These reflections provided leaders and participants in each case with an opportunity to examine more closely their own assumptions about the meeting and to consider alternative approaches or strategies. Students' comments during the discussions revealed their reexaminations of the events as well as their changes in interpretation of the events. Frequently when listening to others' questions and comments, leaders replied "I hadn't thought of that," or "I hadn't looked at it that way when planning for the meeting." Such comments offered evidence that the reflections helped to inform and change students' perceptions of the meetings. One particular student who led the meeting with the parents concerned about their bullied son shared how much he wanted to avoid such tense topics in his work in the future, but he described how much he had learned while watching his partner facilitator allow the different sides to share their frustrations while also focusing on specific, practical changes that needed to be made to address the situation. In multiple reflections, students also discussed what conversations they would have with faculty *before* and *after* the meetings to handle the issues; these were approaches that some had not considered beforehand.

Finally, students' major projects for the course required them to write two reflections on their guidance of the meetings. In the first component, they were required to analyze the meeting events using Bolman & Deal's (2008) frames of reference (structural, human resources, political, and symbolic) and to identify which frame(s) best explained the events that occurred before and during the meeting. In the second component, students summarized the reflection discussion with other students and supervisors and reported how others' comments and questions had informed and changed their interpretations of the events. They concluded by discussing what (if anything) they would do differently in a similar meeting and why.

Drago-Severson (2007) defines transformative learning as "a process of changing our taken-for-granted mindsets and frames of reference ... by making them more open, inclusive, reflective, and integrated. This enables us to envision alternative ways of thinking, and to develop beliefs that can more appropriately guide behavior" (p. 75-76). Students' written papers offered final evidence of how this project had changed their views of the specific class meetings as well as broader strategies to guide their future direction of meetings in schools. Following are examples of comments from their papers that suggest this project not only broadened their perspectives on analyzing different school situations, but it also helped them connect those meeting events to what must happen in the broader school to promote deeper change.

> The principal must continue to analyze his decisions through multiple frameworks throughout his career. A failure to do so will result in similar situations in which two or three sentences spoken at a staff meeting can destroy an entire initiative. (excerpt from first student's written reflection)

> As a result of this "us vs. them" structure (during the role play), there will need to be specific strategies employed that will bring unity back to the staff. In the role play, the principal(s) attempted to do that by guiding the group toward a compromise. The real work, however, would begin after this meeting. For the school to truly heal from this situation, it will take time and commitment to the compromise to rebuild trust and move forward. (excerpt from second student's written reflection)

Both the spoken and written reflections provided initial evidence that through this project's multiple components students stepped beyond their initial perceptions and assumptions to see (a) additional perspectives that were important to consider in planning their responses, (b) alternative strategies to address various situations in their schools, (c) how their future leadership could benefit from these broadened views.

District Partnerships and Collaboration

As programs look for ways to further bridge the gaps between theory and practice, numerous papers have detailed the benefits of partnering with schools and/or district offices (Barnett, 2005; Grogan, Bredeson, Sherman, Preis, & Beaty, 2009; Orr & Pounder, 2011; Sherman, 2006). Specific opportunities for cooperation include allowing districts to partner in program design/redesign (Goldring & Sims, 2005) and allowing practicing administrators to teach in courses and provide more practical perspectives on theory (Aiken, 2001; Milstein & Krueger, 1997). In this section I district three specific areas in which district collaborations have provided rich learning opportunities that connect theory and practice for students.

Realist Public Relations Training

As information flows more and more quickly via social media (e.g., blogs, Facebook, Twitter) and more traditional media such as television, newspapers, and the internet, school leaders increasingly need both basic guidelines and practical strategies to communicate with individuals outside the school, whether they be parents, community members, or members of the press. Multiple students in the program have commented how the rapid evolution of social media has created a large need for places in which educators can discuss the impacts of different policies and decisions. In the course "Schools and Communities" we have partnered with a director of public affairs from a local district to provide intensive training for students to deal with media concerns.

The training takes place over three half-day seminars; the first two seminars focus on traditional media (newspaper and television) followed by a third seminar focusing on social media. Given her extensive experience, this director spends the first class summarizing how a school district handles media relations. She details the ways that different reporters obtain information through parent connections, community contacts, police reports/investigations, emails, and rumors and then contact the district to ask for comment or clarification or to request further information. She describes district policies for what it can/cannot message in response, and what its legal obligation is to comply with formal information requests. She provides numerous personal experiences that not only illustrate these points but impress upon students the importance of being prepared for such events. These initial discussions have generated rich discussions as participants are able to ask for clarification about what to do in specific cases, and she is able to elaborate on how the district can support them when interviews or information are requested from them. Woven through these conversations are a series of simple tips and strategies for a) participating in an interview and b) deciding when to involve the school district when dealing with reporters.

The second seminar enables students to practice what they've learned as the director and a camera crew creates realistic interview situations for the students. During this seminar the director acts as a reporter, interviewing each student while the others watch. The questions range from highly illegal topics (such as rumors that a teacher has been running a dog fighting ring) to district policy issues (such as the principal's view on recently passed school board policy), and the director ranges in her tone of questioning, from more moderate to highly aggressive. We as a class then watch the tapes and reflect both on the reporter's questioning strategy and the students' responses.

In the third and final seminar the director discusses how both social media are evolving and how district policy is changing in response to that. She offers a series of cases that the class is able to discuss and debate regarding how schools should handle social media (for example, should schools have Facebook pages or Twitter accounts, and if so, what policies guide the information on them?). These conversations have been especially rich as students bring a wealth of their own experiences with social media to the class and as rapid changes in these media necessitate ongoing discussions for how to handle them.

These seminars have proven valuable to both the students and the district director. Students have commented often how little information school leaders receive about this very important area, and they have greatly appreciated the opportunity to practice interviews, even if they can be uncomfortable in front of classmates. However, many have reflected that they would much rather practice in a class rather than have their first time on camera be the real thing. This training also enables both the director and students begin to build working relationships that may one day be vital if they work together on high publicity events or issues in the district. Finally, students have commented how much they have appreciated reviewing realistic scenarios that illustrate how theory and district policy guide working with the media and conducting oneself in interviews.

District Supervisor Feedback:
More Meaningful Project Evaluations

Within the Leadership Academy we have partnered with multiple district personnel to teach course content, ranging from media matters (just discussed) to school data analyses to instructional leadership strategies. Research on district partnerships has described how practitioners may teach specific courses or content, but little attention has examined closely one significant benefit for these collaborations: the opportunity for students to receive in-class feedback and evaluations by district supervisors before they move into full positions. For students these can be valuable for two reasons: (a) they receive hear perspectives on their work from more than just their university instructor(s), and (b) they gain insights into individuals who may one day be their direct supervisors. In this section I discuss in detail how district supervisors observed and then evaluated students' performances during the role plays summarized previously.

On the days that students facilitated meetings for the four cases, supervisors for elementary, middle, and high school principals in a local school district attended class and observed the meetings. These supervisors had all presented earlier in the course and were familiar with its content as well as Bolman and Deal's (2008) textbook at the core of the class syllabus. I had briefed them previously regarding the case studies and students' preparation for their roles.

The supervisors' presence influenced the role plays in three ways. First, one supervisor spontaneously took on the role of a district official who unexpectedly joined the meeting to discuss the use of curricular materials focused on standardized test materials versus content that focused more formally on social justice issues. He used his entry into the meeting to emphasize to the participants the district's goal of raising test scores and the need to balance that priority with considerations of other topics. His entrance into the meeting—a very real possibility for school leaders—required students to adjust their discussions to both include him and reiterate the district's interest on the issue at hand, all of which required a level of flexibility to adapt the meeting to new developments.

Second, during the reflections all three supervisors asked questions of the students regarding their decisions during the meetings. Many of these stressed the need to connect directly with specific staff members before and/or after the meetings to clarify issues. For example, one supervisor described how before the meeting regarding the bullied student she would have talked in private with the teacher about appropriate conduct and school policy. She emphasized how this would enable her to express direct concern for the teacher's inattention to bullying/racist comments, and it would allow her to set expectations with the teacher as to how they would respond to the parents' concerns. This supervisor also summarized how she would follow with the teacher after the meeting to evaluate whether or not she had made specified changes from the discussion to be more attentive to the treatment of her students.

Finally, during debriefings on the overall course many students reported that the supervisors' presence had brought a higher level of intensity to the role plays. All of them were highly aware of the fact that their potential supervisors were watching their handling of the meetings, and this added to the already complex challenge of resolving difficult faculty issues. Two students described how stressful this had been, and they cautioned against including supervisors in the observations in the future. And yet a majority of the students (six out of ten) acknowledged that their presence created more realistic conditions in which they as future school leaders would operate. Despite the stress, they agreed that these conditions as well as supervisors' comments and feedback were valuable additions to the experiences.

Aspiring Leaders' Seminars:
Space for the Nuts and Bolts

In our efforts to ensure that the Leadership Academy is grounded in empirical evidence and leadership and learning theory while connecting to the very real challenges and work that school leaders face, we have searched for a place in which district officials and program faculty could cover the practical details and policies that school leaders must understand, whether they be steps for completing IEP (individualized education program) meetings and forms, processes for listing and then hiring for open positions, or documenting disciplinary meetings with students or faculty. Our concern has been that certain courses might dwindle to "tips and tricks" if they focused too tightly on these issues or practitioners' anecdotes, and we therefore limited coverage of more practical policies during classes. However, we have used portions of a year-long seminar to allow specific district personnel to review policies and procedures that leaders will be required to know.

The "Aspiring Leaders Seminar" runs the duration of the school year, and it meets for 1 hour every other Friday. This course focuses on students' completion of various activities during their internship, their documentation of those activities in compliance with standards set by the National Council for Accreditation of Teacher Education, and ongoing reflections on students' internship experiences.

We have also partnered with different district officials to share district policies and guidelines at various points during this seminar. Our collaboration with them came after discussions with the academy students that in future leadership positions they would be required to know particular policies in which they had not been trained (such as documentation and reporting of disciplinary meetings with teachers). We recognized that certain practical issues and policies, while not central to the larger conceptual and theoretical foundations of students' future leadership roles, nonetheless were key to their carrying out their responsibilities.

Working with district personnel and the students, we have identified a wide range of practical details and policies that district personnel discuss periodically during this seminar. They range from discussions of building-level budgeting strategies and requirements, school health and safety issues, personnel policies and practices, details to cover the start of the school year, and changes in federal and state education legislation. During these sessions district personnel have not only presented official steps and requirements (such as documentation), but they have also provided insights and recommendations from their own experience for students to remember in complying with the different policies. These discussions have provided a bridge for the academy to the practical details leaders must face while creating the space for district leaders to advise them closely. They have also provided opportunities for students to provide feedback and recommendations to the district on how it might improve different procedures for documentation or compliance.

The Cohort Model: Space
for Sustained Relationships and Growth

Cohorts have been frequently cited and evaluated as key to effective leadership preparation programs (Barnett, Basom, Yerkes, & Norris, 2000; Grogan et al., 2009; Orr, 2006; Orr & Pounder, 2011). While many of the benefits that participants report include a greater sense of community and support during the program (Barnett et al., 2000; Browne-Ferrigno & Muth, 2003; Norris, Barnett, Basom, & Yerkes, 1996), researchers have not identified conclusive evidence that cohorts have a significant, positive impact on the leadership skills or learning of cohort participants (Barnett et al., 2000). In this section I discuss both specific features of our cohort model and my observations of how these conditions have promoted students' learning over the course of the year.

First and foremost, the cohort model has been integral in developing our students' relationships and support for one another. Beginning with the intensive summer courses in which they see one another for 3-hour classes on a daily basis, they have multiple opportunities to share their motivations for entering the program, their previous experiences, and their views on teaching, learning, and leadership. I started the first course with the cohort with the simple question, "why are you here?" and I gave each student time to share the different experiences that have led them to apply to the program. I also shared my own experiences and reasons for pursuing a doctorate and working with prospective leaders through a university, and I summarized some of my key convictions about learning that had guided my teaching and contributions to the Leadership Academy curriculum. The sharing that started there was key to the numerous discussions that continued throughout the following year—discussions that undoubtedly challenged each student's own assumptions about learning and leadership and contributed to their development as future leaders.

The cohort model allowed conversations to continue across a number of courses, as we returned to comments from previous classes or revised former assumptions. One prime example of these conversations focused on the use of data to evaluate teachers and the school's overall progress toward different goals. During the summer courses we discussed different strategies to evaluate a school's progress toward different goals, whether it be the implementation of professional learning communities, the building of trust between teachers and administrators, communication between faculty and administrators, or improvement in teachers' instructional strategies. These discussions inevitably ended on strategies for collecting data as evidence, a topic to which we returned in the fall in a data-based decision making course. This class allowed the group to return to the summer discussions and examine more closely what types of data would help them evaluate their school's progress. This examination of different evidence continued into the winter during the "instructional leadership" course, and we focused on what data qualified as evidence of quality instruction or student learning. The cohort model not only enabled this discussion to continue across the courses and challenge students' limited ideas of what qualified as data or evidence, but it allowed the students to bring questions back to the group from previous courses or conversations in an effort to answer them more completely in light of new content in the classes.

This model also presented students with a stable reference group in which to reflect on their learning. This dynamic was most evident in discussions at the end of the year in one of the concluding discussions, when I asked students to reflect on how their conceptions of "quality instruction," "student learning," and "school leadership" had changed during the program. Multiple students not only shared what they had learned on different topics from one another throughout the year, but they also reflected that they had benefited from the conversations that had in effect continued throughout the program on these topics within the group and classes. The cohort model had enabled these discussions to continue and deepen over the course of their year together.

The School Internship

Student placements in administrative positions for half- or year-long terms have been used for over 50 years and are now commonplace in effective programs (Barnett, Copland, & Shoho, 2009; Chance, 1991; Orr, 2006; Orr & Pounder, 2011). Frye, Bottoms, and O'Neill (2005) lay out two key sets of opportunities for participants that help leadership programs connect research and theory with practice.

A well-designed internship expands the knowledge and skills of candidates while also gauging their ability to apply new learning in authentic settings as they contend with problems that have real-world consequences. Built right, the internship becomes a sturdy vessel upon which new practitioners can navigate the swift, unpredictable currents that separate classroom and on-the-job reality. (p. 3)

The Leadership Academy faculty have long recognized the importance of this experience to students, and we have carefully structured the internship to maximize students' exposure to practical work and responsibilities while providing opportunities for reflections with their mentors, program faculty, and other district personnel. As I discuss below, we believe that multiple opportunities for reflection both help students learn from their experiences and allow district and program faculty to evaluate students' capacity for applying new concepts and skill sets in a dynamic work environment. Below I describe the specific internship policies we have put in place, and I discuss how these have supported students' learning.

Regular Reflections: Connecting Theory to Practice

As students participate in their internships we require them to engage in two types of reflections throughout the year: regular discussions during the class in which they can share questions, lessons, insights, or concerns from their experiences, and written reflections that connect their work to the course content and leadership standards.

These regular verbal and written discussions have given students a space in which they can relate different dilemmas or questions they have encountered, whether they be working with a challenging student or teacher, identifying teachers with skill sets for advising or coaching other teachers, or resolving differences with a mentor principal. During the conversations students and I make a strong commitment not to share anything outside of the class. This has given them the freedom to ask blunt questions and be candid about questions or frustrations with their experience. Multiple students have noticed that their administrators' organizational strategies differ from their own, or that administrators relate to the faculty in different ways, and our conversations have allowed students to reflect both on how to handle those differences and what to learn about themselves. I have commented that at times students' learning may consist of seeing that their own leadership style is different from their mentors'. These conversations have also deepened over the year as the cohort students have started to trust each other, and in many cases rely on each other to help make sense of their experiences.

The District Partnership: Closing the Loop

One unique feature for the Leadership Academy has been the close district support for the internships. While program faculty have regularly met with and led group discussions about their experiences, school district officials have regularly met with the students on an individual basis to ask about their experiences. These conversations have been central to the district not only for understanding how well its interns are performing and what strengths and weaknesses they possess as future leaders but also how to direct and prepare their mentors to provide challenging learning experiences for them. This feature has been key to closing the feedback loop both interns and district personnel alike, giving both sides opportunities for feedback and dialogue about the quality of the experiences.

CONCLUSION

As we look ahead to potential shortages of school leaders both on a national scale and in particular locations or districts that are harder to staff (Browne-Ferrigno & Muth, 2009; Ringel, Gates, Chung, Brown, & Gosh-Dastidar, 2004) demand continues to grow for programs that can prepare school leaders to move quickly and successfully into entry-level leadership positions (Frye, O'Neill, & Bottoms, 2006). Research into the broader theoretical foundations and effectiveness of these programs is key, as are reports from program faculty that discuss the practical details and nuances that help promote students' learning. These reflections on the programmatic details and learning experiences of both program faculty and their students can aid other program leaders as they develop and refine the curricula and pedagogical strategies in their own courses.

REFERENCES

Aiken, J. A. (2001). Supporting and sustaining school principals through a state-wide new principals' institute. *Planning and Changing, 32*(3), 144-163.

Andrews, R., & Grogan, M. (2001). *Defining preparation and professional development for the future.* Paper commissioned for the first meeting of the National Commission for the Advancement of Educational Leadership Preparation, Racine, WI.

Barnett, B. G. (2005). Transferring learning from the classroom to the workplace: Challenges and implications for educational leadership preparation. *Educational Considerations, 32*(2), 6-16.

Barnett, B. G., Basom, M. R., Yerkes, D. M., & Norris, C. J. (2000). Cohorts in educational leadership programs: Benefits, difficulties, and the potential for developing school leaders. *Educational Administration Quarterly, 36*(2), 255-282.

Barnett, B. G., Copland, M. A., & Shoho, A. R. (2009). The use of internships in preparing school leaders. In M. Young, G. M. Crow, J. Murphy, & R. Ogawa

(Eds.), *Handbook of research on the education of school leaders* (pp. 371-394). New York, NY: Routledge, Taylor, & Francis.

Bolman, L. G., & Deal, T. E. (2008). *Reframing organizations* (4th ed.). San Francisco, CA: Jossey-Bass.

Browne-Ferrigno, T., & Muth, R. (2003). Effects of cohorts on learners. *Journal of School Leadership, 13,* 621-643.

Browne-Ferrigno, T., & Muth, R. (2009). Candidates in educational leadership graduate programs. In M. D. Young, G. Crow, J. Murphy, & R. Ogawa (Eds.), *Handbook of research on the education of school leaders* (pp. 195-224). New York, NY: Routledge.

Chance, E. W. (1991). The administrative internship: Effective program characteristics. *Journal of School Leadership, 1,* 119-126.

Davis, S., Darling-Hammond, L., Meyerson, D., & La Pointe (2005). *Review of research. School leadership study. Developing successful principals.* Palo Alto, CA: Stanford University, Stanford Educational Leadership Institute.

Drago-Severson, E. (2007). Helping teachers learn: Principals as professional development leaders. *Teachers College Record, 109*(1), 70-125.

Frye, B., Bottoms, G., & O'Neill, K. (2005). *The principal internship: How can we get it right?* Atlanta, GA: Southern Regional Education Board.

Frye, B., Bottoms, G., & O'Neill, K. (2006). *Schools can't wait: Accelerating the redesign of university principal preparation programs.* Atlanta, GA: Southern Regional Educational Board.

Goldring, E. B., & Sims, P. (2005). Modeling creative and courageous school leadership through district-university-community partnerships. *Educational Policy, 19*(1), 223-249.

Grogan, M., Bredeson, P. V., Sherman, W. H., Preis, S., & Beaty, D. M. (2009). The design and delivery of leadership preparation. In M. Young, G. M. Crow, J. Murphy, & R. Ogawa (Eds.), *Handbook of research on the education of school leaders* (pp. 395-415). New York, NY: Routledge, Taylor, & Francis.

Hale, E. L., & Moorman, H. N. (2003). *Preparing school principals: A national perspective on policy and program innovations.* Washington, DC: Institute for Educational Leadership.

Hess, F. M., & Kelly, A. (2007). Learning to lead: What gets taught in principal-preparation programs. *Teachers College Record, 109*(1), 244-274.

Jackson, B. L., & Kelley, C. (2002). Exceptional and innovative programs in educational leadership. *Educational Administration Quarterly, 38*(2), 192-212.

Kegan, R., & Lehey, L. L. (2001). *How the way we talk can change the way we work.* San Francisco, CA: Jossey-Bass.

Lawler, P. A. (2003). Reflective activity in practice: Vignettes of teachers' deliberative work. *Journal of Research and Development in Education, 31*(1), 46-60.

Lawler, P. A., & King, K. P. (2000). *Planning for effective faculty development: Using adult learning strategies.* Malabar, FL: Krieger.

Levine, A. (2005). *Educating school leaders.* New York, NY: The Education School Project.

Mezirow, J. (2000). Learning to think like an adult: Core concepts of transformational theory. In J. Mezirow & Associates (Eds.), *Learning as transformation:*

Critical perspectives on a theory in progress (pp. 3-33). San Francisco, CA: Jossey-Bass.

Milstein, M. M., & Krueger, J. A. (1997). Improving educational administration preparation programs: What we have learned over the past decade. *Peabody Journal of Education, 72*(2), 100-116.

Norris, C., Barnett, B., Basom, M., & Yerkes, D. (1996). The cohort: A vehicle for building transformational leadership skills. *Planning and Changing, 27*(3-4), 145-164.

Orr, M. T. (2006). Innovation in leadership preparation in our nation's schools of education. *The Phi Delta Kappan, 87*(7), 492-499.

Orr, M. T., & Barber, M. E. (2007). Collaborative leadership preparation: A comparative study of innovative programs and practices. *Journal of School Leadership, 16*(6), 709-739.

Orr, M. T., & Orphanos, S. (2011). How graduate-Level preparation influences the effectiveness of school leaders: A comparison of the outcomes of exemplary and conventional leadership preparation programs for principals. *Educational Administration Quarterly, 47*(1), 18-70.

Orr, M. T., & Pounder, D. (2011). Teaching and preparing school leaders. In S. Conley & B. S. Cooper (Eds.), *Finding, preparing, and supporting school leaders,* (pp. 11-39). Lanham, MD: Rowman & Littlefield Education.

Ringel, J. S., Gates, S. M., Chung, C. H., Brown, A., & Ghosh-Dastidar, B. (2004). *Career paths of school administrators in Illinois.* Santa Monica, CA: Rand.

Schön, D. A. (1983). *The reflective practitioner.* New York, NY: Basic Books.

Schön, D. A. (1987). *Educating the reflective practitioner.* San Francisco, CA: Jossey-Bass.

Short, P. M., & Rinehart, J. S. (1993). Reflection as a means of developing expertise. *Educational Administration Quarterly, 29*(4), 501-521.

Sherman, W. H. (2006). Transforming the preparation of educational leaders: A case for ethical district-university partnerships. *International Journal of Educational Reform, 15*(3), 309-330.

Shields, C. M., LaRocque, L. J., & Oberg, S. L. (2002). A conversation about race and ethnicity: Struggling to understand issues in cross-cultural leadership. *Journal of School Leadership, 12*(2), 116-137.

Sirontnik, K., & Kimball, K. (1996). Preparing educators for leadership: In praise of experience. *Journal of School Leadership, 6*(2), 180-201.

Talbert, J. E., & Scharff, N. (2008, March). *Leading school improvement with data: A theory of action to extend the sphere of student success.* Paper presented at the American Educational Research Association Annual Meeting, New York, NY.

Talbert, J. E., Mileva, L., McLaughlin, M., Schoener, J., Cor, M. K., Chen, P., & Lin, W. (2009). *Leadership development and school reform through the scaffolded apprenticeship model* (SAM). Standford CA: Stanford University, Center for Research on the Context of Teaching.

CHAPTER 3

SHUTTLE DIPLOMACY

An Interview With
the Principal-In-Residence

Autumn Cyprès

Currently serving as the Cornerstone Principal-In-Residence for the Center for Educational Leadership, Mrs. Betty Sue Sparks is arguably one of the great forces in the educational leadership networks of East Tennessee. As former special education teacher, principal, and human resources director, Mrs. Sparks could have eased into retirement and basked in the glow of her lifetime of contributions to students in the Knoxville as teacher, leader, visionary, and exemplar. Mrs. Sparks' insights help set the stage for a later conversation with Senator Lamar Alexander as she was one of the educators directly influenced by his policy work as the twentieth century drew to a close. Mrs. Sparks also has a unique perspective in that she is one of the first female school administrators in Knox County. Autumn Cyprès, a former principal from Arizona with experience at High, Middle, and Elementary, serves as the director of The Center for Educational Leadership. She and Betty Sue are literally the keystones that ensure the ivory tower of academia and the real world of schools is

Great Leaders Equal Great Schools:
Alliances and Discourse for Educational Reform, pp. 37–53
Copyright © 2012 by Information Age Publishing
All rights of reproduction in any form reserved.

bridged with authenticity. It might be worth noting that while there is a generation between Autumn and Betty Sue, both understand each other very well because both have rich experiences in the realm of school change and reform. What follows below is a transcript of their conversation:

AC: Betty Sue, when did you become a teacher? What year?
BSS: 1969.
AC: Get out! You're not that old!?!
BSS: That was yesterday, what are you talking about?
AC: What did you teach? What was your area?
BSS: I was a special education teacher, and my endorsement was in elementary education and also in special education.
AC: How long were you a teacher?
BSS: Oh, let's see. I started teaching in 1969. I did my student teaching at Linden Elementary School in Oak Ridge. UT had a partnership program with Oak Ridge Schools, and they had to have so many student teachers because of the program that was set up at Linden. So I went in to my student teaching with my own classroom. It was an open space classroom and I taught with eight other teachers. We had I guess 250 fourth-graders, and it was a wonderful experience.
AC: What did you think of the open space concept?
BSS: Well, at Linden I saw how it could work. Subsequently when I was principal at Cedar Bluff Intermediate, it was an open space classroom too. Although it was 15, maybe 20 years later, my experience in Linden prepared me to talk to parents who were concerned the open space classroom that we had. I had to be able to explain to them how we could make it work for their particular child and to meet their individual children's needs. Very shortly after I left Cedar Bluff, walls came up at that building. But we made it work! It was challenging, but some really good things came out of it.
AC: That was a big thing nationally, the open space classroom.
BSS: Yes. And for some children, it was absolutely magical. There were, however, children who had a really hard time attending to what they needed to do.
AC: Because there's so much to look at!
BSS: And very honestly, it was challenging for some teachers too. Because you have to be willing to be open and not threatened by somebody watching you all the time, and be willing to work as a team. For some folks, that was hard.

AC: So there you are in your 20's as a new teacher, experiencing out of the box this idea of a glass house. Do you think that played into your development as a politician? Because one of your skills, Betty Sue, is that when we look at your career and you were the director of human resources, you are an expert politician and diplomat. Do you think part of how you learned that was because you were in this work environment where people always watched each other, or am I just making a leap?

BSS: In retrospect I believe you're right about that. I don't know about the politician business, but in terms of working with other people I think that certainly was an influence and a real important factor for me. Because it did give me an opportunity to watch other people to see their style and I sort of built my own craft, if you will, by taking the things that I do well and try to make sure that I was teaching with my strengths. I think that's important. You have to know what your strengths are and be able to develop those strengths and manage your weaknesses.

AC: You're also someone who is very attuned to self-reflection and being an open book, and taking critique. Do you think part of that came from the experience of being in an open classroom school? Because that means also as a brand new teacher there you are with everybody watching you.

BSS: The feedback that I got in that situation was absolutely wonderful. We met sometimes daily, and at least weekly. Very intense meetings where the master teachers, if you will, were giving us feedback about our teaching. Because it gave them the opportunity to teach next to us and watch us at the same time they also built me up. They talked about the things that I was doing well. When I was able to reach a child somebody noticed. One of the things that still stands out for me; we had a child who had not been able to read. We all knew he was bright, but he just couldn't read. I was given an opportunity to work with him, and using the kinesthetic method of putting the letters on his hand, and that was really kind of "out there" at that time, but I'm telling you it worked for that child. We were able to see him by using large motor movements and tactile kinesthetics we were able to reach him and he was able to start to read. He was reading very close to grade level by the end of the time I left there. That was magical. I can still see him, and see the excitement and see his mother who knew there was something there.

AC: Well said. How long were you in the classroom before you became an administrator?

BSS: I got my own classroom and started teaching at Christenberry
Junior High in August of '69, and I went to a program called
Project Follow-Through in 1976, where we worked with deinsti-
tutionalized kids and getting them acclimated back to the regular classroom. I did the academic component and someone else
did the behavior management component. So I taught, I guess
for 7 years. I was at Fulton High School; I started the special ed
program there, when at that time they didn't have special ed at
the High School level. So I taught there for a half day and went
back to Christenberry. I did that for a year. After the funds ran
out for project follow through I went back to the regular classroom for a couple of years. I taught fifth and sixth-grade at
pond Gap elementary school, it was fun.

AC: So you did that, and then you became an assistant principal?

BSS: No, I was offered a position with a program called Project
MODEL—management of diverse educational levels. What we
did was go into classrooms with teachers who were working with
special ed kids, and we helped teachers to modify the curriculum to meet the needs of the students so that they could go into
the regular classroom and be successful. It was loads of fun, and
I was able to work with lots of new teachers while at the same
time I worked with lots of experienced teachers. I learned a lot
from them. They allowed me to come into their classrooms and
model the techniques. They watched me and then they would
pick up those techniques and use them with the kids in their
classroom. It was an exciting time.

AC: So was it like being a special ed director? Because it was a district level position.

BSS: I was not a director, I was a facilitator. Even as an administrator,
I've always seen myself as a facilitator. What is it that I can do to
help this person? And at the same time, what can you teach me
that I can then turn around and share with other folks?

AC: What put the idea of, "hey, I might want to be an administrator"
in your head? So you're doing this Project MODEL, then what
happened?

BSS: I started graduate school just before I got the position with Project MODEL. And there was a program called the Sex Equity
Administrators Training Institute.

AC: Let's say it again, the Sex Equity Administrators Training Institute.

BSS: Yes, and Norma Mertz and Fred Vandetti were heading that
program up, and the district; Knoxville city, Knox County,
metro Nashville, Memphis, and I think there was one more dis-

trict. Identified five to six teachers who were working in their district who they thought would be good administrators, primarily female. Because that time there weren't very many female administrators.

AC: What year was this?

BSS: I finished my masters in 1981, so that would have been maybe 1979.

AC: So you were tapped. Your superintendent came to you?

BSS: Actually it was an Assistant Superintendent, Dr. Paul Kelley. He had been a high school English teacher at Fulton while I was a student. He had known me through the years and invited me to participate in this program along with other folks in the district.

AC: Do you remember when he had the conversation with you? What was that like?

BSS: I do. Actually, we had the conversation, but Buddy Bean, who was the personnel director, also had a conversation with me. He had been my high school biology teacher. Even in biology, he had paired me up with a student at UT who was in education, and I was invited to come over and spend the night with her in the dorm, and she talked to me about her road to being a teacher.

AC: So you were tapped to be a teacher as a high school student?

BSS: Somebody saw something in me and through the years I've always tried to make it my business to look for talent and to then talk about that talent to the person.

AC: Because that's what happened to you.

BSS: Oh, yeah.

AC: Are there any other teachers in your family?

BSS: My dad was a teacher. He was a welder during the war, and then he started teaching. He worked at Dempster Brothers and then got an offer to teach. After folks started coming home from the war, he taught welding.

Subsequently he went back to school and was the director of a vocational school at Fulton. IT was called the Fulton area vocational training center. So I saw him teaching, and how excited he was about that. I've always wanted to be a teacher. I taught Sunday school from the time I was in junior high. So I've always wanted to be a teacher, and one of the things I found out when I started working with gallop, who studies the best, and one of their interview questions, is tell me about your desire to be a teacher. One of the things that we always listen for is "I've always wanted to be a teacher." So that always reinforced that with me.

AC: I'm the same way. I lined up my shoes and taught them.

BSS: I can't imagine not teaching. I can't imagine not doing that.

AC: So you enroll the Sex Equity Program, which was what they were calling the masters at UT?

BSS: It was. I finished the program with an endorsement as an administrator. We did an internship. It was not as long as our fellows do, it was only one quarter, but I did my internship at Knoxville Adaptive Education Center. As it turned out, the woman who was the principal there moved to Central Office that summer. So I became the principal at KAEC.

AC: Did you expect that to happen so fast?

BSS: No, I did not.

AC: How many kids were at KAEC?

BSS: We had over a thousand kids at that time. It's scary when I think about it. Ages 3 through 21.

AC: That's a big school.

BSS: Every classroom at what was the old Bearden High School was filled, we had 12 portable classrooms, plus we had six classrooms next door at Bearden Elementary School.

AC: Was this for people who would leave that building to be mainstreamed back? A crude way to say it was that this was where they were warehoused? Because that was the time. That's not what we do now, but that was the time.

BSS: Basically yes. But even then I knew there absolutely had to be a better way. Many of the kids were able to go to a vocational training program called Van Guilder at the time. My mom had been the secretary at that school, so I was very close. So a lot of my kids went there to get vocational training, which was wonderful. When I left KAEC to go to a regular elementary school, I took two classrooms with me to Moreland Heights. Just because I knew we could meet the needs of the kids there.

AC: How many years were you at KAEC?

BSS: Five years. After that I went to Moreland Heights Elementary and was there 5 years. It's been kind of a 5-year march for me.

AC: And Moreland heights, was that a mainstream school or was it a special ed school?

BSS: It was a regular elementary school, K-5, with 400 kids. It was wonderful. And there was a strong special ed influence. I will never forget one of my favorite stories. One of the kids who had been at KAEC with me came to Moreland Heights and he got in trouble in the classroom. He was sitting on a bench outside my office and was talking to another little fellow who was in trouble as well. I could hear them talking, and the one kid said "what's she like?," and the kid who had been at KAEC said "you know, it's kind of hard to explain. She doesn't yell or scream, but that old woman means every word she says." I just loved it. I thought you know what, I have arrived.

AC: How old were you when you were an old woman that means every word she says?

BSS: I turned forty at Moreland Heights.

AC: So you were 5 years there, then what happened?

BSS: After Moreland Heights there was another program. The business community realized that we had a lot of at risk kids. So they paid for an at-risk supervisor for the district. So I went to Central Office to be the at risk supervisor. The funds were only available for 1 year, but we raised some grants.

AC: What year was this?

BSS: This was in 1989-1990.

AC: What year did you marry sweet Doug Sparks?

BSS: 1969. I met him while I was doing my student teaching.

AC: And when did you have your kids?

BSS: John came in 1972.

AC: So you're principaling and mommying?

BSS: Well, I took a year off when he was born. But then I went back.

AC: Was it unusual during that time? The Sex Equity Program sounds like it came along at a time when there was a cry to bring more women in the field into leadership positions, and that you were part of that. So how unusual was it to see a colleague that was also a working mother like you?

BSS: Lots of us were doing it at that time. There were women who were in administration, but certainly not as many. At that time there were maybe five or six of us, primarily at the elementary level. Mary Lukanot was a high school assistant principal.

AC: And this is still in the 70s and 80s.

BSS: Yes.

AC: I want to switch gears and talk about the Principal Level Three Certificate that you were one of the very first people to have. You were at Moreland Heights?

BSS: I was. At that time the commissioner Lamar Alexander developed a program. The emphasis was on better schools. It was called the Better Schools Program. The emphasis was on being accountable and willing to accept accountability. That threatened a lot of people. There were a lot of folks who were not really excited about that program. I guess I saw it as a way to be accountable. I wanted that.

AC: It sounds like your whole career you always had critical feedback and were used to have authentic self-reflective evaluations. So this didn't scare you?

BSS: No, it didn't. I've always wanted to be the best I could be. I always felt like I owed that to the people who were counting on me. Certainly that was my family but it was also the children and parents of those children who maybe didn't even know how important and how critical that was.

AC: So that's a big core value for you. Where do you think you got that?

BSS: That's just a part of the fabric of who I am. It was instilled in me as a child as a family child. You will be the very best you can be. My mother expected me to use my talents. You understand, I was not athletically inclined. I took ballet and tap lessons, and I learned later that my teacher encouraged her to save her money. So my mother really pointed out my talents. She knew that I was very articulate, so she expected me to use that and to speak. My grandmother expected that as well. I was maybe this tall and this wide with glasses three inches thick. My grandmother would say, "This is my granddaughter, isn't she beautiful? And she is so smart."

And because my grandmother said it I believed it. I think that's critical for children. I think it's important for children to have an adult who believe in them. It doesn't necessarily have to be a family member, but every child needs to have a caring adult who believes in them.

AC: So when you got this principal certificate, it was to be the best you could be because you wanted to give back. You wanted to show the kids you could be your best, but it also added credibility.

BSS: It did, and it helped me to look at areas where I needed to grow. There was a portfolio that was a critical part of that. Some folks came in and looked at those very carefully, so it allowed me to look at areas where I needed to grow, and to do that.

AC: Did you see it as a ticket to get somewhere higher?

BSS: No.

AC: You really saw it as a thing to make you a better principal.

BSS: To make me a better principal. That's what I wanted to do. As a teaching principal. Even as a principal I continued to teach. Not necessarily in a classroom, but with the staff. To provide professional development and to mentor new teachers.

AC: And that was your favorite thing to do.

BSS: Oh yes. One of my new teachers at Moreland Heights is retiring. But I can still see her. When I watched her with children it was just a thing of absolute beauty. And being able to point out to her what she did so well, was so important to me. I don't know how important it was to her, but I think it might have been important.

AC: When you look back at the process of getting the certificate, that then Governor Alexander had initiated.

BSS: The way you knew you had got it was that your name was published in the newspaper, or it wasn't. That's how you knew. It was in the summer every year. This was the first or second year, I'm not sure. We were at the beach.

AC: Would you get more money if you had a level three certificate?

BSS: Yes, we did.

AC: So that's a nice perk too.

BSS: It was $3,000 a year. And you got the opportunity to work during the summer too. But I really didn't get the money when I moved into HR. We weren't eligible for that money. While it was nice, and I appreciate it, it was not the reason.

AC: So you were at the beach, and you got the newspaper?

BSS: I did. I got the newspaper, and there it was. My name was there. I think it was a phone call from my mom, because she was watching for it. There were two things in my life that I worked so hard for. That was really big for me. Like I said, there was a lot of controversy associated with that. But it was so important for me. I felt like it was something I needed to do.

AC: And the controversy didn't bother you? You didn't care?

BSS: No. There were all sorts of questions about it. I always felt like it had to do with accountability.

AC: Do you think those questions come around every time?

BSS: Sure. It's a cycle. But at the same time, each time the cycle comes around it gets better and better and better. I am so proud of what we are doing today and I look back and see the seeds of all that and think it's really neat to have been a part of that. The career ladder program, I believe, was the beginning of it. Like I said, I know it was controversial. Even today, some of the colleges that I worked with are adamant that it is not a good measure. Having been trough that evaluation process, I felt strongly that it was.

AC: Maybe its like the discussions about unions. Some people don't think that unions are important at all because they think they do their job and don't worry about it. And some people think unions are very important because they're worried they're going

to be beat up, and some people argue its because they're medio-
cre. So you liked the career ladder idea, you got the certificate,
and you only had it a year or two before moving to the district
position?

BSS: I went from Moreland Heights to Cedar Bluff, and I was there a
year before going to the district as the at risk supervisor. Then I
got a phone call from the superintendent asking me to go to
Farragut Primary as the principal there. It was a K-2 school with
16 kindergartens. You haven't lived until you've tried to get that
many kindergarten children on a bus.

AC: That's a lot of kindergartens. Do you remember how many bus-
ses you had?

BSS: Twenty-three. I remember exactly how many buses we had. But
at the same time, we taught procedures and methods. That's
not something I can take responsibility for. Teachers did that
themselves. That was another neat thing, you know I have
found that if you trust teachers and are willing to be involved
with them and support them, they're going to make things
work. They always have for me. We didn't ever lose a child.

AC: Where did you make the jump to the district office to be the
director of human resources?

BSS: I was at Farragut Primary and I became elementary supervisor. I
was in that position for 4 or 5 years.

AC: So elementary supervisor means you worked for the district and
supervised elementary schools.

BSS: Right. There were three of us at the time, so we divided the elementary schools up. We worked the summer learning program
as well.

AC: Why do you think you were picked to be the elementary supervisor?

BSS: I have a passion for what I do. I always have. As I look back at
the opportunities I've had and the facilitating that I've done
with project MODEL and project Follow Through, gave me an
opportunity to lead. When other opportunities came along, I
was given that opportunity as well.

AC: Each one of these, they keep tapping you. You didn't say in your
mind "I want to go be the district elementary person. I want to
be the head of human resources."

BSS: I did apply to be director of human resources. I'd always wanted
to be elementary supervisor. And I had made it known that I
would like to do that, and in the middle of the year got that
opportunity. I left Farragut Primary before school was out. That

was a really hard thing to do, but I was able to go back there and do a little work as well.

AC: Do you think you've been always cognizant of networks? Where do you think you first learned about people who are connected and that you need to make the message clear what you wanted? Where did you firs learn about that?

BSS: Yes. That's something that I've always kind of known. I think it was solidified with Norma Mertz. Talking about defining moments, for me, she provided those defining moments. I have to say, I was not at all happy about some of those defining moments. She was absolutely insistent in the graduate program that we set specific career goals. That was ok with me; I kind of knew what I wanted to do. But, more importantly, she had us make a plan and write that plan out very specifically.

AC: So you had to think ahead in the future and plan your trajectory?

BSS: I was resistant to that. I saw no reason to sit down and write something down like that. But, what it did was help me to think through steps I might want to take. It's hard to say it was intentional, but it really was very intentional. Because I sat down and thought about that. I wanted to be an elementary principal, made a plan, and that happened. I hadn't been in my position very long at all until I got a phone call from Norma, who said it was time to make another plan. Well, I knew I wanted to be HR director. At that time it was called personnel director, but that's what I wanted to do.

AC: So Norma has come in and out of your life to remind you its time for another plan.

BSS: Yes. And I said no. And she said yes, I'm coming to see it. Sit down and write what you need to do. And the day I got to HR I got a phone call from Norma. It's time to make another plan. And at that time I did say no. My next plan will be retirement!

AC: Why didn't you want to make these plans? Why were you so resistant to that?

BSS: When you write it down, it really is intentional. And I think in the back of my mind I was thinking what if I write this down and it doesn't happen? So that was pretty scary. At the same time, I'm pretty sure the hr position wouldn't have happened if I had not had a plan. In working with the fellows, I tell them that story and say to them that it's absolutely important for them to make a plan. The graduate school experience for me came about because I knew I wanted to be a principal, and that was a path to the principalship. You had to do that. But in retrospect, it was a defining moment. To know that if I sit down and make a plan, and follow that plan, chances are going to be a whole lot better.

AC: Because you're acting with intention. You're laying out what you want to do.

BSS: Its very intentional.

AC: we sit down once a year as a large panel to interview people who are interested in this program. I'm there as an academic who grew up in Arizona that's in all truth 10 years younger than you. Maybe a little bit younger, but we'll say ten.

BSS: Let's try 18. I am 64 and proud to be here.

AC: Ok, I'm 18 years younger than you. And we are putting in the book that you look about 44. So I'm arguably from a different generation. We are two different generations of educators and school leaders. There are people on the panel from Knox County who are generations in between you and me. From all different points, you have someone who came from Florida or here, from Boston; you have all sorts of folks. And one of the things that I have found very interesting after doing these interviews is that when we get together and talk abut it, everybody has a kind of same feel for spotting talent. You and I are from different places, and yet we have so much that is very similar. One of the things you've said already is that it hits me when someone is very passionate about their teaching, and I agree. You feel like it's in your bones. When you started talking about making a plan and what it means to be a teacher, I was tearing up because I feel that too, and I know that. So we look for that. What else do you think it is that we see that wows people? Just knocks them off their socks, when you know you're seeing a leader.

BSS: For me, another defining moment was when we started to work specifically with the Gallop organization and look at strengths based leadership. One of the things that I have come to believe so strongly is that you develop specific questions and then you know what the best say. In order to know what the best say, you have to study the best. I don't think that has to be a nationwide thing, it can be in your building. When you develop interview questions, I think it's really important to know how your best teacher would answer those questions. As a leader, you have to be really careful that you are not the one answering those questions. Because you don't want people who look and sound just like you, you want people who look and sound just like the best. So I think its important to know what your best teachers say and how they answer those questions. By doing that, by developing those relationships and knowing what you need to listen for while interviewing an individual, you start to then develop the things that are those ah-ha moments. You know, I'm hearing this, this person I'm talking to really is something. You can't be who you're not. Not for long. And so as you ask those questions, I think its important to say, give me an example. Tell me about a time when, and know what you're listening for.

AC: So part of it is experience and what you just said is that you can't be who you're not. We all kind of have a good BS meter, because you can't be that way for very long.

BSS: Is there substance? Can this person who is so articulate and answers this interview question in such flowery beautiful terms, is there substance? Can this person give me a rock solid example that makes a difference for children?

AC: So the other piece is, you can be charismatic and dazzling, and you and I can think of people right now who are charismatic and dazzling, but they don't have any substance. Part of leadership is have you got that balance.

BSS: Do you look for talent, and do you look for specific credible examples. And good gracious, I've seen in interviewing vocational and technical education teachers, who don't have any experience in a classroom but it's just who they are. They're able to give me real life examples that I know would make a difference in the classroom because of how they treated someone.

AC: I wonder also if the other piece is a person who's got it. Who's really a leader, also knows who they are.

BSS: you have to know, as a leader, you have to have a line that you won't cross. You have to know what those parameters are and be willing to stand up and say no.

AC: And that has to be something you don't say, its something you live. And I think that's also the currency.

BSS: And by saying no, I'm talking about talking to yourself. Now sometimes you have to stand up and say no to everyone else, but to yourself, to say no. This is not what I am about, this is not what's best for kids, and no, I will not be a part of it.

AC: I think that's a huge thing you just shared, because you have to have courage, you have to have a moral compass, and then you have to adhere to it. Because lots of people know when they're doing the wrong thing.

BSS: And check it every day. Because those kinds of questions and examples come up every day in leadership experiences. You have to know what you stand for, and you have to be willing to model that. Even when it's not convenient.

AC: I think this exchange we're having right now is the core of the book, the core of the message of this whole book. About leadership and great leaders equaling great schools. The difference between great leaders and a manager is a leader knows who they are and maintain fidelity to that. You can have great leaders that are different stylistically, but what makes them great is you know how they're going to be on certain things because they're true to their own values.

BSS: When you think about great leaders, think about Churchill and think about Gandhi. Think about how different they were, but bother great leaders. Why? They knew what they stood for and they stood firm to that.

AC: Do you think that's one of the ways you get and give respect When you notice it in another leader? I know I'm that way, and I know you're that way, and I think that's part of the reason you and I gelled quickly. We demonstrated to each other without saying it to each other. We both walked our talk. When I think of the leaders who I would go to war for, it's the same thing. I know they mean what they say and that you and count on them. That's rare.

BSS: Max Depree's book, *Leadership Jazz*, has been so meaningful to me. In that book he talks about leaders being willing to stand up and bear the pain. Are you willing to accept responsibility for what happens? As a leader the folks who are working with you have to know that you're going to be right there with them, right there alongside them, and that you are willing to be held responsible. You are willing to stand up for what's right, you're willing to stand up for making sure that every hid, not juts some children, but all children, get the very best. Even when that's not convenient.

AC: And that is so potent of an idea, of a fact. Because not everybody does that. It's not only inconvenient when the rubber meets the road; sometimes it's just really hard.

BSS: Painful.

AC: Painful is a very good word. And not everybody is willing to go through that. I think that's another thing as I listen to your words and reflect back to the group of people who from all different walks of life, select these fellows, we all end up making jokes around painful experiences of leadership. We all have some story of walking through the fire and eating a plate of crow, and dealing with that. And that's the thing that tests your metal.

BSS: It really is. And being confidant enough in yourself to be willing to say I was wrong. Because let's face it, when you take risks, and leadership is a risk, you can't always be right. You just can't be. But when you build up the collateral with people and are willing to be honest enough to say, "that didn't quite work out the way I wanted it to, let's back up and do that again." Then people know you're telling the truth. They know you're willing to tell the truth even when it's not convenient, even when it hurts.

AC: I think the other thing that's really important that we do well as a team and that you do well is that a really great leader takes the time to make people feel valued in a sincere way. It's not just listening, and listening is worth a whole other book and discussion, but grab leaders really pay attention to what can I do to demonstrate to this person, whether it be a fellow or colleague or teacher or parent or even more importantly a child, that they're unique self is value sand understood.

BSS: And that's the key: understood. When you're able to watch and then point out the things that that person does uniquely and well, and have that person know that you know it and affirm that, it's just such a gift.

AC: That's part of the magic. We all know this, but that's how you get people to buy in and follow the vision.

BSS: It has to be authentic. We've both worked with folks who would talk to you about something that you do well and you know that's really not a strength of yours.

AC: Yeah, I always find that amusing.

BSS: So you have to be willing to get to know that person and to be authentic with adults, but more importantly with children. Children pick up on that in a heartbeat.

AC: I think about the principles I've seen lately where they know the names of the kids in the hall.

BSS: What a gift to a parent, to know that this person knows my child's name. I mean when you're entrusting the most important little individual in the whole world to you, to that person, and you think they don't even know my child's name.
When I first went to Farragut primary, a dad came in who was just a wonderful person. He wanted to talk to me about his child, and he knew that I had lots of children and he also knew that it was important of me to know who they were. I kept their composites with their names on them, and I would take them home at night and memorize them because I wanted to be able

to call those children by their name. When I got on the bus to call somebody down I wanted to be able to call them by name, but I also wanted to be able to go in a classroom and know that child and be able to tell him or her what they were doing good. Having said that, he came in to talk to me about his child, and I had glass on the top of my desk. When we finished our conversation, knowing I had 1100 children in that building, he took a picture out of his wallet and asked if I would mind him putting the picture of his daughter under the glass on my desk. And I said no, I would love it. But you'd better believe I never forgot. Today I can still see that picture, I still have that picture. It pointed out to me that there's nothing better than someone knowing your name. I think that's one of the best gifts you can give anyone, but particularly a child. It's a gift to the child but it's also a gift to the parent. I never forgot that.

AC: Since you're now in the sagacious part of your life, and you talked earlier about the seeds of accountability and the whole cycle. Is there anything you would do differently?

BSS: I wouldn't trade it for anything. I learned from each experience.

AC: You had a chance to retire. How long were you retired?

BSS: Three months, maybe? I had started working with the distinguished professionals program, a nonprofit organization maybe 3 or 4 years after I retired. I realized when I had the spices alphabetized in my kitchen that I just couldn't do that very long.

AC: Dr. Anfara, who has a chapter in here with Dr. Angelle, contacted you and asked if you would like to come and do this. You were in retirement and in Hawaii. Why on earth would you say yes?

BSS: Well, I had been a part of the planning for this program. I went on one of the initial visits when we looked at similar programs in place in Boston and New York City, and it was really exciting. More importantly, Dr. McIntyre looked me in the eye in his office one day, and said to me "will you help me make this a reality?" And I said to him "yes, I will." So how could I say no, when this opportunity came along? What an absolute gift. Never in my wildest imagination did I ever realize that this would be something that I would get to be such a part of. I always saw myself on the side. It's just been the best gift in the whole world to me.

AC: So when you think of what you saw in your head in your visits, because now we're 2 years in and there was no director then;

what's it like now looking back? If you look back now and see what's happened, compared with looking forward at the possibilities, how do they match up for you?

BSS: Every morning I wake up and I think wow; I get to go do what I like to do more than anything else in the world. Who gets to do that? One of my strengths when you look at the Gallop Strengths Finder is futurist. So I'm always thinking about what it could look like in the future. So of course I did have a picture in my head once we got back from New York and Boston. As I look at the center now, I think that it's even better than I imagined. It's even better, and we are just 3 years into this. Thinking about what I'm seeing as I hear the rich discussions when the fellows are in their classes, and when I visit in the schools and see them interact with their mentor principals, and as I talk to the mentor principals, I think about that picture I had in my mind when we started on this journey. The picture has come to fulfillment but there's so much yet that we could do. We have so much farther that we could go. To see the difference the fellows are making in the culture of our district as they go into leadership positions and as they develop those strong networks, as they share their expertise and their stories with other administrators and we see other administrators getting excited about what it could look like with this vision for excellence for all children. I love what I'm doing. Absolutely love it. It's such a gift. I told Dr. McIntyre when he asked me about that, I would do it even if I weren't invited to. That's the thing, to make a difference and love what you are doing. If you are lucky you leave a little something behind that helps the next person.

Part II:
New Leaders
in Action

CHAPTER 4

CRITICAL LEADERSHIP RESPONSIBILITIES FOR CHANGE

Beth Blevins

In 1983, United States Education Secretary Terrel Bell commissioned an 18-month study to determine the status of education in America. The findings titled "A Nation at Risk" reported the American educational system was comfortable with mediocrity and could not compete with the educational systems in other countries (National Commission on Excellence in Education, 1983). After this report, the Clinton administration enacted "Goals 2000," and following that, the Bush administration unveiled "No Child Left Behind." In response, states, districts, and schools adopted a more focused look at instruction and interventions for students not mastering skills. In 2008, the U.S. government spent $62,423,917 on educational reforms (U.S. Department of Education, 2008). As with many hasty responses, some programs were put into districts or schools with no clear research to specify their effectiveness (Bridgeland, Dilulio, & Morison, 2006; U.S. Department of Education, 2008). Like many educators I have witnessed this phenomenon first hand. So it was only natural for me to dedicate some energy into studying what kinds of leadership responsibilities that teachers and administrators perceived as supportive to *authentic* change in a middle school.

Great Leaders Equal Great Schools:
Alliances and Discourse for Educational Reform, pp. 57–78

During the 2009-2010 school year, several students were failing classes at Northwest Middle School in Knoxville, Tennessee. The administration began meeting with students to find out what students perceived as the reason for this dynamic. As students were questioned about failing grades, many said they did not know why they were failing the class or that they could improve the grade to a passing status by "just being nice and following directions in class." In response to this staff members were asked to share with each other and the administration individual grading practices. The results of this exercise were shocking in that there were hardly any consistencies among content areas and grade levels. For some, heavy emphasis was placed on participation (including completing homework) with minimal emphasis on content mastery. For others, content mastery was the only source of grading for the course.

Once the disparity was acknowledged, faculty and administration began discussing the need for a consistent grading procedures document that ensured an accurate reflection of students' mastery of content. The faculty was invited to participate on committee that examined research on effective grading practices and make recommendations for schoolwide procedures. The team consisted of five representatives from the following areas: Related arts (a teacher specializing in a literacy program called Read 180), eighth-grade language arts, eighth-grade math, a seventh-grade language arts, and a teacher from sixth-grade math. The committee met several times to review research and designed a document for grading procedures that included an effort rubric to give specific information regarding the behaviors that either contributed to or inhibited students from mastering content. This recommendation was approved for implementation by the school's principal in May of 2010. Subsequently, the team designed a professional development module that would introduce all Northwest Middle School staff to the new grading procedures. During the 2010-2011 school year the grading procedures committee provided professional development to all staff members and the procedures were implemented beginning August 2010.

Though the grading procedures design and professional development originated from staff members who were committed to the change, implementing the procedures with fidelity was a challenge. Fidelity to the grading procedures included entering three grades per week for each student in a computer program called Gradebook. Some teachers entered three grades per week without reminders from administration, while others did not. For those that entered three grades per week, there was inconsistency in the designation for formative or summative assessment and/or the connection to a state standard. As a response to the lack of fidelity, the administration had to emphasize specific leadership responsibilities to ensure the elements of the new grading procedures were being followed.

The research that follows sought to identify the leadership responsibilities necessary to maintain fidelity to a change initiative. The study that is the heart of this chapter had two phases: the first addressed the responses of administrators compared to teacher responses at Northwest Middle School on McRel's 21 Leadership Responsibilities (Marzano, Waters, & McNulty, 2003; 2005) instrument (see Appendix A for a rubric of leadership behaviors associated with these responsibilities),

The second phase consisted of interviews of teachers and administrators to probe the differences found between the six administrator and 48 teacher responses. In other words: phase one was checking in on the staff and administration to see "what page everyone was on"; and phase two was about discovering why these two groups were "on two different pages." In phase two, 22 teachers were interviewed.

The questions asked were:

- "Are there differences in the behaviors administrators report as important compared to teacher responses?"
- "What are the reasons for any differences in the responses administrators report compared to teacher responses?"
- "What leadership responsibilities are important to support teachers in maintaining fidelity to a change initiative?" (QUAN-qual).

Several terms are used throughout the rest of this discussion specific to school culture. An abbreviated glossary has been placed at the end of this chapter to remedy any questions the reader may have. Limitations of this work center of the bias related to self reporting as well as sample size and context (one school was used as the primary data pool). A notable delimitation of this work is that it does not include the accuracy of how well each grade reflects mastery of a state standard.

WHAT THE LITERATURE SAYS

Many studies have been done on implementing change within schools (Brighton, 2003; Brown & Anfara, 2003; Colantonio, 2005; Finnigan & Stewart, 2009; Gerla, Gilliam & Wright, 2006; Sato & Atkin, 2007; Smith-Maddox, 1999; Stein & Nelson, 2003); however, very few resources are available that tell administrators how to maintain high fidelity after the change occurs in the most efficient and effective way. My literature review followed two lines of inquiry: (1) the conditions and leadership responsibilities needed for implementing change, and (2) the leadership responsibilities needed for sustaining change.

Robert Marzano and colleagues, in *School Leadership That Works* (2005), conducted a meta-analysis and found leadership responsibilities associated with second-order change, or a change that requires a significant break from past practices. Responsibilities identified were ones that best impacted student achievement. This would indicate there may be some fidelity to the change initiative; however, the research did not explicitly focus on the fidelity of the change being implemented. Rather, the focus was on student achievement as an outcome of the change. Any change in a school, whether maintained with fidelity or not, can result in teachers being cognizant of their behavior and student learning. Therefore, change can produce temporary positive or negative impacts on student achievement without the fidelity to the change being the focus. This information is important because if the right conditions are not in place as the change is implemented, the reform initiative could fail, not because it is not an appropriate intervention, but because the conditions to implement the change were not in place. The responsibilities identified as necessary for second-order change were: knowledge of curriculum, instruction, and assessment; optimizer; intellectual stimulation; change agent; monitoring/evaluating; flexibility; ideals/beliefs.

In "Leadership Content Knowledge" by Stein and Nelson (2003), three case studies are reviewed to determine the most important leadership responsibilities needed to support change that has a positive impact on student achievement. The focus of this study was to determine the importance of different leadership responsibilities needed to implement change when it is not in the administrator's area of personal content knowledge and pedagogy. This research is important because if teachers do not feel the administrator has the knowledge necessary to support the change, they will be less likely to implement it in the classrooms. The McRel 21 Leadership Responsibilities emphasized in this article were knowledge of curriculum, instruction, and assessment; involvement in curriculum, instruction and assessment; intellectual stimulation; monitoring/evaluating; and resources.

Finnigan and Stewart (2009) conducted a 2-year qualitative case study involving 331 interviews with teachers, administrators, external partners, and others to determine the administrative responsibilities necessary for moving students in low-performing schools to bring about improvement under pressure. Schools that are in the status of low-performing regarding academic achievement are prone to external pressures for immediate change. This can create a resistance to any reform initiative, particularly because it is usually more than one initiative being implemented to quickly turn around student achievement. This research is important, particularly for the school in this study, as if the conditions are not right to implement the change in a low-performing school then the likelihood of implementing change with fidelity could be compromised. This qualitative data is important for this study as it provided the opportunity for open-ended responses regarding what teachers perceive as effective support during change. The leadership responsibilities identified in this study include: visibility, resources, input, communication, intellectual stimulation, focus, change agent, relationships, flexibility, and culture.

Sarason (1971, 1990) found the need for ensuring conditions are right before a change is implemented. In both *The Predictable Failure of Educational Reform* and *The Culture of the School and the Problem of Change*, Sarason argues that most good change ideas that have not worked were destined to fail because they were launched from the outside the school rather from the ones who would be implementing the change. He contends that a sense of powerlessness in faculty results in, at best, passionless conformity and, at worst, total rejection. In the end, some teachers end up wanting to leave the school or system due to change imposed upon them rather than with them. This research is important because a lack of fidelity to the grading procedures could be a result of a teacher feeling like the change is being done to him or her. The leadership responsibilities connected to Sarason's work are: input; intellectual stimulation; communication; flexibility; focus; outreach; optimizer; and change agent.

Two of the research studies reviewed regarding the conditions necessary for effective change implementation focused on administrative support for maintaining support during a reform initiative as perceived by teachers, with one being focused specifically on the middle school level (Brighton, 2003; Colantonio, 2005). Both studies used teacher interviews and/or reflections to gather information regarding what teachers perceived as effective administrative support when a change initiative was introduced. These findings informed this research by identifying potential differences in the perception of middle school teachers compared with teachers at elementary level. For the middle school teachers, the most important administrative support were the responsibilities identified as change agent, intellectual stimulation, input, relationships, communication, and focus. However, for the elementary level teachers, the support administrators should provide were identified knowledge of curriculum, instruction, and assessment; involvement in curriculum, instruction, and assessment; situational awareness; relationships; and resources. The differences may be due to the middle school teachers feeling they are "experts" in their content area and need more input on the change and focus on the vision to be supported in the change process. Because elementary level teachers are "general curriculum experts", they reported a knowledge of the curriculum and involvement in the curriculum by the administrator were critically important.

Brown and Anfara (2003) claimed that, "to implement an effective change, a principal inspires, challenges, guides, and empowers" (p. 16). They also noted that leaders must:

1. understand the nature, needs, strengths, and limitations of staff members;
2. understand the relevance of the reform in terms of need, practicality and complexity;
3. assess the readiness of staff to become involved;
4. ensure that the necessary resources and support are available, including time to accomplish the task;
5. work collaboratively with a critical mass of diverse constituents (teachers, community members, parents, etc.);
6. understand that change is difficult and will be met with resistance;
7. acknowledge that teachers must "own" the intended reform;
8. ensure that excessive authority is not imposed from above;
9. provide the professional development and education necessary to properly implement the intended reform;
10. remember that structural changes will not ensure fundamental changes in the purposes, priorities, and functioning of a school by themselves; and
11. acknowledge that reform is a developmental process.

This information was important for the research in this study because the participating site is a middle school, and middle school teachers can respond differently to change than elementary or high school teachers. As previously stated, one reason for the difference may be due to the middle school teacher focusing on one content and having 100 or more students per day rather than having their homeroom group of students all day and teaching multiple subjects. Therefore, continuing the look specifically at change initiated at the middle school level was important for understanding any differences in leadership responsibilities that may be specific to middle school. According to the responsibilities identified by Marzano and colleagues (2003), the 11 behaviors listed above fall into the following categories: culture, flexibility, focus, input, optimizer, situational awareness, change agent, relationships, resources, and communication.

In "Supporting Change for Classroom Assessments" by Sato and Atkin (2007), a case study is presented in which the teachers initiated the change. It looked at how change occurs, from inspiration to implementation, and the support teachers need to implement the change. The leadership responsibilities for supporting the implementation schoolwide included relationships, input, resources, knowledge of curriculum, instruction, and assessment, and involvement in curriculum, instruction, and assessment.

In a quantitative study conducted by Gerla, Gilliam, and Wright (2006), the support needed for successfully preparing teachers for change was examined. The study targeted professional development as the most catalyst for initiating change and found that without an intentional focus on preparing and equipping teachers with the knowledge necessary for the new reform initiatives, the effective implementation of the change may be compromised. The study found that providing feedback to teachers as the change is initially implemented was important. The following administrative responsibilities were critical for implementing effective change: knowledge of curriculum, instruction, and assessment, involvement in curriculum, instruction, and assessment, monitoring/evaluating, and communication.

Fullan (2001, 2002) has conducted research on leadership responsibilities necessary to sustain change over time. Though his work does not focus specifically on the fidelity to the change, the research is important for this study as it identifies what behaviors are necessary in a leader for the change to be sustained over time. In *Leading in a Culture of Change*, Fullan (2001) wrote, "All successful schools experience 'implementation dips' as they move forward. The implementation dip is literally a dip in performance and confidence as one encounters an innovation that requires new skills and new understandings" (p. 6).

Effective leaders change their behavior to match the times when implementation of the change initiative is high and when it is low (the implementation dip). This change in support from the administrator creates a sense of security, but requires situational awareness. Fullan (2001, 2002) found that a reculturing in the site of the change had to happen as faculty adopt new behaviors associated with the change. Without this reculturing, the change is seen as a temporary inconvenience rather than a new way of doing things. The leader's behaviors can either support reculturing or prevent it from happening. For the administrative behaviors used in the checklist for the study, the leadership responsibilities include: culture, order, focus, input, affirmation, relationship, change agent, flexibility, situational awareness, and intellectual stimulation.

METHODS AND RESEARCH DESIGN

I selected a mixed methods approach for this study because quantitative data would not have given depth of insight into the type of administrative responsibilities staff felt were most influential in maintaining fidelity to the new grading procedures they were expected to use. Semistructured interviews of 22 teachers (a qualitative methodology) provided depth of information in the form of reflections found in interviews. This married nicely with the checklists geared to promote reflection in terms of McRel's 21 Leadership Responsibilities provided to six administrators and 48 teachers (a quantitative methodology).

BACKGROUND ON THE SCHOOL

Northwest Middle School is a middle school in Knox County School System located in Knoxville, Tennessee. Northwest serves students in grades six through eight. The principal of the school has been in that position for 2 years, with 2010-2011 being her third year assigned to the school. The school qualifies for Title 1 funding due to 77% of the students receiving free or reduced-price lunch. The ethnic diversity of the school is as follows: White, not Hispanic 63%; Black, not Hispanic 27%; Hispanic 8%; Asian/Pacific Islander 1%; American Indian/Alaskan Native <1%. There are five full-time administrators, one part-time administrator shared with another Knox County middle school, 75 staff members, and around 860 students. The mobility rate of the students at the school fluctuates, with enrollment between 780 to 860 throughout the school year. The school has been marked by several disruptive, negative changes over many years. Two years ago, the school was improving in academic progress, but had not met attendance requirements for annual yearly progress. The school was labeled School Improvement 1 under No Child Left Behind and was placed under Corrective Action mandates. These included identifying specific objectives students would master during each 9-week grading period, creating a pre- and postassessment, and designing standards-based grade cards to inform parents of progress with the targeted objectives. This mandate happened during the first year the current administrator was assigned to the building.

Prior to the current administrator being assigned to the school, no principal had stayed in the building longer than 1 year (in the past 7 years); therefore, the school was in crisis. The staff had been left without professional norms for several years. In the community, the school was seen as a place no teacher or student would want to be, if given another option.

In response to the struggles, Knox County Schools made Northwest Middle School a Teacher Advancement Program (TAP) school. TAP is a program that provides professional development and individual coaching for developing teacher effectiveness, using an evaluation model approved by the Tennessee Department of Education. Though TAP had been in place for 2 years prior to my first year in the building, some of the leaders used perceived power inappropriately and there was minimal administrative support or guidance for TAP initiatives.

The staff had, in essence, a "bad taste in their mouths" when it came to supportive administration and with effective implementation of district policies. The new administrator immediately began working to improve academic performance in addition to improving collegiality and professionalism of staff. In the tenure of the current principal, the school successfully adopted Positive Behavioral Intervention Supports (PBIS) to redirect students to appropriate behavior. This behavioral support system reduced office referrals by approximately 40% during the first year it was implemented (2009-2010).

Professional Learning Communities between similar content and grade levels were instituted during the 2008-2009 school year and have continued to improve in structure and content, including vertical teams during the 2010-2011 school year. During the years 2008-2009 and 2009-2010, administration began to include faculty in school-based decisions in leadership meetings, which included team leaders and department chairs in addition to the TAP Master and TAP Mentor teachers. To increase consistency among the different leaders in the building, professional development for leaders began through monthly meetings during the 2009-2010 school year. This leadership structure was used to disseminate information and make school-level recommendations and/or decisions, and greater emphasis was placed on prioritizing teacher-led initiatives beginning the latter part of the 2009-2010 school year. One of the initiatives was the grading procedures recommendations.

For the qualitative data in this study, a purposeful sampling of 22 staff members which included all content areas and grade levels (including related arts and special education) were interviewed by a person who is not assigned to Northwest Middle School to attempt to understand why staff selected the particular responsibilities they felt were most important in helping them maintain fidelity to the new grading procedures. The participants in the qualitative data are shown below in Table 4.1.

DATA COLLECTION

The participants in this study included six administrators and 75 teachers. All of the administrators and staff completed a self-reflection checklist. Of the 75 faculty members, 22 were purposefully selected for interviews. For the initial interviews, teachers were selected based on a range of grade levels and content areas. Also, included in the sample are those who were on the grading procedures committee and those who have

Table 4.1.   Purposeful Sampling of Teachers

Math	Reading	Language Arts	Science	Social Studies	Special Education	Related Arts
6th grade-V, C	6th grade-V	6th grade-V	6th grade-N	6th grade-V	All grades/department chair	Read 180-V
6th grade-N	7th grade-N	7th grade-V, C	7th grade-V	7th grade-N		Health-V
7th grade-V	8th grade-N	8th grade-V, C	8th grade-N	8th grade-V		Technology-V
8th grade-N						Physical education-V
						Art-N

Note: V = teacher with over 5 years of experience. N = teacher with less than 5 years of experience. C = grading procedures committee

expressed concerns over this change. For Phase 1, a checklist identifying McRel's 21 responsibilities of effective leadership was given to the faculty at the school. They were asked to identify which of the responsibilities they provided faculty in support of the new grading procedures. The self-reflection was anonymous and a folder was provided to return the checklist to better ensure accurate reflection. For Phase 2, an interview questionnaire was created to elicit responses from a purposeful sampling of staff members. In the interviews, they were asked to provide feedback regarding what they felt was most beneficial in support from administrators when maintaining fidelity to the new grading procedures. Some questions in the interview protocol (i.e., questions two and seven) were designed to identify the teacher's receptiveness to the change. If a teacher is opposed to change and it is apparent in the response to those two questions, it may impact the other answers. For example, if a teacher reports everything is difficult about the new grading procedures and everyone feels the same way, yet other interviews do not report the same feelings, the leadership responsibilities (if any) that support this teacher may not be reflective of the majority of the sample. A response like this would be considered an outlier and will be identified as such in the findings. To ensure staff members have the opportunity to answer with honest thoughts and perceptions, a person who is not assigned to Northwest Middle School was asked to conduct the interviews. The interviewer was asked to continue interviewing staff members until data saturation was reached. A visual model representing the data collection for this mixed methods approach is shown in Figure 4.1.

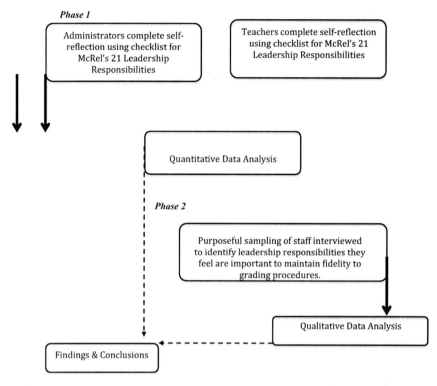

Figure 4.1.   Visual model for the mixed methods research study.

DATA ANALYSIS

During Phase 1, the responses from administrators and teachers were analyzed using a Fisher's Exact Test to determine which differences were statistically significant. After the checklists were collected from both staff and administrators, a Fisher's Test was used to determine the level of significance between the differences of each leadership responsibility identified by staff and administrators. For the Fisher's Exact Test, the alpha level was set at $a = .0024$. A Bonferroni adjustment was made by using .05 divided by 21 (the number of items on the checklist) to provide a more robust level of significance in effort to avoid a Type 1 error that might result in identifying statistically significant differences when they, in fact, the difference is not substantial. During Phase 2, the interviews were analyzed to look for trends to determine possible reasons for differences in administrator and teacher responses regarding the support that best supported fidelity to the new grading procedures. Quotes from teachers were used to support possible reasons for the differences in responses. For the interviews, the behaviors teachers report best supported them in maintaining fidelity to the new grading procedures were both recorded and transcribed. An Excel file was used to capture the leadership responsibilities mentioned during the interviews and quotes were used to explain the reason for faculty responses, which provided insight into the reason for any differences between faculty and administrators. An interview protocol was used to ensure validity and reliability in the responses from staff members.

FINDINGS

The findings from data analysis were organized around the questions in bold type below. What follows is a discussion of the findings and the questions they answered:

Are there differences in the behaviors administrator's report as important compared to teacher responses?

From the list of 21 responsibilities, administrators reported Communication, discipline, flexibility, ideals/beliefs, monitors/evaluations, and relationships were the ones most important to support teachers in maintaining fidelity to change (see Table 4.2). The responsibilities most of the staff felt were important were discipline, input, and visibility. In five of the 21 responsibilities, the difference in what administrators felt were important in maintaining fidelity to the new grading procedures compared to the ones the staff felt were important were statistically significant. The responsibilities that both staff and teachers responded were important were discipline, input, and visibility. The responsibilities that had the most statistically significant differences in administrator and teacher responses were flexibility; ideals/beliefs; monitors/evaluates; and curriculum, instruction, and assessment; and relationships. For all but one of these areas, all of the administrators felt the responsibility was important, but less than one-fourth of the teachers felt it was important.

DIFFERENCES BETWEEN ADMINISTRATOR
AND TEACHER RESPONSES

For the qualitative data, interviews were conducted with 22 teachers who varied in content and grade levels. In these interviews, the participants were asked questions to determine the reasons for differences in adminis-

Table 4.2. Administrator and Teacher Responses

Leadership Responsibility	Administrator Responses		Teacher Responses		
	n of 6	%	n of 48	%	p
Affirmation	5	0.83	12	0.25	.0093
Change agent	4	0.67	4	0.08	.0029
Communication	6	1.00	18	0.38	.0052
Contingent rewards	3	0.50	11	0.23	.1727
Culture	4	0.67	14	0.29	.0873
CIA	5	0.83	7	0.15	.0013
Discipline	6	1.00	24	0.50	.0282
Flexibility	6	1.00	2	0.04	.0004
Focus	3	0.50	12	0.25	.3312
Ideals/beliefs	6	1.00	10	0.21	.0003
Input	5	0.83	26	0.54	.2241
Intellectual stimulation	4	0.67	8	0.17	.0178
K of CIA	5	0.83	18	0.38	.0728
Monitors/evaluates	6	1.00	13	0.27	.0011
Optimizer	4	0.67	9	0.19	.0248
Order	4	0.67	12	0.25	.0563
Outreach	2	0.33	9	0.19	.5900
Relationships	6	1.00	11	0.23	.0005
Resources	3	0.50	15	0.31	.3883
Situational awareness	5	0.83	9	0.19	.0032
Visibility	5	0.83	22	0.46	.1917

Note: This is using a Fisher's exact test, two-tailed with $a = .0024$.

trator responses compared to the teachers. Ten of the 22 teachers said they are following the new grading procedures because it was "the rule" or because "they were told to" rather than it being followed because they believe it will benefit students in reporting academic progress. One teacher said,

> I follow the rules. They told me to [implement the grading procedures]. It's the expectation.

Another teacher said,

> I haven't really been *supported*, just told what to do. I do it, so I don't need the support.

This may be one of the reason for the differences in administrator versus teacher responses. If teachers are following a procedure because it is "a rule" rather than something they believe in, the support they feel would be important would be different from what administrators feel is important for supporting an initiative all agree help students.

All but two of the responses indicated the teachers like the new procedures and feel they bring consistency to grading practices. One teacher said,

> The administrators come in parent conferences and explain the grading procedures. Since we are all doing the same thing, it is a consistent message.

Another teacher commented,

> This new grading procedure has been most helpful in making the expectations clear!

None of the interviewees suggested abandoning the new procedures or indicated there had been no support. In fact, one teacher said,

> It is not like they gave us the procedures and said, 'Okay, go to it. See you in May.'

Most interviewees suggested areas that would really help support teachers ability to maintain fidelity to the new grading procedures. All but one of the interviewees expressed concern over the requirement of three grades per week being entered in Gradebook due to it being difficult to assess students three times per week every week if they are following Knox County's pacing guide for their content. She said,

> The breakdown of three grades per week sometimes is not conducive to the pacing guide.

Three responses suggested administrators could support teachers in maintaining fidelity to the grading procedures by listening to feedback they (or kids are providing). One teacher said,

> They need to listen to feedback from teachers and kids. Administrators don't come to ask where a grade came from, so it [the new procedures] may not be followed completely.

Another teacher commented,

> Checking grades is not the most important thing [regarding support]. Go into classrooms and see what is being done.

This may be the reason for the difference in some of the responses, including monitors/evaluates and communication. All of the administrators felt both was important, but less than half of the teachers marked them as supportive. The teachers may have felt monitoring/evaluating and communication (the way they are currently being addressed) might not be enough to help maintain fidelity to the procedures.

Of the 22 teachers interviewed, every respondent mentioned the emails to remind teachers to follow the new procedures, especially when the grades are not showing in Gradebook, is a form of support. However, five reported the emails are negative and make teachers upset. One said,

> They send nasty emails. Instead of positively supporting us, they negatively support us.

Another teacher said,

> I don't like getting notes about grades. They always sound negative.

Another teacher said,

> Administrators send emails that are sometimes not worded friendly.

For Relationships, only 11 teachers said this responsibility was important for support; whereas, all six administrators highlighted it. Though teachers were asked to identify what would support them, some may have identified what was done rather than what should be done. This may be the reason for the difference in the Relationship indicator in administrator and teacher responses.

> What leadership responsibilities are important to support teachers in maintaining fidelity to a change initiative?

The responsibilities that both administrators and teachers valued as important are input, knowledge of curriculum, instruction, and assessment, and visibility. Having the opportunity for teachers to be involved in the change process supports fidelity once the change has been implemented as it better assures teachers understand the purpose behind the change and are a part of the process. Being knowledgeable regarding the curriculum, instruction, and assessment being taught allows administrators to understand the specific dynamics under which the change is being implemented. Finally, being visible in classrooms keeps administrators aware of what actually is being implemented and provides an opportunity for teachers and students to give feedback regarding the issues they may be having with maintaining fidelity to the change initiative.

The responsibilities that both agree are not as important to the specific change in this study (grading procedures) are contingent rewards, focus, outreach, and resources. Only one of the responsibilities (knowledge of curriculum, instruction, and assessment) indicated as important to second-order change was one both teachers and administrators agree was important for maintaining fidelity to the new grading procedures. The findings of this study show the responsibilities needed to support fidelity to a change are specific to the change and the school where it is being implemented.

CONCLUSIONS AND IMPLICATIONS FOR SCHOOL LEADERS

I found that 48% of the responses administrators and faculty gave for what would best support fidelity to the new grading procedure change at Northwest differed. Only 14% of the responsibilities were identified by both administrators and faculty as important to support fidelity to change.

In reviewing the literature for this study, it became apparent that ensuring the climate is ready for change is critical before a reform initiative is introduced. This leadership responsibility called "Culture" was reported as important by administrators, but most faculty did not identify this as an important leadership responsibility. Ensuring that faculty is a part of the change was another consistent thread woven throughout all of the research in the articles read. This was consistent with both the qualitative and quantitative data from this study. Maintaining focus throughout the implementation of change is also necessary both at the beginning of the change in behaviors to sustaining the change past the "implementation dip." This leadership responsibility was not identified as being important in this study.

Another important aspect of successfully implementing change from these reading is to build relationships with those implementing the change. Relationships was identified by administrators as being important; however, only 23% of the teachers felt this was important to maintaining fidelity to the change in grading procedures.

After analyzing the data for this study, there were three leadership responsibilities that were reported as important to supporting faculty when a change is implemented. To increase fidelity to the grading procedures, soliciting and responding to feedback from faculty will show them you value their input on this change. Being visible both in checking

Gradebook and being present in classrooms to see what is being graded and how instruction supports assessment is important to the faculty as they implement the grading procedures change. Finally, making sure each teacher is held accountable for implementing the new grading procedures by providing consistent feedback, especially positive messages acknowledging when a teacher is following the grading procedures without reminders is critical for supporting fidelity to this change. By focusing on these three leadership responsibilities, the second order change implemented at Northwest should increase the possibility of faculty maintaining fidelity to the change.

In sum the lessons learned in this study were (A) teachers should be able to provide input as to how change should be initiated and how change is implemented. (B) Listening to feedback during implementation is important for maintaining fidelity. And finally (C) being a visible presence in the classrooms and seeing what is happening during the time the change is being implemented is a critical part of that process. This will help support faculty as they try to implement a change initiative with fidelity.

GLOSSARY OF TERMS

- Core Content Areas: Academic subjects including language arts, reading, math, science, and social studies.

- McRel's 21 Leadership Responsibilities: These responsibilities of administrator's were identified by a meta-analysis examining the effects of leadership practices on student achievement. After analyzing studies conducted over a 30-year period, McREL identified 21 leadership responsibilities that are significantly associated with student achievement (Marzano, Waters, & McNulty, 2003)

- Professional Learning Communities (PLCs): This is a weekly meeting where teachers collaborate on instruction and assessment to ensure students learn by focusing on the results, or how they perform on preidentified assessment that connects to the content being taught in the course (DuFour, 2004).

- Positive Behavioral Intervention Support (PBIS): A decision making framework that guides selection, integration, and implementation of the best evidence-based academic and behavioral practices for improving important academic and behavior outcomes for all students. It emphasizes four integrated elements: (a) data for decision making, (b) measurable outcomes supported and evaluated by data, (c) practices with evidence that these outcomes are achievable, and (d) systems that efficiently and effectively support implementation of these practices (OSEP, 2010).

- Read 180: A reading intervention program designed by Scholastic, Inc. used by Northwest Middle School in addition to the core reading class ("Scholastic Read 180", 2010).

- Related Arts: The classes at Northwest Middle School that do not include the core content areas. These classes include Read 180 (i.e., a reading intervention that does not replace the core reading class), technology, physical education, music, health, and art.

- Second-Order Change: A change that requires a significant break from current or past practices (Marzano, 2000).

- Teacher Advancement Program (TAP): Also known as The System for Teacher and Student Advancement, TAP includes four elements that work together to develop educators:
  o Multiple career paths: opportunities for more responsibilities and commensurate pay;
  o Ongoing applied professional growth: continuous on-site professional development embedded within the school day;
  o Instructionally focused accountability: fair evaluations based on clearly defined, research-based standards; and
  o Performance-based compensation: salaries and bonuses tied to responsibilities, instructional performance and student achievement growth (tap, 2010).

Leadership Behaviors Associated with 21 Responsibilities

Responsibilities	*Practices Associated With Responsibilities*
Affirmation	• Systematically and fairly recognizes and celebrates accomplishments of teachers and staff
	• Systematically and fairly recognizes and celebrates accomplishments of students
	• Systematically and fairly acknowledges failures and celebrates accomplishments of the school

Change agent	• Consciously challenges the status quo
	• Is comfortable leading change initiatives with uncertain outcomes
	• Systematically considers new and better ways of doing things
Communication	• Is easily accessible to teachers and staff
	• Develops effective means for teachers and staff to communicate with one another
	• Maintains open and effective lines of communication with teachers and staff
Contingent rewards	• Recognizes individuals who excel
	• Uses performance vs. seniority as the primary criterion for reward and advancement
	• Uses hard work and results as the basis for reward and recognition
Culture	• Promotes cooperation among teachers and staff
	• Promotes a sense of well-being
	• Promotes cohesion among teachers and staff
	• Develops and understanding of purpose
	• Develops a shared vision of what the school could be like
Curriculum, instruction, assessment	• Is involved with teachers in designing curricular activities and addressing instructional issues in their classrooms
	• Is involved with teachers to address assessment issues
Discipline	• Protects instructional time from interruptions
	• Protects/shelters teachers from distractions
Flexibility	• Is comfortable with major changes in how things are done
	• Encourages people to express opinions that may be contrary to those held by individuals in positions of authority
Focus	• Establishes high, concrete goals and the expectation that all students will meet them
	• Establishes high, concrete goals for all curricula, instruction, and assessment
	• Establishes high, concrete goals for the general functioning of the school
	• Keeps everyone's attention focused on established goals
Ideas/beliefs	• Holds strong professional ideals and beliefs about schooling, teaching, and learning
	• Shares ideals and beliefs about schooling, teaching, and learning with teachers, staff, and parents
	• Demonstrates behaviors that are consistent with ideals and beliefs

Input	• Provides opportunities for input from teachers and staff on all important decisions
	• Provides opportunities for teachers and staff to be involved in policy development
	• Involves the school leadership team in decision making
Intellectual stimulation	• Stays informed about current research and theory regarding effective schooling
	• Continually exposes teachers and staff to cutting-edge ideas about how to be effective
	• Systematically engages teachers and staff in discussions about current research and theory
	• Continually involves teachers and staff in reading articles and books about effective practices
Knowledge of curriculum, instruction, and assessment	• Is knowledgeable about curriculum and instructional practices
	• Is knowledgeable about assessment practices
	• Provides conceptual guidance for teachers regarding effective classroom practice
Monitors/evaluates	• Monitors and evaluates the effectiveness of the curriculum
	• Monitors and evaluates the effectiveness of instruction
	• Monitors and evaluates the effectiveness of assessment
Optimizer	• Inspires teachers and staff to accomplish things that might seem beyond their grasp
	• Portrays a positive attitude about the ability of teachers and staff to accomplish substantial things
	• Is a driving force behind major initiatives
Order	• Provides and enforces clear structures, rules, and procedures for teachers, staff, and students
	• Establishes routines regarding the running of the school that teachers and staff understand and follow.
Outreach	• Ensures that the school is in compliance with district and state mandates
	• Advocates on behalf of the school in the community
	• Interacts with parents in ways that enhance their support for the school
	• Ensures that the central office is aware of the school's accomplishments

Relationship	• Remains aware of personal needs of teachers and staff
	• Maintains personal relationships with teachers and staff
	• Is informed about significant personal issues in the lives of teachers and staff
	• Acknowledges significant events in the lives of teachers and staff
Resources	• Ensures that teachers and staff have necessary materials and equipment
	• Ensures that teachers have necessary professional development opportunities that directly enhance their teaching
Situational awareness	• Is aware of informal groups and relationships among teachers and staff
	• Is aware of issues in the school that have not surfaced but could create discord
	• Can predict what could go wrong from day to day
Visibility	• Makes systematic and frequent visits to classroom
	• Is highly visible around the school
	• Has frequent contact with students

REFERENCES

Brighton, C. M. (2003). The effects of middle school teachers' beliefs on classroom practices. *Journal of the Education of the Gifted, 27*(2-3), 177-206.

Brown, K. M., & Anfara, V. A., Jr. (2003). Paving the way for change: Visionary leadership in action at the middle level. *NASSP Bulletin, 87*(635), 16-34.

Bridgeland, J. M., Dilulio, J. J., Jr. & Morison, K. B. (2006). Civic enterprises: The silent epidemic: Perspectives from high school dropouts. Retrieved from http://www.civicenterprises.net/pdfs/thesilentepidemic3-06.pdf

Colantonio, J. N. (2005). On target: Combined instructional supervision and staff development. *Principal Leadership (Middle Sch Ed), 5*(9), 30-34.

DuFour, R. (2004). What is a "professional learning community?" Retrieved from http:// pdonline.ascd.org/ pd_online/secondary_ reading/ el200405 _dufour.html

Finnigan, K. S, & Stewart, T. J. (2009). Leading change under pressure: An examination of principal leadership in low-performing schools. *Journal of School Leadership, 19*(5), 586-618.

Fullan, M. (2001). *Leading in a culture of change.* San Francisco, CA: Jossey-Bass.

Fullan, M. (2002). Leadership and sustainability. *Principal Leadership, 3*(4), 1-9.

Gerla, J. P., Gilliam, B., & Wright, G. (2006). Project summit: A cooperative effort to effect teacher change. *Education, 127*(2), 280-286.

Gravetter, F. J., & Wallnau, L. B. (2011). *Essentials of statistics for the behavioral sciences.* Belmont, CA: Cengage Learning.

U.S. Department of Education. (2008). Reading first impact study interim report. Institute of Education Sciences. Retrieved from http://ies.ed.gov/ncee/pdf/20084016.pdf

U.S. Department of Education. (2008). Appropriations for major programs, by state of jurisdiction: Fiscal year 2008. Institute of Education Sciences. Retrieved from http://nces.ed.gov/programs/digest/d09/tables/dt09_378.asp?referrer=list

Marzano, R. J. (2000). *Transforming classroom grading*. Alexandria, VA: Association for Supervision and Curriculum Development.

Marzano, R. J., Waters, J. T., & McNulty, B. A. (2003). Balanced leadership: What 30 years of research tells us about the effect of leadership on student achievement. Aurora, CO: Midcontinent Research for Education and Learning. Retrieved from http://www.mcrel.org/products/144/

Marzano, R., Waters, J., & McNulty, B. (2005). *School leadership that works: From research to results*. Alexandria, VA: Association for Supervision and Curriculum Development.

National Commission on Excellence in Education. (1983). A nation at risk: The imperative for educational reform. Retrieved from http://www2.ed.gov/pubs/NatAtRisk/index.html

Sarason, S. (1971). *The culture of the school and the problem of change*. Boston, MA: Allyn & Bacon.

Sarason, S. (1990). *The predictable failure of educational reform*. San Francisco, CA: Jossey-Bass.

Sato, M., & Atkin, J. M. (2007). Supporting change in classroom assessment. *Educational Leadership, 64*(4), 76-79.

Scholastic (2010). Scholastic READ 180 | Proven reading intervention software program for grades 3-12. Retrieved from http://teacher.scholastic.com/products/read180/

Smith-Maddox, R. (1999). An inquiry-based reform effort: Creating the conditions for re-culturing and restructuring schools. *The Urban Review, 31*(3), 283-304.

Stein, M. K., & Nelson, B. S. (2003). Leadership content knowledge. *Educational Evaluation and Policy Analysis, 25*(4), 423-448.

The System for Teacher and Student Advancement. (2010). TAP: The System for Teacher and Student Advancement. Retrieved from http://www.tapsystem.org/about/about.taf?page=history

U.S. Department of Education, Office of Special Education Programs. (2010). OSEP technical assistance center on positive behavioral interventions & supports: Effective schoolwide interventions. Retrieved from http://www.pbis.org

IMPLEMENTATION AND OBSTACLES OF ASSESSMENT PRACTICE IN THE SEVENTH AND EIGHTH-GRADE

Paula Jo Brown

This chapter focuses on a study of the obstacles seventh and eighth-grade math teachers encounter as they implement formative assessment practices. The study identifies three areas in which the math teachers will conceivably encounter obstacles: technical, political, and cultural and measures the perceived magnitude of the obstacles.

My review of studies on educational reform including reform of assessment practices agrees that teachers are central to the success of reform efforts (Fullan, 2001). I also found that during the implementation of the reform, teachers would inevitably encounter three types of obstacles: technical, political, and cultural. Johnson (2006) advised that support for teachers implementing reform was needed in order for change to take place. For school leaders to be effective in leading change they must anticipate the obstacles teachers encounter and understand the implications of change. The beliefs, experiences, and knowledge of the individuals or groups expected to execute the change can be a barrier and must be con-

Great Leaders Equal Great Schools:
Alliances and Discourse for Educational Reform, pp. 79–101

sidered in the process. Exploring the obstacles seventh and eighth-grade math teachers encounter while implementing formative assessment practices and identifying the magnitude of those obstacles provide school leaders an opportunity to develop strategies to support teachers in addressing or eliminating the obstacles to change.

SUCCESSES AND DIFFICULTIES

This endeavor has afforded me an opportunity to do something I enjoy immensely. I enjoy learning. Through this work, I have formulated a clear definition and understanding of formative assessments and identified examples of effective formative assessment practices. The results of the study supported prior research identifying technical, cultural and political themes as specific areas wherein teachers experience obstacles in implementing change and provided me as an instructional leader with feedback to better support teachers with the implementation of the change in future assessment practices. If I were to repeat this study, I would strive to include a larger sample of from a variety of different subject areas. I would also increase the number of classroom observations conducted and observe them over a longer time. These improvements would likely yield a more precise image of teachers' knowledge and application of formative assessment practices.

SKILLS AND SKILL SETS UTILIZED

I decided on a sequential mixed method design for this study. This method provided the qualitative means (interviews and classroom observations) to explore obstacles encountered by seventh and eighth-grade math teachers implementing formative assessment practices and the quantitative tools (likert scale) to determine the magnitude of the obstacles experienced by the math teachers. Combining the two approaches allowed me to confirm and complement the findings of each approach, strengthening the conclusion and implications for practice.

The hiring of a new superintendent yielded a new vision for Knox County Schools. The Knox County school board adopted the vision, Building on Strength: Excellence for All Students, December of 2008 as the district strategic plan. This 5-year strategic plan was divided into four goals: focus on the student, engaged parents and community, effective educators, and infrastructure to support student learning.

Within the goal of focusing on the student consisted of higher expectations for learning and the implementation of instructional strategies that produced increased academic rigor. This includes the development of a system of formative assessments to guide teachers' instructional methods and informed student learning. According to the Knox County Schools Five Year Strategic Plan (2009):

> Teachers need to be able to continuously assess student progress toward our academic standards. Unlike summative assessments which provide a "snap-shot" of student achievement at a point in time, usually long after the student has learned the content, formative assessments allow for a virtually real-time check on student learning. (p. 10)

Explanations of formative assessment abound, resulting in multiple and sometimes conflicting understandings (Chappuis & Chappuis, 2007). Because of these differing definitions and views, practices labeled as formative assessment in schools vary. There is a common misconception among administrators and teachers that the test itself is formative. Effective formative assessment programs involve more than the administration of additional tests within an existing program throughout the school year. Chappuis and Chappuis (2007) warned that assessments would produce no formative benefits if teachers and administrators merely administer them, report the results, and then continue with instruction as previously planned.

Due to different mandates such as the No Child Left Behind Act and Adequately Yearly Progress (AYP) goals in math and reading/language arts, schools and classrooms are being held more accountable. As a result, states and school districts were given incentives to implement and expand formative assessment practices to improve student learning (Dorn, 2010). According to Black and Wiliam (1998), when teachers use formative assessment appropriately it is one of the most powerful tools available to guide classroom decisions.

As politicians and the federal government encourage states and school districts to raise learning standards through formative assessments, principals, teachers, students and parents are being asked to develop new ideas about assessing student learning and these measures are used in classrooms. Schools in Knox County were asked to implement a statewide formative assessment schedule designed by the State Department of Education. This schedule evaluates students in reading/language arts and math three times per year. Teams of teachers participate in training sessions after each test administration to develop strategies to assist other classroom teachers in using the results to improve instruction and student learning. The problem is that there is a lack of consistency in what formative assessment should look like in the classroom.

Many researchers and advocates for formative assessments argued that the primary benefit of formative assessments allowed students to control and improve their own learning (Stiggins, 2002). The most common use of the term that we find today assumes that "assessment becomes formative when the information is used to adapt teaching and learning to meet students' needs" (Frey & Schmitt, 2007). Stiggins (2002) suggested that we could realize unprecedented gains in achievement if we turn the current day-to-day classroom assessment process into a more powerful tool of assessment for learning. Chappuis and Chappuis (2007) who use the terms assessment for learning and formative assessment interchangeably, indicated that assessment for learning is formative assessment at its most valuable. Stiggins (2002) disagreed that they were not the same. Instead, he asserted that assessment for learning was significantly more than testing more frequently to provide teachers with evidence so they can revise instruction.

The obstacles encountered by teachers while implementing assessment reform became a major concern for me as I begin to observe classrooms and witnessed no change in instructional or assessment practices. Research has shown that teachers are central to the success of educational reform (Fullan, 2001). Findings from the National Science Education Standards suggested that most teachers were not implementing reform or doing it poorly. I found that many teachers have little knowledge of effective assessment practices for learning therefore; the application of effective formative assessment strategies was nonexistent. What is known from the research is that few teachers are prepared to face the challenges of classroom assessments because teacher preparation programs have placed little or no emphasis on assessment literacy. Principals were of little support since assessment training was virtually nonexistent in administrator training programs. Support for teachers implementing formative assessment reform was needed in order for effective change to take place (Johnson, 2006).

Although the research on the effectiveness of using formative assessment for instructional and intervention decisions was formidable, research on the history of the practice was spotty. Dorn (2010) stated that even with the pressures of high-stakes accountability, the definition of formative assessment was ambiguous, its implementation was inconsistent and the prognosis for future was questionable. There are a number of technical, political, and cultural barriers to implementing any reform. In this study I describe the barriers experienced by seventh and eighth-grade math teachers.

The purpose of this sequential mixed methods study was to explore the obstacles that seventh and eighth-grade math teachers encountered while implementing formative assessments practices. The qualitative phase included interviews and classroom observations to identify obstacles to implementing formative assessment practices within the three types of barriers to reform: technical, political and cultural. The quantitative phase rated the identified barriers on a likert scale of high barrier, medium barrier, low barrier and no barrier.

The sequential mixed methods study in this chapter focused on addressing two questions:

1. What technical, political, and cultural obstacles do Carter Middle School seventh and eighth-grade math teachers encounter during the implementation of formative assessment practices?
2. What is the perceived magnitude of the obstacles encountered by Carter Middle School seventh and eighth-grade math teachers?

One of the limitations involved in this study was the methodology employed to collect data. According to Creswell (2009) bias in the interview data can result from both the researcher (question construction) and the respondent. There can be a tendency within interviews for the respondent to reflect the attitudes or ideas that are perceived to be desired by the researcher. With teacher observations there is always the risk that the events are unfolding differently then how they are being observed.

Another limitation of this study was the method used to collect the data in the quantitative phase of the study. A multipart rubric based on Anderson's (1996) Barriers to Reform study, the Barriers to Implementation of the National Science Education Standards (BINSES) measures the magnitude of the barriers. Although a panel of science education experts determined the validity and reliability of the BINSES rubric, it was created to identify categories and magnitudes of barriers to the implementation of standards based on instruction rather than on formative assessment practices (Anderson, 1996). Within this process the researcher identifies teachers' perceptions of barriers from interviews and observations and places them within the categories of the rubric. Then, the researcher rates each category of barriers as high, medium, low or no barriers to implementing formative assessment practices.

A final limitation of this study was the use of nonprobability sampling methods. A combination of two nonprobability methods was used in this study: convenience and purposeful concept/theory-based sampling. According to Creswell (2009) the use of nonprobability sampling methods limits the ability to generalize findings to other subjects and to larger populations. There is also a greater likelihood of error due to researcher or subject partiality (Creswell, 2009). An identified delimitation of this study is that the sampling was purposefully limited to seventh and eighth-grade math teachers. This grade level and subject area was chosen because of the anticipated impact of implementing formative assessment practices on student achievement in math.

THE LITERATURE

There were very few studies linked specifically to obstacles encountered during the implementation of formative assessment practices. The identified studies focused on educational reform and assessment reform in general. Dorn (2010) used a historical and organizational perspective to explore political dilemmas of formative assessment. In this article, he referenced two case studies indicating how educators understood and responded to different types of formative assessment that were implemented without outside supervision, technical assistance and professional development. Brunner and colleagues (2005) used interviews, classroom observations, and a survey requiring a response to a likert scale in a study of how teachers respond to summaries of student achievement called the Grow Reports.

A study conducted by Johnson (2006) sought to answer the question: "What barriers do science teachers encounter when implementing standards-based instruction while participating in effective professional development experiences?" This question served as the inspiration for the methodology I selected to use in this study.

WHAT IS FORMATIVE ASSESSMENT?

As the literature on formative assessment was reviewed, researchers discussed and identified common characteristics that defined formative assessment. Also included in the discussion was a debate as to whether formative assessment was the equivalent to assessment for learning. This literature review was conducted for the purpose of providing a clear definition of formative assessment and formative assessment practices and to distinguish between formative assessment and assessment for learning during the research process.

The most common description of formative assessment found in the review is that assessments become formative when the information was used to adapt teaching and learning to meet the needs of students (Boston, 2002). Bell and Cowie (2001) defined formative assessments as "the process used by teachers and students to recognize and respond to student learning in order to enhance that learning, during the learning" (p. 537). Students are central to the formative assessment process.

Another term used in the literature on formative assessment is assessment for learning. Stiggins (2002) emphasized, "It is assessment for learning which most directly affects learning" (p. 761). He stressed that if formative assessments were designed to provide feedback only to teachers, then they were not the same as assessments for learning.

Although assessments providing feedback to alter instruction were useful to teachers, and were described as formative, it was not the same formative assessments that help students improve learning. Frey and Schmitt (2007) stated that formative assessments work best when they were treated as assessments for learning and were most effective when students use the information to adjust their own learning behaviors and teachers use the data to adjust their own teaching behaviors. Research revealed that achievement gains were maximized in contexts where educators increased the use of classroom assessments for learning. This included "providing students with frequent informative feedback verses infrequent judgmental feedback, and involve students deeply in the classroom assessment, record keeping, and communication process" (Stiggins 2002, p. 761).

The review of literature suggests that not assessments that not all formative assessments are assessments for learning. Teachers' merely using assessment data to alter instruction was not enough to improve student learning. If formative assessments are to be effective and a true assessment for learning, students must be involved in the process.

FORMATIVE ASSESSMENT PRACTICES

The review of literature revealed a wide range of formative assessment practices. Formative assessment practices, promoted by the National Science Education Standards (NSES) included gathering information on student understanding, analyzing that information, and then using it to guide instruction (Trimble, Gay, & Matthews, 2005).

Stiggins (2002) described assessment practices that teachers implemented to assess for learning as:

- understanding and articulating in advance of teaching the achievement targets that their students are to hit;
- informing their students about those learning goals, in terms that students understand, from the very beginning of the teaching and learning process;
- becoming assessment literate and thus able to transform their expectations into assessment exercises and scoring procedures that accurately reflects student achievement;
- using classroom assessments to build students' confidence in themselves as learners and help them take responsibility for their own learning, so as to lay a foundation for lifelong learning;

- translating classroom assessment results into frequent descriptive feedback (versus judgmental feedback) for students, providing them with specific insights as to how to improve;
- continuously adjusting instruction based on the results of classroom assessments;
- engaging students in regular self-assessment, with standards held constant so that students can watch themselves grow over time and thus feel in charge of their own success; and
- actively involving students in communicating with their teacher and their families about their achievement status and improvement (pp. 761-762).

Black and Wiliam recognized student self-assessment as an essential component of formative assessment practice. "When anyone is trying to learn, feedback about the effort has three elements: recognition of the desired goal, evidence about present position, and some understanding of a way to close the gap between the two" (p. 143). Strategies for addressing the three elements were further emphasized by Chappuis (2005) and Chappuis and Chappuis (2007). In these articles, the authors shared three basic questions that students should be able to answer when formative assessment practices are effective: (1) Where am I going? (2) Where am I now? and (3) How can I close the gap?

OBSTACLES TO EDUCATIONAL AND ASSESSMENT REFORM

The research on barriers to education reform was extensive. Studies on barriers to reform have identified three types of barriers: technical, political, and cultural. Characteristics of the three types of barriers are evident throughout the literature and are used in this study as criteria for identifying teachers' obstacles to implementing formative assessment practices.

The first dimension of Anderson's framework fell in the technical area. This included the teacher's ability to teach constructively and implement reform. It examined the teacher's content knowledge and pedagogical knowledge to determine the impact on implementation of reform. Lack of content knowledge or limited pedagogical knowledge makes it difficult for a teacher to implement instructional reform (Johnson, 2006).

Anderson's second dimension of barriers, related to instructional reform, consist of political issues. Teachers identify the lack of school or district level support as the primary political barrier (Johnson, 2006). Other political barriers identified in the review of literature included resources available such as plan time, equipment, and supplies and materials to implement the reform. Dorn (2010) specifically discussed the political dilemma of school and district policy as a barrier to the successful implementation of formative assessment practices. He suggested that states and school districts should develop policies that encourage an accountability system that is based entirely on structured formative assessments. An example shared is that a state could require that teachers collect formative data weekly or twice a week for children who needed extra monitoring and make monthly instructional decisions based on the information. Dorn (2010) also suggested that teachers and principals be evaluated on their usage of structured formative assessments to make instructional decisions and effectiveness for improving student achievement. The strongest claims for improvement in carefully designed studies have occurred when structured formative assessment coupled with strong guidance instruction (Dorn 2010, p. 328).

Anderson's third feature concerning cultural dimensions was considered the most important to implementing change. This area closely examined teachers' existing beliefs and values regarding teaching. Findings from studies of teacher learning and change identified teacher beliefs as a key aspect in whether or not instructional practices will be changed and how they will be executed and sustained (Fullan, 2001).

In the review of literature associated with cultural barriers to implementing formative assessment, Black and Wiliam (1998) discussed two basic issues as the source of problems associated with changing to a system of formative assessment.

> The first is the nature of each teacher's belief about learning. If the teacher assumes that knowledge is to be transmitted and learned, that understanding will develop later, and that clarity of exposition accompanied by rewards for patient reception are the essentials of good teaching, then formative assessment is hardly necessary. The other issue relates to the beliefs teachers hold about the potential of all their pupils for learning. The "fixed I.Q." view a belief that each pupil has a fixed, inherited intelligence that cannot be altered much by schooling. On the other hand, there is the "untapped potential" view, a belief that starts from the assumption that so called ability is a complex of skills that can be learned. (Black & Wiliam 1998, pp. 145-146)

The literature argued that all students can learn more effectively if the obstacles to learning were removed. Ways of managing formative assessments that work with the assumptions of "untapped potential" do help all students to learn and can give particular help to those who struggle (Black & Wiliam 1998, p. 146).

METHODS

In this study, I attempted to expand the research on formative assessment practices and to close the gap between formative assessment theory and practice. With a dramatic expansion in what districts and states claim is data-driven use of formative assessment, many opportunities exist to study the use of formative assessment in schools under a range of conditions (Dorn, 2010). Since the passage of the No Child Left Behind Act there have been very few studies focused on the implementation of formative assessments and the barriers experienced during practice. Frey and Schmitt (2007) shared an editorial from Bligh (2001) about the gaps between theory and practice in classroom assessments:

> It appears that assessment is an example of a subject where there are two camps: one full of well meaning, earnest teachers and researchers immersed in the language and culture of assessment practice; the other full of well-meaning earnest teachers facing the day to day practical problems of running assessments. (Frey & Schmitt, 2007, p. 413)

The methodology used to explore the barriers of seventh and eighth-grade math teachers during the implementation of formative assessment practices was of great significance. Specifically, this study used a unique sequential mixed methods approach. In this approach one type of data collection was used to build on another.

Qualitative data was collected through interviews and classroom observations to identify barriers to implementing formative assessment practices. Data from interviews and observations was categorized into a multipart rubric to generate quantitative data. Quantitative data was collected using the BINSES rubric to identify the magnitude of the barriers within a likert scale of high, medium, low or no barrier.

Using the sequential mixed methods approach of combining both quantitative and qualitative data allowed me to better understand the research problems. I triangulated the data by identifying the details of the qualitative research (interviews and observations) and measuring the trends of the quantitative research (magnitude of barriers). This methodology provided the most appropriate tools for investigating the obstacles encountered by teachers when implementing formative assessment practices and identifying the degree of those obstacles.

The study took place at Carter Middle School, which is at the center of the rural Carter community where the campus is shared with Carter Elementary School and Carter High School. Average Daily Membership (ADM) is over 800 students and the school has experienced an increase of approximately 40 students each year for the past 2 years. Student demographics include: 83.8% White; 14.2% African American; 1.2% Hispanic;

.4%Asian/Pacific Islander; and .4% Native American/Alaskan. Students with disabilities comprise of 14.5% of the student population. Over 50% of the students receive free or reduced lunch which makes the school eligible for Title I funding under the new Knox County School's guidelines.

The school is on the No Child Left Behind Act list of Targeted Schools for mathematics. Adequate Yearly Progress (AYP) has not been met in math within the sub groups of Students with Disabilities and Economically Disadvantaged. Average daily membership of 92.3% falls below the AYP benchmark of 93% and attendance shows there has been a gradual decrease over the past 3 years. Carter Middle School implemented a statewide formative assessment tool, Discovery Assessment, to provide information to teachers on students' progress of curriculum standards. Students were assessed three times per year in English and math. Teachers analyzed the data to develop formative instructional practices to improve students' performance. Participants in this study included two seventh-grade and 2 eighth-grade math teachers from Carter Middle School. It was the first year of teaching math for two of the teachers, one from each grade level. The other teachers had 15 or more years of experience teaching math. Each of the participants taught one honors math class in addition to their standard math classes. The participants were identified by alphabet codes (participant A, B, C and D) in order to respect the confidentially of their responses.

DATA COLLECTION

One formal semistructured interview was conducted with each participant to collect qualitative information. Responses to researcher developed open ended questions on technical, political, and cultural obstacles to implementing formative assessment practices were digitally recorded to gather information. Clarifying questions were asked as necessary to assist the researcher in obtaining a better understanding of the participants' responses. Classroom observations of the teachers were conducted in 55 minute increments over the course of the study. Four observations were conducted in each teacher's classroom within a 6-week period. The first two observations were announced and the last two observations were unannounced in order to gain a better understanding of the daily formative assessment practices.

A multipart rubric, based on Anderson's (1996) Barriers to Reform, called the barriers to implementation of the National Science Education Standards Rubric (BINSES) was modified to collect quantitative data in this study to identify categories and magnitude of obstacles to implementing formative assessment practices. Modifications included the addition of instructional skills and assessment issues to the rubric identified from the review of literature as specific to implementing formative assessment practices. The rubric for each of the technical, political and cultural areas has a scale of no obstacle, low obstacle, medium obstacle, or high obstacle to implementation. Identification of teacher obstacles was determined based upon interviews and classroom observations.

DATA ANALYSIS

Notes from the interviews and observations were transcribed and analyzed by the researcher. Some analysis occurred during the data collection phase using reflective and marginal remarks. In this method, date was analyzed by comparing incidents resulting from responses to interview questions, observational records, and the categories pertaining to the magnitude of obstacles from the BINSES rubric. The magnitude of the obstacles was determined by the scale of high obstacle, medium obstacle, low obstacle, or no obstacle on the rubric for each dimension.

Technical obstacles included a lack of instructional skills including content and pedagogical knowledge to implement formative assessment practices. Technical obstacles involved classroom management issues, time for planning, instructional and collaboration time, as well as inadequate professional development experiences. These obstacles are described in Table 5.1 below. For each of the individual categories, teachers were identified as having a high obstacle if they experienced obstacles in three of the subcategories, medium obstacle if they had problems with two of the subcategories, and low obstacle if the experienced issue with one subcategory. Therefore, barriers were identified at the "category" level, which included:

1. instructional skills;
2. classroom management issues and roles for teachers and students;
3. assessment issues;
4. time for planning, instruction, and collaboration; and
5. inadequate in-service.

The framework for the political dimension of obstacles to implementing formative assessment practices pinpoints the concerns teachers may have with administrative support at either the building or district level. Concerns included local leadership and support, lack of resources and lack of schoolwide collaboration and in-service opportunities. Table 5.2 provides a description of the political dimension of obstacles.

Table 5.1. Technical Dimension of Obstacles to Implementing Formative Assessment Practices

Category	Instructional Skills	Classroom Management and Roles for Teachers/Students	Assessment Issues	Time for Planning, Instruction, & Collaboration	Inadequate In-Service
Subcategory 1	Content knowledge	Classroom management issues	Challenge of new assessment	Planning time	Teacher pedagogical needs
Subcategory 2	Pedagogical content	Difficulty of new teacher knowledge and roles to implement formative assessment practices	Use of traditional grading system roles	Instructional time	Teacher content needs
Subcategory 3	Ability to implement formative instructional practices	Difficulty of new student roles in formative assessment practices	Use of formative assessment strategies and tools	Time to collaborate with other math teachers	Teacher ability to implement reform
Subcategory 4	Model formative instructional practices	Difficulty of group work	Development of common formative assessments within grade level		

In the political realm, teachers were identified as having a high obstacle if they experienced barriers in three of the subcategories, a medium obstacle if they had problems with two subcategories and a low obstacle if they experienced difficulty in one subcategory. Political obstacles were determined at the "category" level, which included:

1. local leadership and support;
2. lack of resources;
3. schoolwide collaboration for power; and
4. limited in-service.

Table 5.3 describes the cultural dimension of the framework. The cultural dimension included obstacles that are internal to the teacher. These obstacles focus on teacher beliefs and perceptions about teaching, beliefs about alignment of assessments and instructional practices and beliefs about collaboration with peers.

In the cultural realm, teachers were identified as having a high obstacle if they experienced concern in three of the subcategories, a medium if they had problems with two subcategories, and a low obstacle if they had concern in one subcategory. Cultural obstacles were identified at the "category" level, which included:

1. teacher beliefs and perceptions about teaching;
2. assessment issues;
3. lack of collaboration with others;
4. time for planning, instruction and collaboration; and

Table 5.2.   Political Dimension of Obstacles to Implementing Formative Assessment Practices

Category	Local Leadership and Support	Lack of Resources	Schoolwide Collaboration	Limited In-Service
Subcategory 1	Lack of school leadership and support	Lack of curricular resources	Lack of collaboration during school	PD offerings are limited at school
Subcategory 2	Lack of district leadership and support	Lack of instructional resources	Lack of collaboration during staff meetings	Lack of sustained PD at school
Subcategory 3	Parental resistance to reform	Class size and or space issues	Unresolved conflicts among teachers	Lack of administrative support for PD at school

**Table 5.3.   Cultural Dimension of Obstacles
to Implementing Formative Assessment Practices**

Category	Teacher Beliefs and Perceptions About Teaching	Assessment Issues	Lack of Collaboration With Others
Subcategory 1	Existing beliefs and values regarding teaching	Teacher believes state assessment is not aligned with state math standards	Teacher does not collaborate with math teachers in their grade level
Subcategory 2	Value of textbook	Vocabulary and content drill and practice for test preparation	Teacher does not collaborate with other math teachers in school
Subcategory 3	Preparation ethic	Student assignments are assessed for a grade rather than descriptive feedback	Teacher does not collaborate with other math teachers in the district
Subcategory 4	Ideal vs. reality of classroom	Lack of common formative assessment among grade levels	

5.   inadequate in-service.

A science education panel reviewed the rubric and provided input in the final design validated the BINSES rubric. Reliability for the BINSES was tested after each classroom observation for interrater reliability as well as in the analysis of teacher interview data (Johnson 2006, p. 154). The design and use of the rubric was duplicated in this study to provide consistency in validity and reliability of the instrument.

Phase one of the design included the qualitative collection of data: identification of obstacles through interviews with each of the teachers and four classroom observations. Phase two included the quantitative feature of the design: a multipart rubric to determine the magnitude of the obstacles. Blending the two approaches provided an opportunity for the researcher to confirm and complement the findings of each method.

FINDINGS

Results indicated that obstacles were identified within each of the three dimensions (technical, political and cultural) to implementing formative assessment practices by participants. The categories identified as obstacles by participants were somewhat consistent and the magnitude of the obstacles identified within categories were fairly consistent among participants. Table 5.4 provides a summary of the magnitude of the categories of obstacles. Magnitude was considered high if three or more obstacles were identified within a single category, medium if two obstacles were identified within a category and low if one obstacle was identified within a category. A discussion of the findings by category is provided below.

Obstacles were identified by every participant in each category of the technical dimension of obstacles to implementing formative assessment practices. The category of instructional skills was identified as a medium obstacle for participants A, B, and C. Subcategories identified by each of the participants as obstacles were pedagogical content knowledge and ability to implement formative instructional practices. Participant D recognized instructional strategies as a high obstacle, adding the subcategory of content knowledge to what was recognized by participants A, B, and C.

Classroom management issues and roles of students and teachers in the implementation of formative assessment strategies were identified as a medium obstacle for each of the participants. Participant A identified the subcategories of difficulty of new student roles in formative assessment practices and difficulty of group work as specific technical obstacles to implementing formative assessment practices. Participants B, C, and D identified difficulty of the new teacher knowledge and roles to implement formative assessment practices and difficulty of new student roles in formative assessment practices as specific obstacles. Each of the participants identified the category of grading issues as a medium obstacle and shared common subcategory obstacles: use of traditional grading system roles and use of formative assessment strategies and tools.

Although the category of time for planning/instruction/collaboration was identified as an obstacle for all participants, the magnitude of the obstacles received mixed results. Participant A identified this category as a high obstacle recognizing the following subcategories as specific obstacles: planning time, instructional time, and time to collaborate with other math teachers. This category was identified as a medium obstacle for participants B and D and the subcategories identified by both participants were planning time and instructional time. Participant C identified time for planning/instruction/collaboration as a low obstacle, specifically identifying instructional time as the obstacle to implementing formative assessment practices.

The last category within the technical dimension was inadequate in-service. It was also identified as an obstacle by all participants with mixed results. Participant A identified this category as a low obstacle indicating inadequate in-service supporting the teacher's ability to implement formative assessment practices. Participants B and D identified this category as a medium obstacle. Subcategories identified as obstacles by participant B included: inadequate in-service to address pedagogical needs and the participant's ability to implement formative assessment practices. Participant D identified inadequate in-service to address content needs to implement formative assessment practices and to support the participant's ability to implement formative assessment practices. Participant C identified the category of inadequate in-service as a high obstacle. Specific subcategories identified as obstacles to implementing formative assessment practices included inadequate in-service to address pedagogical needs, content needs, and to support the participant's ability to implement reform.

Within the political dimension of obstacles to implementing formative assessment practices none of the categories were identified as a high obstacle by participants in the study. Lack of local leadership and support was identified as a low obstacle for participant C, specifically the subcategory of district leadership and support. No subcategories under lack of local leadership and support in the implementation of formative assessment practices were identified as obstacles for participants A, B, and D.

In the category of lack of resources provided by the school and district in the implementation of formative assessment practices, participant D identified this category as a low obstacle with the subcategory, lack of instructional resources as the obstacle. Lack of resources was identified as a medium obstacle for participants A, B, and C. Specific subcategories identified were lack of curricular and instructional resources.

Collaboration support from the school and district was identified as a medium obstacle for participant A. The subcategories of identified under collaboration support for participant A included lack of collaboration during school and lack of collaboration during staff meetings. With collaboration support being identified as a low obstacle for participants B and C, the specific subcategory acknowledged was lack of collaboration during staff meeting. This category was identified as no obstacle for participant D.

Limited in-service opportunities provided by the school or district to implement formative assessment practices was the final category within the political dimension. This category was identified as a medium obstacle for participant A and the subcategories of limited professional development offerings at the school and lack of sustained professional development were the specific obstacles recognized. Participants C and D identified limited in-service opportunities as a low obstacle, specifically the lack of sustained professional development. Limited in-service opportunities were not identified as an obstacle for participant B.

Every category within the cultural dimension was identified as an obstacle to implementing formative assessment practices. The category of teacher beliefs was recognized as a high obstacle for participants A, B, and D. These participants identified the following subcategories as obstacles: value of textbook, preparation ethic, and ideal versus reality of classroom. Participant C identified teacher beliefs as a medium obstacle, acknowledging the subcategories of preparation ethic and ideal versus reality of classroom as specific obstacles.

Within the cultural dimension the category of assessment issues was identified as a high obstacle for participants A and C. Participant A identified the following subcategories as obstacles: vocabulary and content drill and practice for test preparation, student assignments assessed for a grade rather than specific descriptive feedback, and lack of common formative assessment among grade levels. Participant C identified the subcategories of the belief that state assessments were not aligned with math curriculum standards, student assignments were assessed for grades rather than specific feedback, and lack of common formative assessments among grade levels. Participants B and D identified the category of assessment as a medium obstacle. Both identified the following subcategories as specific obstacles: student assignments were assessed for grades rather than specific feedback and lack of common formative assessments among grade levels.

Lack of collaboration with others to implement formative assessment practices was the final category within the cultural dimension. Participant A identified this category as a high obstacle. Subcategories identified as obstacles for participant A included: teacher does not collaborate with math teachers in grade level; teacher does not collaborate with other math teachers in the school; and teacher does not collaborate with other math teachers in the district. The category of lack of collaboration was identified as a medium obstacle for participants C and D. Specific subcategories identified by each participant included: teacher does not collaborate with other math teachers in the school and teacher does not collaborate with other math teachers in the district.

The results obtained from the identified obstacles on the BINSES Rubric suggested that each of the participants experienced obstacles to implementing formative assessment practices within each of the three dimensions: technical, political, and cultural. These findings were consistent with the implementation of reform study of Anderson (1996), Johnson (2006), and Hargreaves, Earl, and Schmidt (2002). The studies of Anderson (1996) and Johnson (2006) confirmed that teachers experienced technical, political and cultural barriers when implementing educational reform. Hargreaves, Earl, and Schmidt (2002) highlighted risks and issues associated with implementing assessment reform from the technical, political and cultural perspectives.

It was interesting that the obstacles identified by the participants measuring high and medium in magnitude were similar. Common medium obstacles were found mostly in the technical dimension and common high obstacles were mostly found in the cultural dimensions of the rubric.

**Table 5.4.   Magnitude of Obstacles
to Implementing Formative Assessment Practices**

Obstacle	Participant (A)	Participant (B)	Participant (C)	Participant (D)
Instructional skills	Medium	Medium	Medium	High
Management issues/roles	Medium	Medium	Medium	Medium
Grading issues	Medium	Medium	Medium	Medium
Time for planning/ instruction/collaboration	High	Medium	Low	Medium
Inadequate in-service	Low	Medium	High	Medium
Lack local leadership and support	No	No	Low	No
Lack of resources	Medium	Medium	Medium	Low
Collaboration support	Medium	Low	Low	No
Limited in-service	Medium	No	Low	Low
Teacher beliefs	High	High	Medium	High
Assessment	High	Medium	High	Medium
Lack of collaboration with others	High	Low	Medium	Medium
Total obstacles	11	10	12	10

Obstacles identified as low to no magnitude were most common in the political dimension. Implications specific to each of the categories of obstacles are discussed in the following sections.

IMPLICATIONS FOR THOSE WHO LEAD SCHOOLS

The instructional skills category of the technical dimension, which was identified as a medium to high barrier, included participants' content knowledge, pedagogical knowledge, and their ability to implement formative assessment practices. Individual teachers' content knowledge has a powerful influence on teaching practice and classroom culture and demands a high level of pedagogical content knowledge (Johnson, 2006). Lack of content knowledge or limited pedagogical knowledge, according to Anderson (1996), makes it difficult for a teacher to teach constructively and effectively implement new instructional strategies required for reform.

Assessment issues was another category within the technical dimension identified as a medium barrier by each participant. Although grading was not identified as an obstacle from the analysis of the interview responses, the fact that participants identified quizzes as formative assessment practices demonstrated issues based on the research with grading. I observed teachers returning graded practice homework to students and reviewing the missed items in class. When teachers assessed student learning for purely formative purposes, there was no final mark on the paper and no summative grade in the grade book (Chappuis 2005, p. 16). The giving of marks and the grading function were overemphasized, while the giving of useful advice and the learning function were underemphasized (Black & Wiliam 1998, p. 142). One of the formative assessment strategies identified by Chappuis (2005) to support students in knowing what to do to close the gap between where they are and where they need to be, emphasized providing students an opportunity to practice revising their work before they are held accountable to a final grade.

The final category identified as an obstacle within the technical dimension was inadequate in-service to support the participants' ability to implement formative assessment practices. Responses from the interviews indicated that the four participants averaged 4 hours of professional development in formative assessment practices from October 2010 to February 2011. The quantity of in-service or professional development hours was strongly linked to teachers' effectiveness in changing instructional practices. It was reported by Johnson (2006) that professional development programs with durations of less than 80 hours were ineffective in changing teacher practices. Effective professional development opportunities that initiated change required multiple opportunities to learn, practice, and interact, as well as actually using the new skills (Johnson 2006, p. 151). One day workshops, semester courses, and institutes did not provide teachers with the opportunity to develop new strategies and instructional methods. Sustained experiences lead to changes in instructional practices.

Political obstacles were the hardest for teachers to control (Johnson, 2006). The magnitude identified political obstacles in this study measured from no obstacle to medium obstacle. Three out of the four participants identified the category of lack of local leadership and support as a no obstacle with the fourth classifying it as a low obstacle. Lack of resources was identified as a medium obstacle from three of the four participants and was the category within the political obstacle with the highest magnitude. According to Anderson (1996) lack of resources such as equipment, consumable supplies, and curriculum materials were barriers to reform and potential problems for teachers enacting new instructional methods.

Political obstacles have implications for both the school and the district administration. Resources such as physical space, equipment, consumable materials and curricular materials were all necessary. Fullan's (2001)

research on change in teaching practices and on professional development stressed the importance of adequate time for planning, instruction,
and collaboration between teachers within the school context as keys
reform success. Participants in this study did not identify lack of support
from school and district level leadership as a barrier, These results were
contradictory to Johnson's (2006) study. Teachers must be empowered
through shared decision making of policy related to the implementation
of reform. Principals must be actively involved in the implementation of
formative assessments practices and understand the needs of teachers for
resources of time, materials, and space.

Participants identified more categories within the cultural dimension
with a magnitude of high obstacles than any other dimension. The category of teacher beliefs was identified as a high obstacle by three of the
four participants. The fourth participant identified teacher beliefs as a
medium obstacle. Assessment issues were identified as high in magnitude
by two participants and medium in magnitude by two participants. The
results suggest that participants were experiencing obstacles within several areas of the cultural dimension. Their beliefs about the values of the
textbook in the implementation of formative assessment practices, preparing students for the test and the next level of math, and ideal vs. reality of the classroom were all concerns. Other areas in conflict with the
participants' beliefs appeared to be whether state assessments were
aligned with curriculum standards, changing the practice of assessing for
a grade rather than for descriptive feedback and developing common formative assessments within grade level. Anderson (1996) advocated that
the cultural dimension is the most crucial and important factor in implementing change. According to Johnson (2006), the cultural realm of
Andersons' framework, compared to the first two dimensions, was the
most difficult thing to change and control. Findings from studies of
change identified teacher beliefs as a significant aspect in whether or not
instructional practices would be changed, how they would be implemented and whether the change would be sustained (Fullan, 2001). In
order to change beliefs and instructional practices, teachers needed multiple opportunities to apply and experience formative assessment practices in the context of their own classroom (Johnson, 2006).

Obstacles identified within each of the dimensions provided an opportunity for instructional leaders to make the implementation of formative
assessment practices more technically effective, more politically empower-
ing, and more culturally reflective. Acknowledging there were obstacles to
implementing reform such as the implementation of formative assessment practices was the first step in fostering change. This study identified
several categories of obstacles to implementing formative assessment
practices and the magnitude of the obstacles in the implementation of

formative assessment strategies. The next step for instructional leaders would be to closely examine all identified obstacles to determine how their negative effects can be reduced or removed.

According to findings in this study categories within the cultural dimension were identified as having the greatest magnitude of obstacles. The category specifically identified as a high obstacle was teachers' beliefs concerning curriculum, instruction, assessment, learning, and the implementation of formative assessment practices. Based on the evidence presented in this study and research on the implementation of reform, teacher attitudes and beliefs are the most difficult to change and have the greatest influence on the success of reform. In conclusion, the following strategies are recommended to reduce obstacles to implementing formative assessment practices.

1. To change beliefs and in turn instructional practices, teachers need multiple opportunities to practice and experience formative assessment strategies within the context of their own classroom.
2. Teachers must be provided the opportunity through ongoing sustained professional development to strengthen content and pedagogical knowledge necessary to implement formative assessments practices.
3. Adequate time should be provided for teachers to plan instruction utilizing formative assessment strategies.
4. Collaborative relationships must be formed for schoolwide efforts in implementing formative assessment practices.

This study has presented findings related to obstacles seventh and eighth-grade math teachers encountered while implementing formative assessment practices. The magnitude of the identified obstacles was determined to provide additional support to the findings and implications for instructional leaders. Through additional research, instructional leaders can learn more about the obstacles encountered during the implementation of formative assessment practices and ways to facilitate successful implementation.

REFERENCES

Anderson, R. D. (1996). *Study of curriculum reform. Vol. 1: Findings and conclusions.* Studies of Educational Reform. (ERIC Document Reproduction Service No. ED 397535)

Bell, B., & Cowie, B. (2001). The characteristics of formative assessment in science education. *Science Education, 85*, 536-553.

Black, P., & Wiliam, D., (1998). Assessment and classroom learning. *Assessment in Education Principles, Policy and Practice, 5*(1), 7-73.

Black, P., & Wiliam, D., (1998). Inside the black box: Raising standards through classroom assessment. *Phi Delta Kappan, 80*(2), 139-148.

Bligh, J. (2001). Assessment: The gap between practice and theory. *Medical Education, 35*, 312.

Boston, C. (2002). The concept of formative assessment. *Practical Assessment, Research and Evaluation, 8*, 9.

Brunner, C., Fasca, C., Heinze, J., Honey, M., Light, D., Mandinach, E., & Wexler, D. (2005). Linking data and learning: The grow network study. *Journal of Education for Students Placed at Risk, 10*, 241-267.

Chappuis, J. (2005). Helping students understand assessment. *Association for Supervision and Curriculum Development, 63*(3), 39-43.

Chappuis, S., & Chappuis, J. (2007). The best value in formative assessment. *Educational Leadership, 65*(4), 14-19.

Creswell, J. W. (2009). *Research design: Qualitative, quantitative and mixed methods approach* (3rd ed.). Thousand Oaks, CA: SAGE.

Dorn, S. (2010). The political dilemmas of formative assessment. *Exceptional Children, 76*(3), 325-337.

Frey, B. B., & Schmitt, V. L. (2007). Coming to terms with classroom assessment. *Journal of Advanced Academics, 18*(3), 402-423.

Fullan, M. (2001). *The new meaning of educational change.* New York, NY: Teacher College Press.

Hargreaves, A., Earl, L., & Schmitt, V. L. (2002). Perspectives on alternative assessment reform. *American Educational Research Journal, 39*(1), 69-95.

Johnson, C. C. (2006). Effective professional development and change in practice: Barriers science teachers encounter and implications for reform. *School Science and Mathematics, 106*(3), 150-161.

Knox County Schools. (2009). *Building on strength: Excellence for all children. Strategic Plan.* Knoxville, TN: Knox County Schools.

Stiggins, R. J. (2002). Assessment crisis: The absence of assessment for learning. *Phi Delta Kappan, 83*(10), 758-765.

CHAPTER 6

DATA REFLECTION

How Looking Within Helps Middle School Teachers Improve Instruction

Jonathan East

THE RATIONALE FOR SELECTING THIS PROJECT

At the risk of stating the obvious, improvement in student achievement happens through the day-to-day methods of delivery and tasks that teachers ask of their students; however, we often fail to collect data and ensure that the instructional strategies we know to be highly effective make it to the students in the classroom. Much of the work in administration at the school, district and state levels involves creating plans and professional development with the hopes that these expectations trickle down to the daily practices where content and skills are developed in students. However, our plans often fall short of full actualization because we fail to involve teachers in the planning process with regards to setting explicit and measurable goals, and if we do make it this far, it is difficult to systematically collect data to measure the changes we hope are happening in the classroom. I wanted to implement a system of tracking this data on effec-

Great Leaders Equal Great Schools:
Alliances and Discourse for Educational Reform, pp. 103–119
Copyright © 2012 by Information Age Publishing
All rights of reproduction in any form reserved.

tive instructional strategies and involve teachers in both reflecting on the data and making the plans to implement changes to their daily practices.

SUCCESSES AND DIFFICULTIES

The outcomes of the project were revitalizing not only in the positive results of increasing summarizing and note taking strategies, increasing the level thinking according to Bloom's Taxonomy, and reducing the amount of whole group instruction, but also in the rich dialogue and teacher collaboration around these topics of instructional methods.

The one area where positive change was not made in the outcomes of this project was increasing the use of cooperative grouping with students: with this data the observation showed no change. As I have reflected on the possible reasons for this change, I realized that the cooperative grouping was the most prescriptive strategy that had to meet specific criteria to be marked as observed. Teachers did not have the in-depth training they needed to fully implement this specific strategy. As a result of these findings, we realized that professional development in this strategy would be required to create a significant increase in its use.

Through the use of systematic data collection and paired sample t tests, I was able to see changes in the data over a long period of time that might have been difficult to see without the use of these tools and the understanding of how to use them. The ability to facilitate collaboration within a team of teachers, as well as provide them with the data and time to reach their own conclusions and create their own solutions was a critical skill necessary to building capacity in the team for sustainable change.

With all the data that we collect on student achievement through classroom grades, benchmark assessments and state tests, very little, if any, data are collected regarding the actual instructional strategies in use in the classroom. As an assistant principal and a member of the school's administrative team, it is important to understand the types and quality of the teaching methods being used in our schools. It is also important for teachers to understand what the research shows are the most effective instructional methods and how to use these strategies in their classrooms. However, research has also shown that affecting sustainable changes in organizations is most effective when teachers are involved in the decision-making and are engaged in planning and implementing the changes in the organization. This single site, quantitative, quasi-experimental study explores the current practices of middle grades teachers and attempts to increase their use of effective instructional practices of teachers.

There is a large body of research regarding what the best practices and classroom instructional strategies for the middle level learner are (Marzano, Pickering, & Polluck, 2001). However, other studies have shown that many teachers in the classroom do not always implement these strategies into their lessons. While many teachers work diligently to provide quality instruction for their students, by refraining from using what the research has shown to be highly effective strategies in delivering their instruction, there is a loss in efficiency of the time and energy that teachers spend teaching. In a time of increased accountability for student growth in learning, teachers must reflect on their practices and implement research-based instruction to optimize their time with children and realize their highest levels of efficiency.

The study at the heart of this chapter is to examine the extent to which an approach of reflecting collaboratively on data regarding current instructional strategy usage can effect teacher practice. To achieve this goal, it was necessary to observe teachers in practice to determine the level of implementation of instructional strategies currently in use. After compiling the data, a group of teachers were presented with the data regarding their practices in the classroom. They were asked to reflect on the data, identify areas they felt would impact student learning the most and create target goals they would work toward in the second round of classroom observations. Finally, I observed teachers after the collaborative reflection session and measured to see if they were able to attain their goals.

In order to achieve the purpose of this project, the following research questions were addressed:

1. What goals and actions for changing instruction did teachers make after reflecting on classroom observation data?
2. Did teachers' use of instructional strategies change once the action plan was created and implemented?

Delimitations

There were several delimitations that confined the design of this project. For this study I selected teachers from a single grade level, sixth-grade, in the school. The participants were selected based on my perceptions that they would have the greatest level of participation and willingness to make changes to their instructional practices. The work was also limited to observing teacher instructional practices through classroom observations; no data regarding student learning outcomes were evaluated.

Limitations

There are several limitations inherent in this study and its design. First, the classroom observations were "snap shot" observations in which I and the observers only spent 3 to 5 minutes per visit. This is a limitation because lessons were not observed in their entirety and we may not have observed instructional strategies that were used during parts of the lesson not observed. Second, while all the observers attended the training on use of the observation instrument, and we all spent approximately 1 month observing and debriefing in groups to calibrate how we conducted the observations and used the instrument, it is still possible that the level of interrater reliability of the observers could be low. Another limitation of this study is that the researcher conducting this study serves in a supervisory role to the participant of the study that could affect the behaviors and outcomes of the study. Last, because the study takes place at a single site, the generalizability of the results of the study may also be limited.

While we know to a large degree what strategies are effective in delivering instruction to middle level learners, we also know that these strategies are not always put into action in the classrooms (Gaines, Teague, Wilson, Beavers, Henly, & Anfara, 2010). This work attempts to explore the effectiveness of collecting observational data and allowing teachers to reflect on the data and create goals for increasing the implementation of research-based instructional strategies. Finding ways to get teacher practice to change from its current state of lower implementation of best practices to a place where best practices are the norm in school classrooms is valuable information for policy makers, district level officials, site based administrators and classroom teachers. All of these stakeholders have a vested interest in continuing to improve student learning outcomes and performance.

HIGHLY EFFECTIVE INSTRUCTIONAL
STRATEGIES AND THE LITERATURE

It is important to understand what the research says are the highly effective instructional strategies for delivering middle-level content. It is also important to understand what the research says regarding teacher involvement in indentifying changes that are needed to effectively implement and sustain those changes to daily practice. This section will review the literature on instructional practice and the components of effective structures for data reflection.

The National Middle School Association (NMSA), in its most recently released position paper entitled *This We Believe: Keys to Educating Young Adolescents,* recognizes that the quality of the teacher and instructional strategies used is paramount in ensuring quality educational experiences for the middle-level learners. NMSA (2010) discusses several examples of the types of research-based strategies that should be used at the middle school level including working with student in setting goals and objectives, using experiments, providing students with feedback, reinforcing effort, cooperative grouping/peer collaboration and other delivery methods that are engaging and require higher order thinking skills. They recognize that some instruction will need to be direct instruction through lecturing, but the majority of the learning needs to be through more hands-on, student-centered learning strategies.

Drawing from the work of NMSA (2010) and many others, Gaines and colleagues (2010) found many similar themes of high quality instructional practices in their review of literature concerning developmentally appropriate instructional practices for middle-level students. Some of these themes include students and teachers collaboratively setting goals and objectives, differentiating instruction for individual students, continuous assessment and feedback to inform instruction, cooperative grouping, high student engagement and peer teaching opportunities. These researchers, among others, make a strong case that the quality of the instructional strategies used in the classroom matters.

The instructional strategies and practices I observed in classroom observations were based on the strategies evaluated in the meta-analysis study conducted by Marzano and colleagues (2001) and presented in the book *Classroom Instruction That Works: Research-Based Strategies for Increasing Student Achievement.*

Findings from Marzano's work identified nine broad categories of instructional strategies used by teachers that the research has shown to have a high likelihood of producing a greater effect on student achievement. The categories include: Identifying similarities and differences, summarizing and note taking, reinforcing effort and providing recognition, homework and practice, nonlinguistic representation, cooperative learning, setting objectives and providing feedback, generating and testing hypotheses, and cues, questions and advance organizers. These strategies were used as "look for's" as I observed classrooms.

LEARNING IN CONTEXT

If we know which strategies promote effective learning, but we also know that these strategies are not being used in classrooms at a high enough frequency, how do we make an effective change to practice that lasts? Creating sustainable change in any large organization can be a daunting task—especially when you take into consideration that many members of that organization have established the behaviors that allow them to do their work over long periods of time and might be resistant to change. The education field is no exception. Many teachers who have been teaching for a number of years often fall into a rhythm of practices and methods to which they have grown accustomed. They know which lessons they need to teach, and they have ways of teaching those lessons that they feel are effective or at least comfortable in many cases. How does one go about the very difficult task of working with individuals or organizations to examine their practices? What are the most effective ways of creating a need for change that is both nonthreatening and sustainable?

Fullan (2002) gives some insight into effective approaches for fostering a culture of continued learning and growth through what he calls "learning in context". He explains that "learning in context" happens when members of an organization examine the problems and issues and design and plan solutions with others within the organizations. This is in contrast to the approach of bringing in an outside agency to examine and offer solutions or going outside the organization to find solutions. Fullan (2002) explained:

> Learning in context has the greatest potential payoff because it is more specific, situational, and social (it develops shared and collective knowledge and commitments). This kind of learning is designed to improve the organization and its social and moral context. Learning in context also establishes conditions conducive to continual development, including opportunities to learn from others on the job, the daily fostering of current and future leaders, the selective retention of good ideas and best practices, and the explicit monitoring of performance. (p. 20)

This approach to using the power of the individuals within the organization and the inherent benefits associated as result of this approach is why I have reviewed the literature on strategies for organization members to reflect on data collaboratively and create solutions through action planning.

Reflective Practice

One component of support can be found in a form of individualized professional development known as reflective practice. Researchers have distilled two types of reflective practice: reflection *in* action and reflection *on* action. The first refers to a thought process in the moment that helps to create decisions in the moment, and the second refers to the practice of reflection on data after actions have been made (Sarsar, 2008). The reflection on action is the approach that is valuable to the improvement of teaching practices and can be summed up by the questions suggested by Wagner (2006): "What do I know and already do well? What additional skills do I need? And how can I be more effective?"

Organizational Learning

Although the teaching profession is not traditionally rooted in collaboration (Good, 2006), by combining the individual reflection with collaboration with peers, we arrive at some very powerful and potentially sustainable practices that can have an impact on strategies and student learning (Good, 2006). This combination of reflection with groups of peers is also known as organizational learning (OL) (Ingram, Louis, & Schroeder, 2004). OL is organized into five steps, which include: (1) learning from past experience, (2) acquiring knowledge, (3) processing on an organizational level, (4) identifying and correcting problems, and (5) organizational change (Ingram et al., 2004).

Organizational Learning results in a transcendence of the sum of individual learning in the organization and compounds the impact and effectiveness when members of the group begin learning together and make unified changes in their practices that are aligned with one another (Ingram et al.). According to Good, these forms of research or action research initiate reflection and inquiry by teachers and have an impact on changing personal beliefs and practices of educators. Teachers have reported very favorably to the practice of reflecting as individuals and within groups, stating that the process offers opportunities for teachers to interact with each other and have the opportunity to take on leadership roles (Good, 2006).

Barriers

Though noteworthy, these reflective practices and general use of data exploration are not without their shortcomings whether perceived or real. The first and most obvious barrier to reflective practice with peers is the limitation of *time* with their peers. In many cases it is very difficult to find the time for peers to collaborate (Good, 2006). In some studies, teachers have reported a frustration with the process, stating that the time spent on researching solutions seemed ancillary to the roles and responsibilities of what is perceived as the traditional role of the teacher (Good, 2006). Teachers found that there had to be a trade-off between teaching or carrying out other instructional responsibilities of teaching, such as planning or grading, collecting and analyzing the data.

Aside from the time constraints, Wagner's (2006) study reported that a common response found in interviews was that teachers had a mistrust of data and/or the use of data, noting that they felt that data were often used to justify and push through decisions that were already made in the minds of administrators and supervisors. Some of these educators also expressed a fear of using data because of the risk that data will be used in a judg-mental way that might have punitive consequences (Wagner, 2006).

Methodology

At the beginning of the year, teachers were given a brief explanation of the study and an explanation of the observation instrument that the researcher would be using. Base-line data were collected for the first 4 months of the study. At the midpoint of the study, teachers were pre-sented with their composite grade-level data as well as national data of the same grade level using the same instrument. Teachers were given a series of guiding questions (see Appendix) and asked to reflect on changes in practice they felt were most necessary and would have the greatest impact on student learning. Teachers created a series of goals, and the researcher collected post intervention data to measure for signifi-cant changes in the data.

SITE

The work of this project takes place at Gresham Middle School in East Tennessee, which sits atop a hill on a 15-acre tree and lawn-covered cam-pus overlooking Fountain City, a community of Knoxville, Tennessee. Fountain City is beautiful historic area with a large fountain at the center of the city for which Fountain City was named. Gresham has a history that runs deep with the citizens of Fountain City, many of whom attended the school when it was Central High or in its present form as Gresham Mid-dle.

Gresham Middle's enrollment fluctuates from 800 to 900 students in any given year due to a relatively high rate of mobility. It has approxi-mately 300 students in the sixth-grade, 271 in the seventh and 250 in the eighth, and nearly 60 highly qualified educators serve its students. The major ethnicities represented in our student population are as follows: 73% White, 19% Black, and 6% Hispanic. The teaching staff is comprised of 52 teachers varying in experience from first year teacher to 30-plus year veteran.

Based on the Tennessee Comprehensive Assessment Program or TCAP scores, Tennessee's NCLB metric for student achievement, Gresham Mid-dle students perform at an average level compared to other Tennessee middle schools. However, over the last several years Gresham has scored highest in growth in Math, Reading, and Science as compared to other Knox County middle schools. The school is in "good standing" by making the cut scores for proficient and advanced in all subjects and subgroups of students according to Adequate Yearly Progress.

Sample

Ten teachers from Gresham Middle School were selected to participate in this study. All ten teachers were sixth-grade teachers who taught the core academic classes, including two teachers from of each of the following subjects: math, science, language arts, reading, and social studies. The participants were selected based on the researcher's perceptions that they would have the greatest level of participation and willingness to make changes to their instructional practices.

Data Collection

The classroom walk-through observation tool that was used in this study is an instrument called *Power Walkthrough: Classroom Observation Software*. This system is a digital template that works through the use of personal digital devices such as the Apple ipad, iPhone, Blackberry, or other similar digital device. The mobile software allows the user to select from checklists and drop-down menus to choose the strategies observed and stores the data which can be viewed in a variety of customizable reports online. Eliminating paper observation reports which would need to be entered into a spreadsheet and managed makes the process of collecting this amount of data a manageable and efficient process, thereby allowing the user to focus on the instruction and less on data entry. For detailed information about the instrument used contact the Mid-Continent Research for Education and Learning at www.mcrel.com.

There are four individuals who were trained on the use of this tool and conducted the observations. Each of the observers attended a 7-hour interactive webinar that shows the users of the Power Walkthrough (PWT) how to operate the software, but more importantly, how to identify the strategies and other items that are the selectable fields listed in PWT software. Each observation took no longer than five minutes, and the collected information includes the following major sections: affective strategies, primary strategy, secondary strategy, level of Bloom's taxonomy, context of learning, teacher use of technology, student use of technology, evidence of learning and a short student interview. However, for the purposes of my work, we focused on the: affective strategies (setting objectives, providing feedback, reinforcing effort and providing feedback), primary strategy, secondary strategy, level of Bloom's taxonomy, and context of learning (whole group, individual, small group or cooperative grouping).

Before the observations began, the administration met with teams and explained that the purpose of observations is to collect schoolwide data about the instructional practices in use in our building in order for the faculty to make decisions about changes they feel are necessary, possible professional development foci, instructional strengths within our building and effectiveness of professional development. We emphasized that these data would not be used in a evaluative way to make decisions regarding teacher retention or dismissal, but we did provide a disclaimer that we would address any issues that we felt needed to be addressed in the course of conducting walkthroughs as we would any other time we are in the classrooms and other school locations.

To increase the interrater reliability of the observers, we made observations in pairs and in threes for approximately 1 month. After each observation, we would debrief outside of the classroom to discuss and come to consensus about what was observed and what should be marked on the template. The reason for making observations together and debriefing in the beginning was to continue to develop the observers' skills and ability to correctly identify what was happening in the classroom and ensure higher interrater reliability.

We conducted 90 observations to establish a baseline before we began the collaborative reflection session. We made 92 observations after the collaborative reflection sessions began for a total of 182 observations schoolwide by the end of the study.

After five to eight observations were collected on each teacher, I met with teams and shared the data with them. While I had my own opinions about what the data said, I tried to remain objective and allowed the teams to see the data and construct their own conclusions about it. The team and I worked through a series of questions that helped them to analyze and identify areas of strength and areas they would like to affect change in strategies. (see Appendix) Once they identified a specific area they wanted to improve, they constructed SMART (Specific, Measurable, Attainable, Results-oriented, Time-based) goals and developed an action plan for how they were to accomplish the goals. I served as support for achieving these goals through providing teachers with materials, engaging in conversations about the goals and providing teachers with the time to meet and discuss the data.

We continued to conduct observations and met with individual teachers. Near the end of the year, the initial baseline data collected was compared to the data collected after the collaborative reflection sessions to measure if there was a significant change in the areas the team set as their goals. After all observations were complete, two-tailed paired sample t test with a significance of .05 was conducted using SPSS to determine if there was a statistically significant increase or decrease in the number of occurrences of the identified strategies during the observations conducted after the teachers set their goals.

FINDINGS

Which goals and actions for changing instruction did teachers make after reflecting on classroom observation data regarding the instructional strategies used? After looking at and discussing their aggregate data on instructional strategies from the first 4 months of the study and comparing it to national data from the same grade levels and subject areas, the teachers identified three areas that they agreed would have the greatest impact on student learning. These areas were: increasing the level of Bloom's taxonomy within the classroom activities, increasing the occurrence of summarizing and note taking strategies, increasing the number of occurrences of cooperative grouping strategies and decreasing the occurrence of whole-group instruction.

Through their discussions, teachers came to a consensus that the most educationally impactful strategy that was measured by the instrument was the level of Bloom's taxonomy, also referred to throughout this study as higher order thinking skills, and cognitive demand. They agreed to set a goal to increase the overall cognitive demand in their classrooms by a statistically significant difference during the post intervention observation period that was approximately 6 weeks long.

The team set a goal of increasing the frequency of the note taking and summarizing at a statistically significant difference by the end of the post intervention observation session, which lasted approximately 6 weeks. As an additional action step, one teacher agreed to compile a resource of summarizing techniques that the teachers could use to aide them in achieving their goal. The teacher made copies and disseminated the resource to all teachers within a few days of the collaborative reflection session.

The team identified a third and final goal of reducing the number of occurrences of whole group context and increasing the number of occurrences of cooperative grouping strategies to deliver content used during classes. They identified this strategy because they stated that they were "surprised" at the high frequency of whole group occurrences, as it had been reported in the data. They agreed to decrease the number of occurrences of whole group instruction as used in their classrooms as Team Goal 3 and increase the number of occurrences of cooperative grouping strategies as Team Goal 4, both by a statistically significant amount by the end of the post intervention observation session.

Did the teachers' use of instructional strategies change once they had a chance to reflect on the data and create goals and actions? Changes in instructional strategies were measured using four sets of pre/post data. For each set of data, a two-tailed paired-sample t test was calculated at an alpha level of .05. Below are the tables and results from each of the four strategies.

In regards to Team Goal 1, increasing the level of Bloom's taxonomy, the first paired sample t test was calculated for the level of cognitive demand in the classrooms during observations before and after the collaborative reflection session using Bloom's levels of higher order thinking as the metric for statistically significant difference. Each of the six levels of Bloom's taxonomy was weighted one through six respectively, and an average Bloom's Index was calculated for each teacher. The results showed that there was a significant difference in the scores for Bloom's Index before intervention ($M = 2.45$, $SD = .54$) and after intervention ($M = 3.20$, $SD = .52$) conditions; $t(9) = -3.29$, $p = 0.009$. These results suggested that providing teachers data regarding classroom instruction strategies and allowing them to set goals for improving instruction has a significant effect on increasing the cognitive demand of the classroom.

In regards to Team Goal 2, increasing use of summarizing and note taking strategies, the second paired sample t test was calculated for the percentage of time the summarizing and note taking strategies were used in the classrooms during observations before and after the collaborative reflection session to measure if there was a statistically significant difference. The results showed that there was a significant difference in the percentage of summarizing and note taking strategies before intervention ($M = .07$, $SD = .09$) and after intervention ($M = .26$, $SD = .16$) conditions;

**Table 6.1.   Level of Bloom's Taxonomy—
Pre- and Postcollaborative Reflection Session**

Teacher	Bloom's Index Pre	Blooms Index Post
Teacher A	2.11	2.67
Teacher B	3.17	3.14
Teacher C	2.50	3.00
Teacher D	3.00	3.38
Teacher E	1.75	3.86
Teacher F	2.60	4.00
Teacher G	1.67	3.14
Teacher H	2.88	2.67
Teacher I	2.00	2.50
Teachers J	2.88	3.67

$t(9) = -3.18$, $p = 0.011$. These results suggested that providing teachers data regarding classroom instruction strategies and allowing them to set goals for improving instruction had a significant effect on increasing the occurrence of a predetermined instructional strategy of summarizing and note taking used in the classroom.

In regards to Team Goal 3, reducing the amount of whole group context, the third paired sample t test was calculated for the percentage of time instruction was delivered through a whole group context during observations before and after the collaborative reflection session to measure if there was a statistically significant difference. The results showed that there was a significant difference in the percentage of time instruction was used in the whole group context before intervention ($M = .5$, $SD = .16$) and after intervention ($M = .10$, $SD = .15$) conditions; $t(9) = 7.00$, $p = 0.001$. These results suggest that providing teachers data regarding classroom instruction strategies and allowing them to set goals for improving instruction had a significant effect on decreasing the occurrence of whole-group strategies used in the classroom.

In addition to decreasing the amount of whole group instruction strategies, the team set a goal to increase the number of cooperative grouping strategies. The fourth and final paired sample t test was calculated for the percentage of time instruction was delivered through a cooperative grouping context during observations before and after the collaborative reflection session to measure if there was a statistically significant difference. The results showed that there was a significant difference in the percentage of time instruction was used in the cooperative grouping context before intervention ($M = .04$, $SD = .06$) and after intervention ($M = .10$, $SD = .15$) conditions; $t(9) = -1.2$, $p = 0.258$. These results suggest that

**Table 6.2.   Summarizing and Note Taking Strategies—
Pre and Post Collaborative Reflection Session**

Teacher	Summarizing and Note Taking Pre	Summarizing and Note Taking Post
Teacher A	0.06	0.07
Teacher B	0.00	0.29
Teacher C	0.22	0.30
Teacher D	0.06	0.50
Teacher E	0.00	0.29
Teacher F	0.00	0.31
Teacher G	0.25	0.14
Teacher H	0.00	0.00
Teacher I	0.07	0.25

**Table 6.3.   Whole Group Context—Pre
and Post Collaborative Reflection Session**

Teacher	Whole Group Pre	Whole Group Post
Teacher A	0.78	0.33
Teacher B	0.40	0.33
Teacher C	0.50	0.00
Teacher D	0.43	0.17
Teacher E	0.33	0.00
Teacher F	0.40	0.25
Teacher G	0.67	0.14
Teacher H	0.70	0.33
Teacher I	0.50	0.00
Teachers J	0.29	0.00

**Table 6.4.   Cooperative Grouping Context—
Pre and Post Collaborative Reflection Session**

Teacher	Cooperative Grouping Pre	Cooperative Grouping Post
Teacher A	0.00	0.00
Teacher B	0.20	0.00
Teacher C	0.00	0.20
Teacher D	0.00	0.00
Teacher E	0.10	0.00
Teacher F	0.00	0.00
Teacher G	0.00	0.14
Teacher H	0.00	0.00
Teacher I	0.00	0.40
Teachers J	0.10	0.33

providing teachers data regarding classroom instruction strategies and allowing them to set goals for improving instruction did not have a significant effect on increasing the occurrence of using cooperative grouping context to deliver instruction.

SUMMARY, CONCLUSIONS AND RECOMMENDATIONS

The goals the teachers selected followed a very logical pattern. They identified Bloom's taxonomy as the indicator in the data that had the greatest impact on student learning. They selected this as a goal, but then followed up by adding summarizing and note taking as a goal that would help to achieve an increase in Bloom's Taxonomy. In response to the reflecting question "What did you see in the data that is surprising or unexpected?" (see Appendix), the teachers expressed that they were surprised by the amount of whole group instruction that the data showed, and they set a goal to decrease the amount of whole group instruction. Again, in a logical progression they set a follow-up goal to increase the amount of cooperative grouping used in their classrooms.

The results from the paired sample t tests of the pre and post mean scores showed a statistically significant difference in all cases with the exception of Goal 4, increase use of cooperative grouping. Goal 1, "increase Bloom's index" showed a large increase from pre to post, as did Goal 2, "increase summarizing and note taking." Goal 3, "decrease the amount of whole group instruction," showed a large decrease. The effect size as determined by calculating Cohen's d for results of the first three goals' t tests were all in the "large" range, above .08. However, there was not a statistically significant increase in the use of cooperative grouping.

A key element to this study was allowing the teachers to reflect on the data and set their own goals as a team as opposed to the researcher establishing the particular strategies to improve. In this way, teachers began to "own" the process by evaluating their own work and setting their own direction for improvement. This approach built trust in the participants and established capacity-building versus judgementalism as Fullan (2008) describes in *The Six Secrets of Change*. Because the participants identified their own areas to strengthen, they were less likely to feel judged by an extrinsic metric imposed by the researcher; but rather, they realized a goal that they set for themselves in the context of their work. The findings of this study support the literature on collaborative reflective process which states that change in practice can be accomplished most effectively by allowing teachers to identify the areas in which they need to improve and allowing them to create the solutions to those needs (Sarsar, 2008).

A second key element of this study was that the data collection and intervention were set in the context of "the real work" of the participants. Fullan (2002) states that the most effective professional development provides teachers chances to learn in context, allowing the teachers opportunities to learn from others on the job and to create their own solutions. While it was not part of the data collected, I did observe teachers having conversations about ways they were using the resources that were provided, and I was able to engage teachers in many conversations about their teaching practices and how they were making changes to their practices to achieve their goals. These conversations and interactions created a rich environment in which teaching and learning was the focus.

To any administrator who is trying to develop a culture that encourages collaboration and one that focuses on shifting teaching methods to research-based methods, I would recommend creating a system for collecting data on how content is delivered in the classroom. Be transparent about the observations and let teachers know that the purpose of the observations is to collect data about strategies in use in the building so that the teachers can identify strengths and areas to strengthen. This process of observation data collection should be separate from the evaluation process in order to build the trust that is necessary to collect and share the data with the team.

In addition to creating a system for tracking teaching practices, teachers must be provided time to reflect and collaborate with one another regarding this data in order to identify areas that individual teachers as well as entire faculties need to grow. Allow teachers to set their own goals and provide a metric to measure whether or not they reach their goals. I would also recommend sharing the data in aggregate form to the whole group of teachers so that teachers begin to understand what strategies are being used across the building as compared to the strategies each teacher uses individually in their own classroom. This data creates some healthy pressure to make changes to teaching practices for individuals who may be unaware of what the rest of the school is doing.

APPENDIX—MEETING PROTOCOL AND GUIDING QUESTIONS FOR REFLECTION

1. What data stand out to you as you first look over the information about strategies used in our classrooms?

2. What do you see in the data that is surprising or unexpected? What did you expect to see that is not present in the data?

3. Do you feel that this data is an accurate representation of the strategies and practices in your classroom?

4. How would you describe the relationship between:

    (a) Context and Bloom's?
    (b) Instructional strategies and Bloom's?
    (c) Evidence of learning and Bloom's?

5. According to the data, in what areas is this grade level particularly strong? Are there areas that you would identify as areas to strengthen?

6. How does the Gresham Middle School Data compare to the National data for sixth-grade classrooms?

7. Select one or more aspects of the data that you feel would impact student learning the most and create a SMART (Specific, Measurable, Attainable, Realistic, and Time-bound) goal to address the change you would like to see happen between now and the end of the year. Are there any additional resources you would need in order to achieve this goal?

REFERENCES

Fullan, M. (2002). The change leader. Retrieved from http://www.cdl.org/resource-library/articles/change_ldr.php

Fullan, M. (2008). *Six secrets of change: What the best leaders do to help their organizations survive and thrive.* San Francisco, CA: Jossey-Bass.

Gaines, C. B., Teague, G. M., Wilson, N. L., Beavers, J. L., Henley, V. L., & Anfara, V. A. (2010, November). *Middle grades instructional practices.* Paper presented at the Mid-South Educational Research Association, Mobile, AL.

Good, R. B. (2006, December 16). *Analyzing the impact of a data analysis process to improve instruction using a collaborative model.* Retrieved from EBSCOhost

Ingram, D., Louis, K., & Schroeder, R., (2004). Accountability policies and teacher decision making: Barriers to the use of data to improve practice. *Teachers College Record, 106*(6), 1258-1287.

Marzano, R. J., Pickering, D. J., & Pollock, J. E. (2001). *Classroom instruction that works: Research-based strategies for increasing student achievement.* Alexandria, VA: Association for Supervision and Curriculum Development.

National Middle School Association. (2010). *This we believe: Keys to educating young adolescents.* Westerville, OH: Author.

Schön, D. A. (1983). *The reflective practitioner: How professionals think in action.* New York, NY: Basic Books.

Wagner, K., (2006). Benefits of reflective practice. *Leadership 36*(2), 30-32.

CHAPTER 7

YES WE CAN!

The How and What of Improving Language Arts and Literacy Achievement

Kimberle Harrison

The focus of this chapter is to examine the effectiveness of customized, site-based professional development activities in the subject areas of language arts and reading used to increase student achievement in the third and fourth-grades.

As a former special education teacher, my entire career was focused on working with students with learning differences. It was my responsibility to teach students to read proficiently despite the learning challenges they faced. During my administrative internship, I was placed in a school where the students faced many different challenges that impacted their academic performance. The entire school population was 100% free and reduced lunch, 43% English language learners and a community where most parents did not graduate from high school. State testing yielded poor achievement scores in reading and language. It was our challenge as an administrative team, as a staff and a community to restructure our literacy program and professional development to meet the various learn-

Great Leaders Equal Great Schools:
Alliances and Discourse for Educational Reform, pp. 121–139

ing needs of our students. As we created and implemented a tailored literacy framework for our students in third, fourth- and fifth-grades, we needed collect data to determine the success of the framework and professional development to support student growth.

The success that came with this project was that there was an increase in student growth in reading and language arts from 2010 to 2011. The most significant gains came in the subject area of language arts. Through an interview process teachers evaluated the literacy framework and weekly professional development training. Common themes were revealed through teacher responses. This information provided professional development opportunities for the next school year. The challenges we faced were starting this framework and professional development in late fall and there were other interventions that may have also impacted student performance.

The skill sets that were necessary for this project required a deep understanding of literacy and language arts curriculum, state standards, and knowledge of students and their learning styles. I also needed to have an awareness of the various teacher skill sets to support and increase student performance. I used extensive data analysis of state testing scores in reading and language arts dating back 8-10 years. The data analysis examined trends based on literacy programs, demographics and various support systems through the years. The interview process required knowledge of questioning, recording and analyzing the responses from teachers. That process provided some very critical information that could impact future professional development for the school.

Today educators have a variety of opportunities to obtain skills in quality literacy teaching ranging from differentiated instruction to phonemic awareness, phonics fluency, vocabulary, language arts, and comprehension. Fisher and Frey (2007) stated that the challenge of improving achievement in literacy is to make certain that all teachers at the whole-school level have the knowledge, skills and dispositions necessary to ensure that their students develop increasingly sophisticated understandings of literacy. Kennedy and Shiel (2010) found that effective literacy teachers and effective professional development have helped schools beat the odds and succeed in helping the majority of their students perform well in literacy despite their socioeconomic status. Both urban elementary school studies identified a strong correlation between effective on-site professional development and increased literacy achievement in low socioeconomic schools. This relationship between customized, site-based teacher professional development and achievement in literacy was the focus of this single site, mixed methods study at Lonsdale Elementary School.

Mitchell and Castle (2005) found that many principals expressed the broad concept that "instructional leadership is basically teaching people how to teach people and improving instruction for students." DuFour, DuFour, Eaker, and Many (2006) stated that educators in professional learning communities acknowledge that deep insights and understanding come from action, reflection and continual improvement. Knox County Schools had embraced Marzano, Pickering and Pollock (2001) nine instructional strategies in the 2010-2011 school year to promote and develop a common language throughout the entire school system. These trends in how teachers learn to teach, the growth of shared professional development, and Lonsdale's 4 years of participation in the Teacher Advancement Program (TAP) provided a solid foundation for the objectives of this study.

The purpose of this single site, mixed methods study was to examine the effectiveness of the customized, site-based professional development activities in the subject areas of language arts and reading used to increase student achievement in third- and fourth-grades. The intent of this study was to explore teacher perceptions of the effectiveness of the customized, site-based professional development with the primary emphasis on language arts and literacy. A qualitative approach using teacher interviews helped examine the perceptions and effectiveness of the customized, site-based professional development. This was necessary to better understand the advantages/disadvantages and the successes/failures of the customized professional development and its impact on student performance. Finally, a detailed analysis and comparison of Tennessee Comprehensive Assessment Test (TCAP) scores from 2010 to 2011 examined student growth in literacy for third- and fourth-grades.

The study was guided by the following research questions: What are the perceptions of the staff when examining the effectiveness of site-based professional development as a key strategy to improve literacy and will the use of site-based professional development increase student achievement in language arts and reading as measured by Tennessee Comprehensive Assessment Test?

As the state-mandated *First to the Top* and *Knox County's 5-Year Strategic Plan* maintained focus on increasing student achievement based on current data, this study focused on the significant relationship between professional development activities and instructional strategies/interventions utilized to increase proficiency in language arts and literacy. In their individual studies (Fisher & Frey 2007; Kennedy & Sheil, 2010; Musti-Rao, Hawkins & Barkley, 2009; Peck, 2010), explored the change process of taking marginal urban schools to high achieving schools through collaborative, customized, on-site professional development. The study of Lonsdale Elementary School encompassed the latest trends in research and continued the quest for increasing literacy achievement in at-risk urban schools.

Historically, professional development was "one-stop shopping" or "one size fits all," meaning that everyone in the system had the same professional development opportunities/activities without considering the varying needs of individual schools. With the new state standards and student expectations at an all-time high, it was incumbent upon administrators and educators to meet the specific needs of each school and its student population. Administrators must examine the professional development for their own school and customize it to meet the needs of the students. Based on the needs of the students at Lonsdale Elementary School, the administration restructured the professional development to focus on language arts and literacy in third through fifth-grades.

This study focused on three aspects of creating success for literacy in urban schools: site-based professional development, literacy in urban schools, and research-based instructional strategies. The choice to work on these three components was a result of evaluating Lonsdale Elementary School's past and present achievement in literacy with an emphasis on language arts. Current TCAP data revealed a need to reexamine the curriculum and instructional methods utilized at Lonsdale Elementary, therefore, the results instilled a sense of urgency to research successful literacy programs in urban schools.

As stated previously (Fisher & Frey 2007; Kennedy & Sheil, 2010; Musti-Rao, Hawkins & Barkley, 2009; Peck, 2010), explored the change process of taking marginal urban schools to high achieving schools through collaborative, customized, on-site professional development. Fisher and Frey (2007) found in their study at the Rosa Parks School, in San Diego, California, that learning is social and that collaborative learning for both educators and students improves achievement. When the school faculty understood core beliefs about literacy and instructional framework, they worked together as a team and moved beyond practices of individual teachers.

Historically, teachers have participated in conferences or staff development sessions and bring back yet another strategy to add to their list. There was never a cohesive plan for literacy development. This study showed that access to quality professional development, learning communities and peer coaching versus "seagull consulting" (they fly in, drop something off, and fly away) improved teacher focus on key literacy beliefs and framework.

Danielson (2002) supported the concept of teachers working cooperatively and states "teachers must form teams and plan their instruction to maximize student learning of the curriculum." DuFour and colleagues (2006) stated that focus on results is essential to team effectiveness. When teams work together to establish measurable goals, collect and analyze data, then teachers monitor and adjust their teaching to achieve desired outcomes. When looking at how literacy teachers make a difference in urban schools, teachers' subject knowledge, pedagogy, and relationships with students were all factors that contributed to the success of the students in these teachers' classrooms. Lazar (2006) stated that teachers who have succeeded in challenging environments have demonstrated the following instructional practices: (1) coaching children in how to apply phonics to everyday reading, (2) organizing small group instruction, (3) staging independent reading opportunities, (4) coaching during reading, (5) asking higher level questions, (6) having children write in response to reading, and (7) communicating with parents.

Fisher and Frey (2007) identified English Language learners as a factor in their study with regard to an instructional focus on oral language, storytelling and think-pair-share. According to the Fisher and Frey study, developing an instructional framework was paramount in guiding teachers to make sound instructional decisions. The literacy framework focused on grade level content standards in reading, writing, and oral language as the core curriculum. The framework also included the following components: direct instruction/modeling (focus lessons), guided instruction, collaborative learning, independent practice with conferring, and assessment. Peck (2010) supported the theory of a focused framework and students taking ownership of learning. Peck's study found that student ownership of learning translated to students valuing literacy and using reading and writing at home, school and in community settings. In addition, Musti-Rao and colleagues (2009) brought attention to the apparent lack of effective instruction that meets the unique needs of the culturally and linguistically diverse population often found in urban schools. Learning to read in English is a complex process that involves cognitive, linguistic, sociocultural and educational components (Burns & Helman, 2009). Early intervention, which includes explicit, systematic, and intensive reading instruction, remains imperative to succeed in urban school settings.

Tate (2003) identified 20 instructional strategies that engaged the brain and increased learning and achievement in the classroom. Some of Tate's strategies echoed Marzano's instructional strategies as well as Howard Gardner's research on multiple intelligences. Additional strategies included project-based instruction, music, movement, humor, story telling, mnemonic devices, technology, and field trips. Marzano (2001) stated that all instructional strategies must be provided to teachers via high-quality staff development to effect change. Just knowing the strategies was not enough. Administrators needed to provide opportunities for adequate modeling and practice, accurate and timely feedback, allowances for differences in implementation, and celebrations of success. Reeves (2009) found that prioritizing instructional strategies, especially those which focus on literacy, was imperative since "educators are drowning under the weight of initiative fatigue" (p. 14).

Upon review of the literature, current studies supported the validity of the case study at Lonsdale Elementary School and the literacy framework, which was created and implemented. Like other urban schools, Lonsdale Elementary School was in a constant state of improvement and change. The Tennessee School Improvement Planning Process (TSIPP) provided a detailed structure to set goals and objectives that helped align resources to improve student achievement. The most recent goal was to decrease the number of students by 10% who score basic on the TCAP reading component. In order to meet this goal, the choice was to focus on customized site-based professional development, improve literacy and incorporate research-based instructional strategies. This was supported by current research and was based upon the leadership team's evaluation of school data and the need for academic improvement in literacy/language arts.

The design for this research was a single site, mixed methods approach using teacher interviews and analysis of TCAP results. This study was completed in two phases. Teachers were interviewed using a semistructured questionnaire, which was constructed using components from Thomas Guskey's professional development evaluation framework. Results of teacher interviews were used to investigate if the professional development activities were beneficial to student outcomes the areas of language arts and literacy in third- and fourth-grades as observed and reported by each teacher.

The second phase used a quantitative approach to analyze achievement scores in reading and language on the TCAP in 2010 and 2011. Reporting Category Performance Index (RCPI) scores were compared and measured for student growth. Data was analyzed using an independent samples t test through a computerized analysis system. Student growth was also reported in terms of means, standard deviations and categorical data such as below basic, basic, proficient and advanced.

The design of the mixed methods study was to use a qualitative approach to gather information regarding teacher perception of the effectiveness of the professional development at Lonsdale Elementary School, the strengths and weaknesses and its impact on future professional development. A total of seven teachers from third and fourth-grades were interviewed using a semistructured interview protocol based on the Guskey's three key components to evaluate professional development experiences. A quantitative approach consisted of data analysis of the Tennessee Comprehensive Assessment Test (TCAP) results, which examined possible relationships between customized site-based professional development and student achievement in literacy/language arts. Were the current instructional approaches and literacy framework working successfully?

Lonsdale Elementary School in Knoxville, TN, had a diverse population of 324 students where 100% of the school was on free and reduced-price lunch and 43% of the students were identified as English Language Learners. Academically, Lonsdale was a school in good standing from 2003-2010. Educational levels varied among parents and guardians. A survey conducted by Knox County Schools in the fall of 2004 indicated that many of our parents had an education of eighth-grade or less. One hundred percent of Lonsdale students received free meals in accordance with Provision 3 of the National School Lunch Program. Many businesses, churches and community organizations partnered with Lonsdale Elementary to assist in meeting the needs of students and to support their educational experience.

The administration and Teacher Advancement Program (TAP) Leadership Team examined the TCAP data for the 2009-2010 school year. With a combination of new state standards and new TCAP, current data revealed that 80%-85% of Lonsdale students in third- through fifth-grade were identified as below proficient in reading. After further examination of the data, results showed that two thirds of the TCAP Reading Assessment tested language, writing and research skills. This revelation instilled a sense of urgency within the school, thus the TAP Leadership Team devised a plan of action to address the skill deficits in language, writing and research.

The first step began as the TAP Leadership Team reviewed and grouped the state performance indicators (SPI) into three different categories. The categories included the following: skills introduced through the basal series, skills reviewed through exposure, and skills taught through direct instruction. The TAP mentor teachers presented the categories of skills introduced to their respective grade levels in weekly cluster meetings. During cluster meetings, teachers began to dissect the TCAP practice test questions and aligned each question with the language, writing and research strands of the state performance indicators. The TAP Leadership Team then created a notebook, which included the state performance indicators, grade level expectations and pacing guide for each strand. The pacing guide included time frames, resources and lesson plans for each objective. Lesson plans were created and field-tested by the TAP mentor teachers each week.

In this study, convenience sampling was used as the participants consisted of the following: 48 third-grade students (2010), 44 third-grade students (2011) and 4 third-grade classroom teachers; 43 fourth-grade students (2010) and 50 fourth-grade students (2011) and 3 fourth-grade classroom teachers.

Upon review of 2009-2010 TCAP and Discovery Education scores, data revealed an urgent need for restructuring the literacy framework to meet the unique needs of the students. The third and fourth-grades were involved in a total restructuring of the literacy framework with a strong emphasis on language arts instruction. The customized, site-based professional development under the TAP model provided the teachers with strategic and purposeful goals and objectives to ensure acquisition of literacy/language arts skills.

The first phase of research used the Constant Comparative method to analyze interview responses that were collected. The length of each interview varied from 20 minutes to 40 minutes. Interviews were then transcribed verbatim and the transcriptions were examined and coded for repeated themes from each of the respondents. These themes were reported and supported by direct quotes taken from the transcriptions. The analysis of these themes provided insight for the administration as to address the professional development needs for the 2011-2012 school year.

The second phase of the study used a quantitative approach to analyze and compare achievement scores in reading and language on the TCAP in 2010 and 2011. Data analysis compared 2010 RCPI reading and language scores to 2011 RCPI reading and language scores on the TCAP completed by third and fourth-grade students. The research focused on student growth in the areas of reading and language arts. Data was analyzed using an independent samples t test through a computerized analysis system. Student growth was also reported in terms of means, standard deviations and categorical data such as below basic, basic, proficient and advanced.

Teacher interviews were conducted in April 2011 to determine teacher perceptions of customized, site-based professional development and its relationship to literacy achievement.

Teacher interviews were conducted to third and fourth-grade teachers in order to dig deeper into the advantages/disadvantages or success/failures of the sited based professional development in language arts and literacy. Teacher perceptions of the site-based professional development were analyzed to examine patterns and trends within responses. Results were shared with administration and staff at cluster meetings by the end of May 2011 and used to guide future professional development at Lonsdale Elementary School.

The first component of this case study examined teacher perceptions of the effectiveness of the customized, sight-based development activities and structure to improve literacy at Lonsdale Elementary School. The interviews were structured around key components from Guskey's (2000) model to evaluate professional development for this year. The three components were as follows: (1) participants' reaction to the professional development, (2) participants' learning from the professional development and, (3) how did the organization support professional development? More probing questions are included under each component of the interview protocol (see Appendix A). Identified themes for each component were reported and supported by specific quotes from multiple teachers.

When asked to identify the positive aspects of the professional development activities, seven out of seven teachers shared several positive comments. The most common theme of the positive aspects was how the lesson plans and materials were very student-centered and incorporated technology to hold students' interest.

Examples of responses are as follows:

Teacher #2: The most positive thing is that it is student-focused. The most effective method has to begin with "hands-on" learning, not just worksheets, but interactive (PowerPoint activities) for the students.

Teacher #4: I liked that they were student-based, directly based from student needs. This was something we could take and use immediately. Here is a week of lessons, videos and TAP did a great job of integrating technology to get students excited.

Teacher #7: I really enjoyed teaching grammar this year. I've never taught it in such a structured way. The kids started liking grammar because they generally don't feel positive about it ... the kids would get upset if we didn't have our TAP grammar lesson for the day.

When asked about the negative aspects of the professional development activities, there was an overriding theme of time constraints regarding the professional development activities. A total of five teachers noted that more time was needed to implement the professional development activities. It should be noted that of the seven teachers interviewed, 3 teachers were TAP mentor teachers who helped construct the professional development activities for third, fourth and some fifth-grade teachers. This information impacted the outcome for this particular theme. Another important factor, which could have impacted the responses, was the professional development structure started in mid October, and teachers were under time constraints to construct a plan as well as teach all of the language/literacy skills before TCAP testing in April.

Examples of responses are as follows:

Teacher #4: We need more planning time and more time to develop lessons.

Teacher #5: We started late. We need to set up a calendar to chart out a plan for next year.

Teacher #7: I wish I had more time to plan. We came up with it (structure/ plan) later in the game.

A very interesting theme was noted when asked how to improve the professional development for next year and four out of seven teachers mentioned vertical planning between grade levels. Some teachers pointed out the aspects of vertical planning to gain a better understanding of grade level expectations.

Some examples are as follows:

Teacher #2: We need to look at second-grade and where they end and we need to look at where we end and where fourth-grade is going to begin.

Teacher # 6: We need to reach out to other professionals within teaching. We need to look at SPIs for third-grade and fifth-grade and what they have learned and what my fourth-graders will need for fifth-grade.

Teacher #1: We need more sharing with each other between grade levels to know what skills students need to start the year.

When asked how teachers used the professional development activities in their classrooms this year, the primary theme was how teachers adjusted their instruction based on the pre/post test data and also how they incorporated the language skills into other content areas.

Responses are as follows:

Teacher #4: I analyzed test questions and the obstacles students had difficulties with. I'm ahead of the curve for next year.

Teacher #7: The TAP language structure was a great way to assess student learning. I've adjusted my instruction and grammar allowed me to provide more small group centers.

Teacher #5: It helped with sharing pre/post test data, which correlated to TCAP. It helped students to verbalize and label their learning in other areas.

Teacher #6: It helped me hone in on those language skills in different content areas. I brought language skills into reading. For example, we'll pull pronouns, adjectives, adverbs and other parts of speech instead of teaching it in isolation.

When asked about the impact on student learning, the majority of teachers saw improvement in student performance based on observations, daily work and class participation as well as growth in pre/post test data.

Teacher responses are as follows:

Teacher #6: I notice students are more engaged in language than at the beginning of the year. Their writing has gotten better. They are using vivid details with better sentence structure, capitalization and punctuation.

Teacher #1: I can see a big improvement in students' pre/post test data. They liked the competition so they could bring up their scores. They are recognizing language skills in other areas.

Teacher #5: It really impacted student learning. We should teach other subjects in this manner. If we had the time, all out teaching should be this way!

When asked how this would be used next year, all seven teachers wanted to use this structure and focus on language in their classrooms. Teachers wanted to expand the activities and incorporate this structure into other content areas.
Responses are as follows:

Teacher #1: Our team felt very positive about the professional development for this year. We are meeting this summer to make files, games and activities to make it fun. We are going to work on reading SPIs and create more hands on materials.

Teacher #7: I would like to add more PowerPoints, hands on activities and more technology to my lessons for next year.

Teacher #6: I want to continue with the language but add to cross-curricular things to make an impact. I want to make those connections with math as I am departmentalizing and teaching math next year.

Finally, looking at organizational support through both administration and grade level teams, six out of seven teachers felt supported by administration and six out of seven teachers felt supported by their respective grade level teams.
Examples of responses are as follows:

Teacher #1: I felt very supported by the administration. I liked that the principal, assistant principal and TAP master teacher came into my classroom because the students wanted to share what they were doing. It helped drive students to do their work and they looked forward to the classroom visits.

Teacher #2: I felt very supported by the administration. There were clear expectations to where we need to be and gave us a focus.

Teacher #6: Yes, the administration identified the need and gave us the tools that were necessary.

Teacher #5: Initially, the team wasn't supported because it was being built. We were all working from scratch. We didn't know what needed to be supported, but it will come next year. The administration did give us the go ahead to try something new.

Teacher #7: Amazing!!! My team was very complimentary of the lessons considering the short time frame. We shared ideas with one another and worked collaboratively with one another.

Overall, the interview process provided a deeper understanding of teacher perceptions regarding the professional development and its impact on student performance. This information was very insightful and has impacted the professional development plans for the next school year.

The customized, site-based professional development plan was created to meet the unique needs of our students. The ultimate goal as mentioned in the Tennessee School Improvement Planning Process (TSIPP) was to decrease the number of students scoring basic by 10% in reading. The quantitative data analysis of the TCAP scores from 2010 to 2011 provided some insight as to whether or not the professional development plan was successful.

The two components of the TCAP that were measured were the TCAP reading composite and TCAP language composite for both third and fourth-grades in 2010 and 2011. Categorical data using Reporting Categories Performance Index (RCPI) scores and proficiency levels were used to analyze reading and language arts data. Data was also reported using mean scores, standard deviations, and independent samples t test information.

TCAP RCPI Reading cut scores in 2010 for third-grade were 41 Basic, 72 Proficient and 89 Advanced. Reporting of the 2010 student reading scores were as follows: 50% of third-grade students were Below Basic, 35% of third-grade students were Basic, 13% of third-grade students were Proficient, 2% of third-grade students were Advanced. The mean reading score was 46.18 with a standard deviation of 19.70.

TCAP RCPI Reading cut scores in 2011 for third-grade were 39 Basic, 70 Proficient and 88 Advanced. Reporting of the 2011 student reading scores were as follows: 27% of third-grade students were Below Basic, 57% of third-grade students were Basic, 11% of third-grade students were Proficient, 5% of third-grade students were Advanced. The mean reading score was 52.22 with a standard deviation of 18.52.

In comparison of the third-grade TCAP reading scores from 2010 to 2011, there was a significant change of 23% who moved from below basic in 2010 to basic in reading for 2011. There was a change in percentage of students who moved from proficient to advanced by 3% in 2011. The overall mean score for reading increased by 6.04 from 2010 to 2011 (see Appendix A for graphs). Student growth for third-grade showed a 13.8% increase from 2010 to 2011. The independent samples t test yielded $p = .134$, which was beyond the level of significance at $p > .05$. Even though third-grade students showed growth from 2010 to 2011 in reading, statistically speaking, there was not a significant amount of growth to make the correlation between the professional development and student achievement.

TCAP RCPI Language cut scores in 2010 for third-grade were 37 Basic, 67 Proficient and 85 Advanced. Reporting of the 2010 student language scores were as follows: 46% of third-grade students were Below Basic, 40% of third-grade students were Basic, 8% of third-grade students were Proficient, 6% of third-grade students were Advanced, and 10% of third-grade students had higher language scores than reading scores. The mean language score was 43.69 with a standard deviation of 19.21.

TCAP RCPI Language cut scores in 2011 for third-grade were 46 Basic, 75 Proficient and 90 Advanced. Reporting of the 2011 student language scores were as follows: 30% of third-grade students were Below Basic, 48% of third-grade students were Basic, 18% of third-grade students were Proficient, 4% of third-grade students were Advanced, and 45% of third-grade students had higher language scores than reading scores. The mean language score was 53.29 with a standard deviation of 18.76.

In comparison of the third-grade TCAP language scores from 2010 to 2011, there was a 16% decrease of students who were below basic in language from 2010 to 2011. There was an increase of 10% of students who were proficient in language from 2010 to 2011. There was a slight decrease in advanced students from 6% to 4% from 2010 to 2011. The overall mean score for language increased by 2.23 from 2010 to 2011. Student growth for third-grade showed a 22% increase from 2010 to 2011. See Appendix B for graphs. The independent samples t test yielded $p = .017$, which was below the level of significance at $p > .05$. Third-grade students showed major growth from 2010 to 2011 in language, statistically speaking, there was a significant amount of growth to make the correlation between the professional development and student achievement. Another trend that was observed was the number of students who had higher language scores than reading scores for each year. In 2010, 10% of third-grade students had higher language scores whereas in 2011, 45% of third-grade students had higher language scores than reading scores.

TCAP RCPI Reading cut scores in 2010 for fourth-grade were 46 Basic, 75 Proficient and 90 Advanced. Reporting of the 2010 student reading scores were as follows: 49% of fourth-grade students were Below Basic, 40% of fourth-grade students were Basic, 7% of fourth-grade students were Proficient, 4% of fourth-grade students were Advanced. The mean reading score was 50.55 with a standard deviation of 18.95.

TCAP RCPI Reading cut scores in 2011 for fourth-grade were 44 Basic, 74 Proficient and 91 Advanced. Reporting of the 2011 student reading scores were as follows: 36% of fourth-grade students were Below Basic, 44% of fourth-grade students were Basic, 18% of fourth-grade students were Proficient, and 4% of fourth-grade students were Advanced. The mean reading score was 54.92 with a standard deviation of 18.21.

In comparison of the fourth-grade TCAP reading scores from 2010 to 2011, there was a significant decrease of 16% who moved from below basic in 2010 to basic in reading for 2011. There was a 9% increase in the percentage of students who were proficient and no change in advanced category for 2011 (see Appendix B for graphs). The overall mean score for reading increased by 4.37 from 2010 to 2011. Student growth for fourth-grade showed an 8% increase from 2010 to 2011. The independent samples t test yielded $p = .261$, which was beyond the level of significance at $p > 0.05$. Even though fourth-grade students showed some growth from 2010 to 2011 in reading, statistically speaking, there was not a significant amount of growth to make the correlation between the professional development and student achievement.

TCAP RCPI Language cut scores in 2010 for fourth-grade were 46 Basic, 75 Proficient and 90 Advanced. Reporting of the 2010 student language scores were as follows: 49% of fourth-grade students were Below Basic, 40% of fourth-grade students were Basic, 7% of fourth-grade students were Proficient, 4% of fourth-grade students were Advanced, and 53% of fourth-grade students had higher language scores than reading scores. The mean language score was 51.06 with a standard deviation of 18.93.

TCAP RCPI Language cut scores in 2011 for fourth-grade were 45 Basic, 75 Proficient and 91 Advanced. Reporting of the 2011 student language scores were as follows: 34% of fourth-grade students were Below Basic, 44% of fourth-grade students were Basic, 18% of fourth-grade students were Proficient, 4% of fourth-grade students were Advanced, and 62% of fourth-grade students had higher language scores than reading scores. The mean language score was 56.7 with a standard deviation of 18.65.

In examining the fourth-grade TCAP language scores from 2010 to 2011, there was a 15% decrease of students who were below basic in language from 2010 to 2011. There was an increase of 4% of students who were basic in language and an 11% increase of students who were proficient from 2010 to 2011. There was a no change in advanced students from 2010 to 2011 (see Appendix B for graphs). The overall mean score for language increased by 5.64 from 2010 to 2011. Student growth for fourth-grade showed a 10% increase from 2010 to 2011. The independent samples t test yielded $p = .153$, which was beyond the level of significance at $p > .05$. Even though fourth-grade students showed growth from 2010 to 2011 in language, statistically speaking, there was not a significant amount of growth to make the correlation between the professional development and student achievement. Another trend that was observed was the number of students who had higher language scores than reading scores for each year. In 2010, 53% of fourth-grade students had higher language scores whereas in 2011, 63% of fourth-grade students had higher language scores than reading scores.

Urban schools have very specific needs and challenges that requires strategic planning and training to meet the unique needs of the students and the community. New and innovative instructional and curricular plans have been tailored to address the issues of schools in urban settings. One approach that has proven successful is using customized site-based professional development to improve teacher knowledge through collaboration, having common language, instructional practices and common goals throughout the school.

The findings in this case study indicated that the customized, site-based professional development program that was constructed this year had an impact on the overall reading and language TCAP scores for both the third and fourth-grades for the 2011 school year. For example, 10% of third-grade students in 2010 had higher language scores than reading scores. In 2011, there was an increase of 35% of third-grade students who had higher scores in language than reading. The same trend appeared in fourth-grade as well. In 2010, 53% of fourth-grade students had higher language scores than reading scores. In 2011, there was an increase of 9% of fourth-grade students who had higher language scores than reading scores. Overall TCAP scores increased from 2010 to 2011 in both third and fourth-grades. However, statistically speaking, the only significant impact was revealed in the third-grade language scores. All other areas did not show statistically significant changes. This indicated that the professional development plan at Lonsdale Elementary did have a positive impact on student achievement in the areas of reading and language; however, it cannot be the sole contributor to the increase in student achievement.

There were a number of questions that were raised throughout this study. First, these results are comparing two different cohorts of students in both third and fourth-grades. This study did not examine student growth over time or review value added scores of teachers. What were the implications for the next school year? Based on teacher interviews, this structure can expand to the next level. Teachers were excited to move in this direction as well as expanding lessons, materials and technology that would enhance the current literacy/language instruction and structure that was already in place. This study had great implications for professional development plans for next year. Teachers and Administration are making plans for vertical planning between grade levels to ensure students are prepared to enter the next grade level. Discussions began to move toward teacher training on student-based strategies to compliment the current literacy/language structure already in place. As teachers analyzed student data from pre/post tests during the cluster meetings, discussions were directed toward creating formative assessments every four and a half weeks to determine if students were retaining information and provide more review opportunities for students. Another advantage for next year was the fact that the lessons were already designed and would begin at the beginning of the school year; therefore, little time would be wasted to develop a plan to address the needs of the students.

Overall, the mixed method study that is the heart of this chapter provided insight as to the teacher perceptions of the customized professional development and the impact it had on student performance. The qualitative data provided a number of directions for the professional development plan for the next school year and suggested that the customized, site-based professional development activities had a positive impact on student performance.

APPENDIX A

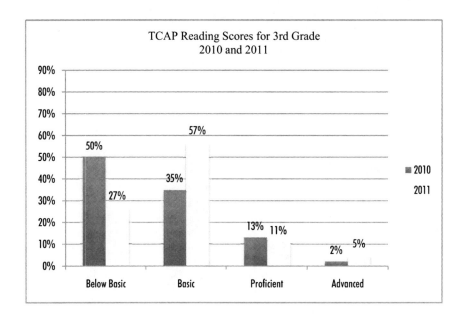

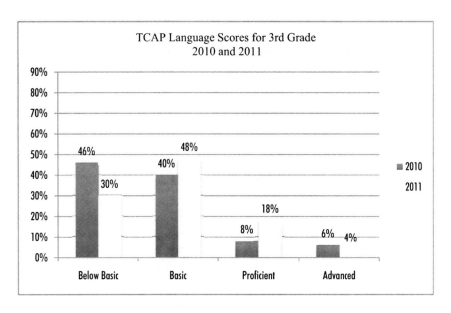

APPENDIX B

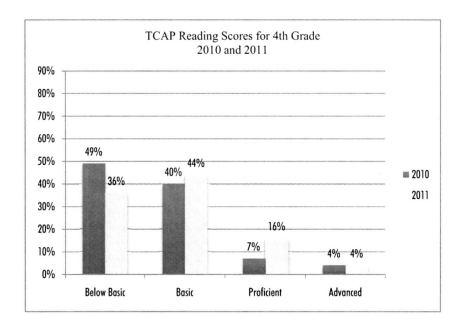

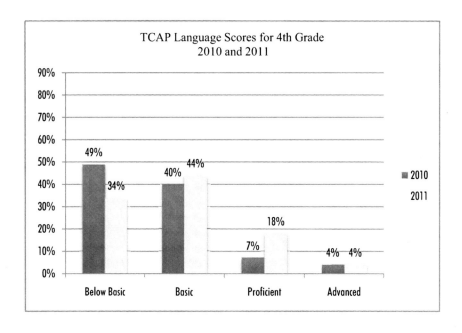

REFERENCES

Burns, M., & Helman, L. (2009). Relationship between language skills and acquisition rate of sight words among English language learners. *Literacy Research and Instruction*, *48*(3), 221-32.

Danielson, C. (2002). *Enhancing student achievement: A framework for school improvement*. Alexandria, VA: Association of Supervision and Curriculum Development.

DuFour, R., DuFour, R., Eaker, T., & Many, T. (2006). *Learning by doing: A handbook for professional learning communities at work*. Bloomington, IN: Solution-Tree.

Fisher, D., & Frey, N. (2007). Implementing a schoolwide framework: Improving achievement in an urban elementary school. *The Reading Teacher, 61*(1), 32-43.

Guskey, T.R. (2000). *Evaluation professional development*. Thousand Oaks, CA: Corwin Press

Kennedy, E., & Shiel, G. (2010). Raising literacy levels with collaborative on-site professional development in an urban disadvantaged school. *The Reading Teacher, 63*(5), 372-383.

Lazar, A. (2006). Literacy teachers making a difference in urban schools: A context-specific look at effective literacy teaching. *Journal of Reading Education, 32*(1), 13-21.

Marzano, R. J., Pickering, D., & Pollock, J. (2001). *Classroom instruction that works: Research-based strategies for increasing student achievement*. Alexandria, VA: Association of Supervision and Curriculum Development.

Mitchell, C., & Castle, J. B. (2005). The instructional role of elementary school principals. *Canadian Journal of Education, 28*(3), 409-435.

Musti-Rao, S., Hawkins, R., & Barkley, B. (2009). Effects of repeated readings on the oral reading fluency of urban fourth-grade students: Implications for practice. *Preventing School Failure, 54*(1), 12-23.

Peck, S. (2010). Not on the same page but working together: Lessons from an award-winning urban elementary school. *The Reading Teacher, 63*(5), 394-403.

Reeves, D. B. (2009). *Leading change in your school: How to conquer myths, build commitment and get results*. Alexandria, VA: Association of Supervision and Curriculum Development.

Tate, M. L., (2003). *Worksheets don't grow dendrites: Twenty instructional strategies that engage the brain*. Thousand Oaks, CA: Corwin Press.

CHAPTER 8

STUDENT LEADERSHIP TEAMS

The Key to Sociopersonal Development

Alisha B. Hinton

Student leadership programs and councils have most often been left to the upper grades of middle and high schools. It is assumed that these students had more flexibility in their academic schedules and the independence to perform leadership opportunities at times outside the typical school day. Too often, elementary-aged students were neglected in the area of leadership development. Time and resources were not utilized in a way that allowed these students a voice and presence in the functioning of the elementary school. Administrators, teachers, and parents created and organized activities and events in which elementary students participated. These events may be schoolwide, grade level, or take place in individual classrooms. In each case, adults took the lead in the development of the activities, while students reaped the benefits at the end of the project. Instead of inviting students to enjoy the end result, the intent was for students to develop, plan, and implement programs and campaigns that benefited the school, as well as support their own leadership development.

Elementary-aged students had limited access to leadership opportunities in the elementary school setting. Students were often on the receiving

Great Leaders Equal Great Schools:
Alliances and Discourse for Educational Reform, pp. 141–151
Copyright © 2012 by Information Age Publishing
All rights of reproduction in any form reserved.

end of most school-based activities, having little to no say in the development or organization of service or learning activities. The lack of an organized student leadership group in the elementary school setting contributed to the lack of sociopersonal development in students. Sociopersonal skills are those related to a person's commitment to individual well-being and volunteerism, and the opportunity for a citizen to determine his own needs and to influence decisions that affect him. A student leadership team may help to facilitate the participation of students in meaningful roles within their elementary school. Students may play major roles in mentoring peers at multiple grade levels, targeting and developing service-learning projects for the school and community, and performing service-related tasks for the base school.

The purpose of the single-site, qualitative case study that grounds this chapter was to explore the sociopersonal development of students in fourth-grade who participated in an intermediate student leadership team. The voluntary leadership program incorporated leadership lessons of self-awareness, creativity, ability to inspire, ability to listen, and opportunities to reflect. Service-learning projects at both the school and community level allowed students opportunities to practice these leadership skills. In sum, the research questions that guided this effort were:

1. How does participation in a student leadership team affect the sociopersonal development of the fourth-grade student representative?
2. What are fourth-grade teacher perceptions of student sociopersonal development as a result of participation in a student leadership team?

Limitations within this effort research project were those associated with a qualitative study. Bias on the part of the participants in response to the survey questions was one limitation. Data collected from this study were not generalizable to other schools or grade levels due to the single data collection location. Because the researcher was an administrator at this school, participants may be more inclined to report favorably regarding this new initiative.

Opportunities for student leadership development at all levels of a student's academic career were an integral aspect of growing the whole student. At the elementary school level, student leadership was often overlooked as too time intensive or not relevant to the required curriculum. This study targeted the meaningful integration of a student leadership team at the elementary school level for the purpose of increased student sociopersonal development. Administrators and teachers who

wanted to create a student council at their school benefited from the findings of this study.

In order to better understand the efforts being made to understand the
problem some definitions are in order:

- Student Leadership Team—an extracurricular organization for students in an elementary school to learn leadership skills and participate in service-learning projects.
- Sociopersonal Development—a commitment to individual well-
  being and volunteerism, and the opportunity for citizens to determine their own needs and to influence decisions that affect them.

Student leadership and the development of students beyond the
required curriculum was often overlooked in elementary school settings.
Too often, administrators, staff, and parents took the lead in organizing
events or learning activities that would more greatly benefit students, if
given the chance. Students in the intermediate grades of three though
five should be allowed the opportunity to practice what they learn in the
regular curriculum. Whether they organize community-service or school-
based projects, students should have the advantage of developing their
leadership skills at the school level. A student council could also be of
benefit to the school's administration and faculty. Tasks that were often
seen as additional time constraints to school staff may be provided as
excellent learning opportunities to students. Student leadership team
members had the power to contribute additional perspective to the school
community and school growth. As a member of the student leadership
team, students were provided the format to practice leadership skills and
positively impact the school and community.

Research on student leadership programs and effectiveness focused on
four categories; importance of leadership groups for students at the school
level, how to support curriculum through increased leadership opportunities, examples of opportunities to incorporate leadership activities, and the
benefits offered to student participants. A majority of the available research
pointed to the positive effects of student leadership in public schools.

SIGNIFICANCE OF STUDENT LEADERSHIP

The importance of offering student leadership opportunities, as reported
by Ponder and Lewis-Ferrell (2009), is seen in the small "butterfly effects"
throughout a school. These small changes in leadership development can
lead to a chain of events that produce large-scale effects for the school as a
whole (Ponder & Lewis-Ferrell, 2009). Beyond the school environment,

participants are exposed to activities that develop students beyond the confines of the school. Students learn how their actions affect processes at the school level, while at the same time preparing them to make decisions that will be put to practice in the community. Karen A. Roland (2008) offers that a student's community involvement may be enhanced by the participation in school-based citizenship programs. The student's awareness of self-help and societal engagement are heightened by the knowledge gained in school leadership roles (Roland, 2008). The insight gained in school, leads to increased preparedness as global citizens (Ponder & Lewis-Ferrell, 2009).

CURRICULUM ENHANCEMENT

A student leadership program is not a self-contained initiative. Projects and activities should support the regular academic curriculum. Connections should be put in place to extend student learning beyond the foundational curriculum. Roland acknowledges the importance of integrating student leadership with educational programming, which recognizes intercultural education (Roland, 2008). In addition to the importance of raising globally responsible adults, student leadership programs should focus on building students who can analyze, reflect, and evaluate their experiences (Ohn & Wade, 2009). These skills can be supported and applied through an integrated approach in reading, writing, social studies, science, math, and technology standards (Ponder & Lewis-Ferrell, 2009). Opportunities to learn and apply leadership responsibilities may also come about through various examples and contexts.

EXAMPLES OF STUDENT LEADERSHIP OPPORTUNITIES

Research offers numerous avenues in which to integrate student leadership into the regular education curriculum. Many of the ideas offered are integrated into the regular school day through instructional strategies and projects. The goal is to move toward a shared vision to create an environment that generates new ideas and supports creativity (Daft, 2007). The strategies presented in the research lead to the common theme of integration. Peer support and collaboration is also one strategy that is offered by Roland to increase citizenship (2008). Students may serve on student councils, governing boards, or diversity committees (Levinson, 2009). Susan Leshnower (2008) offers one strategy of incorporating storytelling into the development of a shared vision for student learning. Students who are given an academic goal can use acting out or storytelling to relay that vision to others. Another way to integrate leadership development is through teamwork activities. These activities prove to strengthen student leadership through role play or simulation (Leshnower, 2008). Regardless of the activity offered, Roland says these opportunities can be direct or indirect instruction, empathic development in the student, and community building (Roland, 2008). Through the integration of these instructional approaches, student benefits are broad.

STUDENT BENEFITS

The benefits to students involved in leadership development programs are both academic and social. Roland offers that student involvement in citizenship or character education programs can support a school goal of community building. The relationships formed can have a profound effect on students in the educational setting (Roland, 2008). These students exhibit enhanced motivation and enthusiasm toward school (Ponder & Lewis-Ferrell, 2009). These attitudes lead to increased attendance due to the involvement with student leadership projects (Ponder, 2009). Overall benefits for the students include; the capacity to think critically, respond with sensitivity and understanding to perceived differences, negotiate conflicts and protect and defend human rights (Cogan & Derricott, 2000). Socially, students are motivated and energized to look toward the future in a promising way that provides them with meaning (Daft, 2007).

The design for this study was a qualitative, single-site case study. Research focused on two specific areas: fourth-grade student representatives' perceptions of sociopersonal development and fourth-grade teachers' perceptions of student growth as a result of participation in the student leadership team. By using a qualitative method, the researcher was able to conduct interviews with all research participants. This allowed the researcher to determine common themes found in the feedback provided.

This study took place at A. L. Lotts Elementary School, a large, suburban school, serving children from Kindergarten through Grade 5. Total school enrollment was roughly 1,100 students as of August 2010. The facility included 52 regular education classrooms, seven of which were located in portable buildings. There were two comprehensive development classes, two resource classes, and one personal accountability class. Other support services included: one curriculum coach, one gifted and talented coach, two speech teachers, and part-time physical and occupational therapists. Related arts were also provided to each student. There were three music teachers, three physical education teachers, two art teachers, two guidance teachers, and one media specialist.

After school hours, the facility was used for a variety of community functions such as Boy Scout and Girl Scout meetings, sports team practices, election voting, and afterschool and summer day care programs. Student enrichment programs were also offered to students after school hours. Math Olympiad, cross-country, and yearbook club were programs in which students participated.

Lotts had a very active and supportive Parent-Teacher Association. For numerous consecutive years, PTA membership had been 100%. Lotts' PTA sponsored a fall festival during the fall semester, Scholastic book fairs twice a year, and afterschool student enrichment programs during the fall and spring semester.

Lotts was located in an upper-class suburban community, with many families moving to the area for employment reasons. Although the majority of the student population is Caucasian, there were a wide variety of minority populations identified in the school as reported in Table 8.1.

A. L. Lotts' preliminary 2010 achievement levels for grades three through five in reading and math were well above state proficiency targets. The state Reading/Language Arts proficiency target for 2009-2010 was 32%. The state Math proficiency target for 2009-2010 was 20%. These percentages were the minimum proficiency expectations for the state during the initial year of more rigorous curriculum standards and assessment.

A. L. Lotts' combined proficient and advanced levels for reading and mAs administration and faculty planned for the 2010-2011 school year, school goals were developed to address the needs of all students. Students scoring in the 11th-25th percentile in reading and math were targeted to receive additional support within the classroom. Educational assistants (EA) continued to support the classroom teachers in working with small groups and individual students. Along with the EA support, curriculum coaches worked alongside classroom teachers to develop research-based

Table 8.1.   Racial Demographics of A. L. Lotts' Student Population

Ethnicity	Percentage of Students
White	84
Asian	9
Black	3
Hispanic	3
Other	1

Table 8.2.   Proficient/Advanced Achievement Levels

Grade Level	Reading Achievement	Math Achievement
Third-grade	67%	66%
Fourth-grade	69%	66%
Fifth-grade	72%	63%

lessons. These strategies ranged from collaborative projects to more indi-vidualized instruction to better meet student needs.

This site was chosen as the research site due to convenience for the researcher. The researcher was currently the assistant principal at Lotts and understood the current needs of the school and student body.

Participants for this research consisted of fourth-grade student repre-sentatives and fourth-grade teachers. Fourth-grade was selected based on the grade ranges that will participate in the student council at Lotts, grades three through five. These students had one remaining school year at Lotts. This allowed the researcher to continue to track their sociopersonal development and progression as they returned as fifth-graders for the following school year. This also provided a sufficient sample size from which to collect data. Their feedback helped to develop a more meaningful program for the 2011-2012 student council participants, many of which may be student participants from this year. The eight fourth-grade teachers of these students also contributed data as participants, providing their perceptions of the students' socioper-sonal development based on involvement with the student leadership team.

FINDINGS FROM INTERVIEWS

After analyzing the interviews gathered, two main themes emerged for research question one and one main theme for the second research ques-tion. Below is a discussion of each:

Increased Leadership Opportunities

When both students and teachers were interviewed, a recurring theme in their answers was the increased opportunities for student leadership. These opportunities allowed the students to increase their involvement in the overall school culture and dynamics. Student representatives com-mented on how they felt they were now a part of the school in a way they had not before the Student Leadership Team (SLT). Many teachers com-mented on how student leadership had been a void at A. L. Lotts. One teacher commented that she felt that student leadership was a bit of a vacuum at A. L. Lotts compared to other schools in which she had taught. With the introduction of a SLT, students now had more opportunities to engage in leadership programs and services. Examples of teacher comments related to increased leadership opportunities include:

Teachers #1: It (Student Leadership Team) gives them the opportunity to do things to better the school and to work with the community in a leadership type of position.

Teacher #2: The SLT offers students the opportunity to work with others, to be a leader because she [student representative] has the opportunity to talk with our class and share.

Teacher #3: I think it SLT offers a chance to develop leadership skills: decision-making, responsibility, seeking others' opinions on issues, becoming aware of their [student representatives] function as a leader.

Teacher #7: The SLT offers them (student representatives) the chance to think of the school as a whole. It gets them to stretch their thinking of our school as a community and them as a part of that community.

Of the eight teachers interviewed, a general consensus was reached in regards to the implementation of the Student Leadership Team and increased leadership opportunities. Student representatives also commented on the expanded opportunities they had as part of the SLT. A few student comments include:

Student #3: I've enjoyed all the projects. I liked when we interviewed the adult leaders. I learned that the PTA President likes to help people and she listens to others.

Student #4: I feel like we're learning a lot of skills that will help you when you try to lead something. We learned how to organize something or how to have everyone working on a project. I liked making the posters for the clothing drive.

Student #5: I think the interview and the posters were the most helpful. We can know what other leaders do and how they help. It can help us learn how to be leaders.

Heightened Self-Perception as a Leader

The second theme that helped to clarify the impact of an SLT on sociopersonal development of student representatives is their heightened self-perception as leaders in the school. When asked if they felt like a leader and why, each of the eight student representatives responded with positive comments. The student comments include:

Student #1: I really feel like a really big leader because I got to be with people and when they have troubles, I can listen to their ideas.

Student #2: Being a part of the group has helped me. I can learn from what the fifth-graders have learned and help the third-graders. I think I'm a student leader because I stand up for my ideas and I'm trying to work on seeing more details in my plans.

Student #3: I see myself as a leader because I'm on the SLT and we like to help people. I help my teacher and other kids in my classroom.

Student #5: I think I'm a leader because I help other people if I can and I'll give my opinion on things. They can help me and I can help them.

Student #6: I think I am a leader. Like when we play tag, I give out some ideas. I think I am pretty confident to share my ideas.

Improved Confidence Within the Classroom

The overwhelming theme in teacher responses in regards to the second research question was improved confidence in the student representatives. Although many teachers stated that the student representative had intrinsic leadership qualities prior to his or her participation in the Student Leadership Team, those qualities where strengthened and better defined in the classroom. One teacher shared how the student representative has come into her own and bloomed in the classroom. Examples of teacher comments related to improved confidence within the classroom include:

Teacher #3: She's become a little more mature in a very short period of time. Before it was this laughing, giddiness. She's stepped up and been a little more serious. As a leader, she has changed.

Teacher #5: I have noticed that she has improved as far as communicating with others about what she's been doing and she's improved skills as far as standing in front of the group and saying I need some feedback. Without a purpose, she wouldn't necessarily do that.

Teacher #6: In the classroom they rarely get to share their ideas. It's an opportunity for them to get to showcase their ideas and what they can do.

Two teachers responded specifically on how the experience in the Student Leadership Team has increased the already present leadership skills in their students. The comments include:

> Teacher #7: He is a natural leader in a very quiet way, more example than words. He will make suggestions quietly. This was a good opportunity for him to become more outspoken and more confident.

> Teacher #8: She is more personal and seems to have really stepped up. She's become more assertive. She approaches me with a sense of responsibility. I don't have to ask her for help.

After conducting personal interviews with student representatives and their respective fourth-grade teachers, both research questions were adequately answered. Student representatives also shared a sense of encouragement in the program's implementation. In addition to answering the two research questions, student representatives also shared ideas on how to improve the program for next school year. What I found when interviewing teachers was perhaps a sense of encouragement and satisfaction in the implementation of the Student Leadership Team and the growth in their student representative. One teacher summed up the SLT as, "the opportunity to develop relationships with the administration and learn to communicate with others. This is the first step to building a foundation on how to get things done." Another teacher shared, "Every student ought to be responsible in some way to his or her school. Even if it's the smallest effort, would make them more aware of why they're here and it's not just a place they come to from 8:30 to 2:30."

IMPLICATIONS FOR PRACTITIONERS

This single-site, qualitative case study explored the sociopersonal development of students in fourth-grade who participated in an intermediate student leadership team. The program incorporated the leadership lessons of self-awareness, creativity, ability to inspire, ability to listen, and ability to reflect with service-learning projects at both the school and community level.

Research findings showed that a student leadership team at the elementary school level helped to develop the student representative's sociopersonal development. There were numerous positive implications of a student leadership team for the elementary administrator. Students who participated in a student leadership team have the tools to make better choices in and out of the classroom. This could lead to fewer behavior referrals or discipline issues within the classroom. Students are also exposed to opportunities to practice appropriate leadership skills with one another or community members.

Specifically, for the teachers and administrators at A. L. Lotts Elementary, the successful implementation of the Student Leadership Team filled a void at the school. Student representatives brought a sense of energy and new ideas to the school culture. The students strengthened an already strong academic program at A. L. Lotts with strong school and community service. If elementary practitioners were searching for a way to energize students while developing future leaders, an elementary student leadership team may be the right answer.

REFERENCES

Daft, R. (2007). *The leadership experience* (4th ed.). Mason, OH: South-Western.

Leshnower, S. (2008). Teaching leadership. *Gifted Child Today, 31*(2), 29-35.

Levinson, M. (2009). Taking action: What we can do to address the civic education gap. *Social Studies Review, 48*(1), 33-36.

Ohn, J. D., & Wade, R. (2009). Community service-learning as a group inquiry project: Elementary and middle school civiconnections teachers' practices of integrating historical inquiry in community service-learning. *The Social Studies, 100*(5), 200-211.

Ponder, J., & Lewis-Ferrell, G. (2009) The butterfly effect: The impact of citizenship education. *The Social Studies, 100*(3), 129-135.

Roland, K. (2008). Educating for inclusion: Community building through mentorship and citizenship. *Journal of Educational Thought, 42*(1), 53-67.

CHAPTER 9

INTERVENTIONS THAT WORK

A Look at Student Attendance and Achievement

Renee Kelly

The focus of this work is on how an academic and a social intervention positively impacted the attendance and achievement of high-risk middle school students. Student engagement at its most basic level starts with attendance and I was shocked to learn approximately every nine seconds a student becomes a dropout. To my surprise, high school dropouts can be identified as early as first grade based on their attachment to school and their attendance rates (Alexander, Entwisle, & Horsey, 1997). In the study that is the heart of this chapter, I analyzed the effectiveness of both academic and social interventions to determine if the attendance and achievement of the students would be impacted. A paired samples t test was used to examine the attendance and achievement of the high-risk students before and after both interventions.

SUCCESSES AND DIFFICULTIES

As a woman of color, my experience includes stories from my ancestors which noted that "education was the great equalizer"; I know that they

Great Leaders Equal Great Schools:
Alliances and Discourse for Educational Reform, pp. 153–172
Copyright © 2012 by Information Age Publishing

marched, boycotted, and picketed so that I could have an opportunity to obtain a "first class" education. Moreover, as someone who truly enjoys the social interaction that accompanies attending school, I was equally dumbfounded as to the reasons that one would forgo a chance to "hang out" with friends in an instructional setting. I was also surprised to learn that little research has been done in the area of social interventions to increase high-risk students' attendance and achievement considering that most children are naturally and incredibly social beings (Alexander, Entwisle, & Horsey, 1997).

After reflecting on the literature, I concluded that our obsession as a society with "racing to the top" via increased student achievement has caused us to omit and ignore the realization that we all have a basic need to belong at school before we are motivated to produce academic results in the classroom. The implications of this endeavor prompted me to initiate daily "Principal's Check-Ins" with our high-risk sixth-graders at West Valley Middle School. It is imperative that I identify and connect with these students to ensure that they attend school. Moreover, as a caring and committed adult at school, I make certain that they are engaged in the learning process through a strategic accountability plan supported by our teachers and their parent(s). Although I was internally motivated to succeed in school, the venture taught me that a caring school community can make a difference in the attendance and achievement of high-risk students. While the rigor of the curriculum remained static, the relevance of the instructional material appeared to increase due to the peer interaction and adult accountability for both groups. Ultimately, the high-risk students in the social intervention group experienced greater gains in attendance and achievement than their peers who were exposed to the academic intervention. The sample t-test results revealed that relationships matter!

What the Literature Says
About Attendance and Achievement

America's schools are faced with the incomprehensible task of educating and preparing all students to compete in a global economy. In addition to increased responsibilities related to preparing students academically, schools are similarly experiencing increased accountability concerning the attendance of students. Currently the attendance and achievement of every public school student in the United States is monitored and used to determine the Adequate Yearly Progress (AYP) of the school based on the federally mandated requirements of the No Child Left Behind Act (NCLB) of 2001. While attendance policies are made at the state and local levels, student attendance was not considered a measurable indicator of a school's success until 2001 when it was outlined and detailed in NCLB. School attendance and achievement as defined by NCLB requires that all public schools have a 92% annual attendance rate and proficient academic performance by all students. The No Child Left Behind Act requires that localities keep detailed records of truancy. Additionally, it supports drug and violence prevention activities designed to reduce truancy and improve attendance rates in schools. Consequently, identifying strategies to increase student attendance and achievement have recently become meaningful topics worth researching based on the relationship between student attendance and AYP status according to NCLB. To that end, school boards, superintendents, principals, teachers, and parents are extensively searching for ways to engage children in the learning process at its most basic level by encouraging them to attend school on a consistent basis.

Understanding absenteeism in a school setting is critical to eliminating it and the negative behaviors associated with it (Dube & Orpinas, 2009). Compounding the matter of students not attending school is the fact that high school graduation rates are equally measured by NCLB and are also considered in the AYP equation. Hence, graduation rates are frequently and openly discussed in academic conversations in lieu of attendance rates and academic performance because for many, the graduation rate is an indicator of the culmination of a student's successful academic experience. However, as high school graduation rates continue to climb in the United States, dropout rates also continue to increase (Neild, Balfanz, & Herzog, 2007). Years of research imply that excessive school absenteeism is an indicator of anxiety, depression, and risky behaviors, such as dropping out of school (Dube & Orpinas, 2009).

Neild and colleagues (2007) found that chronic absences also led to academic underachievement and social isolation. In particular, their work mentioned that a sixth-grader who had one of the four signals (a final grade of F in mathematics, a final grade of F in English, attendance below 80% for the year, or a final mark of unsatisfactory behavior in at least one class) had at least a 75% chance of dropping out of high school: (Neild et al., 2007). Most students do not drop out of school because of a major life event or because they have no desire to get a diploma. Rather, they usually quit because of school failure and they typically send strong distress signals to educators for years prior to dropping out. In fact, most students attend school for 1 or 2 years after they have decided to dropout, which suggests that there is a window to intervene and positively influence their school experience and improve their attendance (Neild et al., 2007).

In some cases, students send the message as early as the elementary school years that they are potential candidates to drop out of school based on their school attendance. Alexander and colleagues (1997) found that children's engagement behaviors in the first-grade, such as attendance issues (i.e., tardiness and absences) and in-school behavior accounted for more variance (12%) than their attitudes (i.e., self image, satisfaction with school and locus of control); however, attachment to school in the first-grade was a significant predicator of student dropout. In terms of attendance, dropouts averaged 16 absences in the first-grade, compared to 10 absences for graduates. Each additional absence was estimated to increase the likelihood of dropout by 5% (Alexander et al., 1997).

Purpose Statement

The purpose of my study was to determine if the attendance and achievement of high-risk, middle school students increased because of an academic intervention or a social program. The focus to improve the attendance and achievement of students, particularly in the middle grades, was not a new as evidenced by the passage of NCLB in 2001. In 1989, the Carnegie Council of Adolescent Development's Task Force on Education of Young Adolescents prepared a report, which focused on the recommendations for a new structure for middle grade education. The program task force proposed eight essential principles that addressed issues pertaining to middle grade schools that ranged from dividing middle schools into smaller learning communities to promoting school and community partnerships (Picucci, Brownson, Kahlert, & Sobel, 2004). One of the principles specifically mentioned organizing "middle grade schools to ensure success for all students" (Picucci et al., 2004, p. 2). This principle specifically lent itself to the notion that when grouped for meaningful interactions, middle schoolers can succeed despite their previous learning experiences. In essence, the middle school concept advised that successful middle schools advocate: (1) a belief in excellence and equity for all, (2) a challenging curriculum with high expectations and the provision of expert instructional methods that prepare all students to achieve at higher levels, (3) a collaborative school culture that shares a developmentally and intellectually appropriate purpose, and (4) a partnership involving parents and the larger community in supporting student learning (Picucci et al., 2004).

Subsequently, school attendance and student achievement were tremendously influenced by the adoption of the middle school concept. Ideally, all schools should establish a unique setting where learners can achieve socially and academically provided they have the necessary skills and are well adjusted. For some young adolescents, the middle school setting provides a place where they can develop a relationship with a teacher, which has the potential to be the most significant relationship in their lives. For the educator, it may possibly be one of the final attempts by to engage a student in the learning process through consistent attendance before high school (Hall-Lande, Eisenberg, Christenson, & Neumark-Sztainer, 2007).

Most techniques practiced to improve school attendance assume that students are not intrinsically motivated and hence, condition students to attend school until the rewards and/or consequences prove to be ineffective. Interventions that address the underlying issues associated with academic failure and social isolation could potentially increase student attendance, as well as improve student achievement (grade point average).

Many high-risk, middle school students have poor attendance, low academic achievement, and high discipline referrals. According to research conducted at Johns Hopkins University, high-risk students in sixth-grade were defined as high-poverty students who failed English or math, whose attendance fell below 80% or who received an out-of-school suspension (or failing behavior grade) (Zinth, 2009). As a result, interventions are needed to ensure that these students remain on the path to graduation. Over the course of the last 10 years, educators, legislators, and parents have recognized and verbalized the need to ensure that students attend school. The problem is that most of the strategies used to increase attendance focus on short term gains through positive reinforcement and/or negative reinforcement, which fail to give the student the appropriate skills and necessary motivation needed to create a positive school experience. This project examined if an academic intervention or a social program could positively influence the attendance and achievement of high-risk, middle school students with diverse needs. The research questions were:

1. Does the attendance of high-risk, middle school students increase because of an academic intervention or social program?
2. Does the achievement of high-risk, middle school students increase because of an academic intervention or social program?

Limitations

There was one limitation to my study. The attendance and achievement data collected for the research was based on information provided by the Student Teacher Attendance Report (STAR) used in the Knox County, Tennessee school district. STAR is an electronic student management program that is readily available to Knox County Schools' employees. The data collected in STAR could be incorrect due to human error.

Delimitations

There were three main delimitations to the study. First, the sixth-grade students who were the subjects of the study were selected from only one grade level team (i.e., Team 6-1). Second, the participants in the study were selected by their teachers to participate in the research during the first 6 weeks of school based solely on the teachers' observations of poor attendance, disengagement in classroom activities, and/or limited or inappropriate social interaction with peers. The final delimitation of the study involved the school's guidance counselor implementing the social program with periodic support and assistance from the researcher. The guidance counselor was the only staff member at that the research site who was formally trained to implement the social program. As a result, he was exclusively responsible for conducting the social intervention sessions with the targeted students.

Significance of Study

In spite of the limitations and the delimitations of the study, my project is significant to both educators and administrators. It is noteworthy to educators because it provides suggestions and strategies for improving the attendance and achievement of high-risk students through various interventions based on the diverse needs of the learners. Likewise, the study has implications for administrators because it provides recommendations for approaches that may improve students' attendance and achievement, hence increasing the likelihood of meeting AYP requirements under NCLB. The research of Alexander and colleagues (1997) suggests that when a child develops a positive relationship with a concerned adult in an academic setting, the student substantially increases his/her likelihood of experiencing academic success while experiencing a sense of connectedness to the learning community. In view of that, most research pertaining to students' attendance and interventions has largely focused on the benefits of academic interventions, but a gap exists in the research regarding the advantages of utilizing academic interventions, as well as social interventions, to increase the attendance and achievement of students.

The focus of this research endeavor was to determine if the attendance and achievement of high-risk students in the middle grades was positively impacted by an academic intervention or a social skills program. The purpose of the research was to support, or refute the notion that relevant and rigorous interventions that are supported by caring adults result in improved student attendance and achievement.

We know that academic interventions are often used to improve student attendance and achievement. Yet, we do not know whether a social intervention will increase students' attendance and achievement. As a result, I opted to study the impact of an academic and a social intervention on the attendance and achievement of 20 high-risk, sixth-grade, middle school students.

The literature indicates that numerous authors (Fuchs, Fuchs, & Compton, 2010; Poynton, Carlson, Hopper, & Carey, 2006) have investigated the impact of academic interventions on the attendance and achievement of middle school students. Nevertheless, few researchers (e.g., Graham, Bellert, Thomas, & Pegg, 2007) have examined the specific relationship between the implementation of a social intervention and the corresponding improvement in the attendance and achievement of middle school students. Thus, the literature review revealed a gap in the research. The void in the literature further substantiated the need to examine the impact of a social intervention on the student outcomes of attendance and achievement.

Review of the Literature

In terms of the significance of relationships, the research reviewed suggested that there was a positive correlation between the attendance of students and healthy relationships with a caring adult (Anderson, Christenson, Sinclair, & Lehr, 2004). A substantial body of literature also indicated that there was a relationship between poor student attendance and the high school dropout rate (Alexander et al., 1997; Campbell & Brigman, 2005; Neild et al., 2005; Picucci et al., 2004). Most notably, the review of the literature revealed that information regarding school refusal and dropout prevention were prevalent.

Academic Interventions

After reviewing the literature on academic interventions in the middle grades, several strategies seemed to emerge as commonly used approaches that provided middle school students with additional academic support. The academic interventions mentioned in the literature were typically implemented during school in an attempt to increase student participation while avoiding an extended school day (Fuchs et al., 2010; Poynton et al., 2006). Likewise, teachers were often used to provide instruction during the interventions, but other support staff members were employed to meet the various academic needs of the students without adding additional hours to the school day (Anderson et al., 2004.)

Social Interventions

At the other end of the spectrum concerning the literature on social interventions, Neild and colleagues (2007) researched a successful approach in a Philadelphia middle school that used a daily referral process that was managed by teachers to improve the attendance of students. The daily check-ins resulted in student accountability for missing assignments as well as positive student-teacher relationships. Additionally, the findings of Rosenfeld, Richman, and Bowen's (2000) research concluded that social relationships mattered based on the findings that middle school and high school students who perceived high support from parents, friends, and teachers had better attendance, spent more time studying, exhibited fewer inappropriate behaviors at school, enjoyed school more, participated in school more, and earned better grades.

Hall-Lande and colleagues (2007) examined the importance of peer relationships relative to school attendance. The researchers concluded that adolescence was a challenging time in the lives of most children, and it was a time when students desire a sense of independence yet long for meaningful, social connections with peers. As a result, middle school students form group associations that provide psychological support and a sense of belonging that can positively or negatively impact school attendance. Thus, educators were urged to encourage and to nurture these relationships.

Anderson and colleagues (2004) focused extensively on social interventions that improve middle school attendance. While not responsible for developing the program, the researchers examined "whether the closeness and quality of relationships between intervention staff and students involved in the Check & Connect program were associated with improved student attendance at school" (Anderson et al., 2004, p. 98). Specifically, "Check and Connect" is an intervention model designed to promote student attendance through relationship building, problem solving, and persistence" (Anderson et al., 2004). According to the study, participants "were referred to the program for exhibiting a consistent pattern of absences and tardies during elementary school (i.e., absent or tardy 12% or more of the previous school year and months prior)" (Anderson et al., 2004, p. 101). The employed an experimental design and used quantitative data to determine the findings of the research. The literature relative to the "Check and Connect" study suggested that higher quality relationships were associated with improved attendance at school (Anderson et al., 2004). The results of the research mentioned that the findings were not surprising "given what we know about positive adult-child relationships and child outcomes" (Anderson et al., 2004, p. 108). This study was unique because it was among the first to demonstrate a link between the quality of relationships between students and intervention staff as an important school outcome. These results were particularly promising given that "the students included in this program, by design, were at high-risk for educational failure" (Anderson et al., 2004, p. 108).

Organizational Structure

The literature review unearthed an interesting article that detailed the role that the organizational structure of a school may play in school refusal. According to Hartnett (2007), the organizational structure and culture of a school may contribute to absenteeism. Organizational school structures endorse and reward some social groups (i.e., "Jocks") while ignoring and shunning others (i.e., "Burn-outs") may create a culture of prejudice fueled by nonacceptance. In his work, Hartnett (2007) proposed that when a culture of inclusion has been created, school attendance should increase. Harnett's (2007) research was simple in theory, yet difficult to implement. Ultimately, he recommended that changing a culture of nonattendance required establishing personal relationships with students.

Academic and Social Intervention

One of the few interventions reviewed that addressed both the academic and the social skill needs of students was the SSS model (Student Success Skills) by Campbell and Brigman (2005). The group intervention concentrated on the improvement of student achievement and student success skills (i.e., academic, social, and self-management skills). School counselors were used to implement the intervention with 240 students (12 students from 20 schools) who scored in the mid to low range in math and reading achievement. The model required that the counselors use a structured, group approach to aid students in the development of these three skills (academic, social, and self-management), which were considered essential for a successful experience in school. While the purpose of the SSS model project was to measure the impact of group counseling on student achievement and behavior, as opposed to student attendance, the students that participated in the study were consistently present at school, which accounted for their ability to participate appropriately in the study. The results reported by Campbell and Brigman (2005) were promising and showed a positive correlation the between treatment group and improvement in both academic performance and behavior. The findings of the researchers indicated that the students targeted in the study experienced achievement gains in the reading and math content areas based on their standardized test scores and the successful implementation of the SSS model with elementary and middle school students.

Overall, the literature on the matter demonstrated that work has been done examining the impact of academic interventions on middle school students' achievement and attendance. However, few researchers have considered the implications of social interventions on students' school attendance and achievement. I believe that there are tremendous short and long-term implications for student attendance and achievement, as well as high school completion if students consistently attend school as a result of their academic and social needs being met in the middle grades. The gap in the literature and the research created an opportunity to explore an academic and a social intervention that could potentially improve the attendance and achievement of high-risk, middle school students.

Methods

My study employed a quantitative, experimental design. The experimental study used in the research was a repeated-measures design with an intervention in which measurements were taken on all subjects before and after the treatments. The data source used was STAR. Study participants were assigned student numbers for confidentiality. A computer program, Statistical Package for the Social Sciences (SPSS), was used to statistically analyze the information from the data source. The data source STAR, was chosen because it allowed for a broad source of data.

DATA COLLECTION

Data collection consisted of 12 weeks of STAR attendance and achievement history of the study participants. Attendance and achievement data were examined for a period of 6 weeks before and 6 weeks after the interventions employed by the researcher. The academic and social interventions were implemented for 12-week period. Attendance and achievement data for the study were provided by the school's attendance secretary and focused exclusively on 20 high-risk, middle school students selected for the study. While there were differences in the students' pre and postintervention data, all students were identified as high-risk based on their attendance and achievement history which can be found in Appendix A. Once the collected data was entered into SPSS, the researcher analyzed it. The interpretation of those findings became the basis for a framework determining the differences that existed between the attendance and achievement of the participants in each program. This framework provided a platform for explaining the various ways that an academic or a social intervention impacted the attendance and achievement of high-risk students in the middle grades.

Sample

The subjects in the study were 20 sixth-grade students in Knox County, Tennessee enrolled at Bearden Middle School (BMS) on Team 6-1. Twelve of the subjects were males, eight were females, 13 were Caucasian, and seven were African American. The participants were selected by their classroom teachers based on classroom observations, attendance records, mid term grades, and discipline referrals during the first 6 weeks of the school year. Each student was considered high-risk because of low attendance, poor grades, and/or high discipline referrals. Team 6-1 was composed of six teachers: three Caucasian males and three Caucasian females. All six teachers were involved in selection of the students for the study. The teachers' educator licensure information indicated that they were all highly qualified in their subject areas for grades kindergarten through six, and two of the teachers had highly qualified status through grade eight.

Site Description

BMS is in the heart of West Knox County Tennessee and has 11 elementary feeder schools. Over the last 3 decades, school rezoning placements in West Knox County have affected many families. Students were rezoned to Bearden Middle School due to inner-city schools closing and population growth in other parts of the county. During the 2010-2011 academic year, approximately 44% of the students at BMS received free or reduced-price lunch. Bearden Middle was designated as a Title I school in 2009-2010.

Staff and Student Characteristics

There were 74 teachers at BMS during the time of the research. Fifteen members of the faculty and administration had more than 20 years experience. Fifty members had less than 20 years of teaching experience. Specifically, 20 teachers had 0 to 5 years of experience, 15 teachers had 6 to 10 years of experience, 18 teachers had 11 to 15 years of experience, seven teachers had 16 to 20 years of experience, four teachers had 21 to 25 years of experience, four teachers had 26 to 30 years of experience, two teachers had 31 to 35 years of experience, and four teachers had 36 to 40 of experience. Similarly, 24 teachers (32%) had bachelor's degree, 48 teachers (65%) had master's degrees, and two teachers (3%) held education specialist's degree.

In terms of student enrollment, BMS had approximately 1050 students in grades sixth through eighth during the 2010-2011 academic year with a teacher-student ratio of 14.2:1. Due to the transient nature of the student population, the total number of students varied from day to day. In 2011, there were 298 sixth-graders, 408 seventh-graders, and 344 eighth-graders. Moreover, there were 561 males and 489 females. The breakdown of percentages of students is as follows: Asian (1.55%), African American (22.78%), Hispanic (5.15%), American Indian (0.31%), Pacific Islander (0.21%), and White (70.0%). Attendance was computerized on a daily basis with a follow-up report for teacher review. The average attendance rate ranged from 97% to 88%.

Sources of Information

Attendance and achievement data were collected for the study by accessing STAR. STAR is an electronic student management program that tracks the attendance, achievement, and behavior of the students in the Knox County, Tennessee school district. For the purpose of this study, the researcher reviewed the attendance rates and the grade point averages of the students in the study before and after the interventions. Grade point averages (GPAs) were used for this research because they are typically used to measure student performance and achievement in an academic setting. The sources of evidence used were attendance and grade documents generated by STAR. The strengths of the data sources used were that attendance records and grade cards were readily available and accurate documents. The weakness of the sources used was that human error could result in the reporting of inaccurate data. The site was selected based on the researcher's ability to collect data where the events researched would occur.

Interventions

The academic intervention used for the study was Focus 30, and the social intervention utilized was the WhyTry program. A sample of 10 high-risk, sixth-grade middle school students participated in Focus 30 and 10 high-risk, sixth-grade middle school students took part in the WhyTry program. The social intervention, WhyTry, was being piloted, schoolwide at one other Knox County middle school. The academic intervention involved students participating in a teacher-directed lesson for 30 minutes on a weekly basis. Similarly, the social intervention involved students engaging in a guidance counselor directed program for 30 minutes on a weekly basis.

Each 45 minute class period was reduced by 5 minutes on the designated intervention day (Wednesday) to account for the 30 minutes needed to implement the interventions. The lessons taught during Focus 30 targeted math and reading skills and were designed by building level reading and math instructional coaches. Teachers received the lessons 1 week in advance of the intervention session. Math interventions were held the first 2 weeks of each month followed by reading interventions the remaining 2 weeks of each month.

Focus 30 was an academic strategy used schoolwide at BMS and was based on a variation of Tier 1 of the Response to Intervention (RTI) model. The RTI model is a method of academic intervention used in the United States that was designed to provide early, effective assistance to children who are having difficulty learning. RTI seeks to prevent academic failure through early intervention and frequent progress measurement. The RTI model is based on a three-tier process and relies on academic assessments and evidence-based targeted interventions to improve the academic achievement of students. In Tier 1, research-based instruction is used by the classroom teacher for high-risk students in a whole class setting. Instruction typically lasts for 15 to 20 minutes daily. In Tier 2, general education instruction is also used by the classroom teacher along with specialized interventions in a small group (two to four students) setting for 20 to 30 minutes daily. Tier 3 involves special education instruction that is designed to supplement, enhance, and support Tier 1 and Tier 2 and is provided to individual students or small groups for 45 to 60 minutes daily. Researchers advised that evidence that supports the RTI approach is beneficial in helping all students succeed academically because the model provides every student the additional time and support needed to learn at high levels (Fuchs et al., 2010).

Equally, the WhyTry program was based on a model that is used nationally. WhyTry was implemented by the BMS guidance counselor on the same designated day (Wednesday) as the academic intervention and was observed and evaluated by the researcher frequently. The WhyTry program is a strength-based approach to helping youth overcome their challenges by improving outcomes in the areas of truancy, behavior, and academics. The program is based on sound, empirical principles such as Solution Focused Brief Therapy, social and emotional intelligence, and multisensory learning. The goal of the approach is to teach social and emotional principles to students in a way that they can understand and recall. The program uses a series of ten visual analogies to engage students. Each visual aid introduces a principle to the students such as resisting peer pressure, obeying laws and rules, and decisions have consequences. The ten pictures are reinforced by music, physical activities, and hands-on group activities so different learning styles are addressed. The mission of the program is to answer the reoccurring question of high-risk students, "Why try in life?" According to the founders of WhyTry, the key to successfully implementing the program lies in the ability to connect a caring and concerned adult with a student in crisis (www.whytry.org).

DATA ANALYSIS

 A paired-samples t test was run in the computer program SPSS to examine the statistical significance of the interventions. Attendance and GPA data from STAR were analyzed by the researcher using descriptive statistics (mean and standard deviation). The data were reviewed by the researcher for discrepancies. The data used were an accurate measure of the study participants' attendance and achievement. Student attendance was recorded and reported in STAR electronically on a daily basis by homeroom teachers. To ensure accuracy, the BMS Attendance secretary confirmed recorded absences by notifying all teachers via email on a daily basis of students' absences. In terms of achievement, GPAs were correlated with achievement and, in this case, were calculated based on the grades provided by teachers. Therefore, grades documented in STAR by content area and Related Arts teachers were used for the study.

In summary, the Attendance secretary at Bearden Middle School provided STAR data to the researcher before and after the interventions with respect to the attendance and achievement of the 20 high-risk, sixth-grade students that were selected to participate in the study. A paired-samples t test was run using the computer program SPSS to determine if the interventions implemented during the study statistically impacted the attendance and achievement of the sample students. The data used in the research were valid based on the reliability of the information provided by STAR. The analysis of the data led to the findings that will be presented in two parts: attendance findings and achievement findings.

FINDINGS

The questions that guided this study were:

1. Does the attendance of high-risk, middle school students increase because of an academic intervention or a social program?
2. Does the achievement of high-risk, middle school students increase because of an academic intervention or a social program?

In this study, preintervention and postintervention data were collected on each of 17 students regarding their attendance and achievement 6 weeks before and 6 weeks after a 12 week treatment period. Of the original 20 participants, two of the students in the academic intervention group did not complete in the study due to transfers to other schools. One of the students in the social intervention group did not complete the study due to a long-term suspension.

Attendance

Means and standard deviations for baseline and postintervention attendance and achievement by intervention group are presented in

Table 9.1. Intervention Groups: Pre and Post Attendance and Achievement Mean Scores

		Paired Samples Statistics			
		Mean	*N*	*SD*	*Std. Error Mean*
Pair 1	Social_Term_1_GPA	1.6044	9	.79762	.26587
	Social_Term_4_GPA	2.0011	9	.77056	.25685
Pair 2	Social_Term_1_Abs	4.78	9	4.295	1.432
	Social_Term_4_Abs	3.89	9	3.371	1.124
Pair 3	Academic_Term_1_GPA	1.0838	8	.59888	.21174
	Academic_Term_4_GPA	1.2588	8	.48393	.17109
Pair 4	Academic_Term_1_Abs	4.75	8	3.576	1.264
	Academic_Term_4_Abs	11.38	8	6.610	2.337

Table 9.1. The absences for the study were calculated from STAR attendance data based on the number of days that the study participants did not report to school or were dismissed from school prior to 11:15 a.m. The absences of Term 1, the 6 week period prior to the interventions, were compared with postintervention absence data which were gathered at the completion of Term 4, the 6 week period following the interventions. The study's sample evidence noted in Table 9.1 revealed preintervention absence means equal to 4.8 respectively for the social intervention group and the academic intervention group. However, the post-absence means were 3.9 for the social intervention group and 11.4 for the academic intervention group. Statistically speaking, the sample means as well as the standard deviations were not approximately the same. A paired-samples t test procedure was used to test the quantitative research hypotheses by evaluating whether the mean of the differences between the variables was significantly different from zero. Additional statistical findings of the study are presented in Appendix B and Appendix C.

Achievement

A paired-samples t test was also used to test the quantitative research hypotheses with respect to the achievement of the participants in the study. The results in Table 1 also included the means and standard deviations for the baseline and postintervention achievement data for both intervention groups. According to the data provided by STAR, the social intervention group had a preintervention mean GPA of 1.6 while the academic intervention group began the study with a mean GPA of 1.1. At the conclusion of the 6 week period that followed the interventions, the social intervention group had a mean GPA of 2.0, and the academic intervention group had a mean GPA of 1.3. While the achievement of both groups appeared to be positively impacted by the interventions, the social intervention group experienced significant grade point average gains with a slight variance in the standard deviation.

DISCUSSION

This portion of the research primarily focused on my findings in relation to the literature and the implications for practice. While a wealth of research and knowledge exists with respect to academic interventions in the middle grades, little is known about the impact of social interventions on middle school students. Fostered from the findings in this study, I would encourage further research and exploration on the correlation between social relationships and improved attendance and achievement in the middle grades.

The results of this research challenge those that solely promote the benefits of academic interventions in the middle grades. Yet, it does not refute the literature and research that supports positive student outcomes (e.g. improved attendance and achievement) that result from significant and helpful relationships between educators and students. The literature proposes that there is a positive correlation between the attendance of students and meaningful relationships with a caring adult (Anderson et al., 2004). Additionally, Anderson and colleagues (2004) acknowledged that "attendance is the most basic engagement behavior—if students are not present, they cannot learn, establish relationships with teachers and peers, or experience other forms of engagement at school with learning. Furthermore, students' attendance in school has been associated with student achievement" (p. 98). Thus, the findings of this research support and fill a void in the literature in the respect to people and not programs make a difference in the attendance and achievement of students. While the sample size for this study was relatively small, the findings are significant because the mean achievement of both groups improved, and the attendance of the social intervention group improved considerably.

Implications

The intentional effort to improve the attendance and achievement of middle school students strategically started in 1989 with *Turning Points: Preparing American Youth for the 21st Century* and continued with the passage of NCLB in 2001 and persists today. Consequently, this research may aid students, parents, educators, and instructional leaders in the middle grades with leveraging social interventions to increase attendance and closing the achievement gap of high-risk students. Specifically, educators and school administrators that are desperately seeking ways to support their high-needs students while making AYP may now have the potential means to differentiate instruction as well as interventions. Because other variables may have impacted the attendance and achievement of the participants during the study, future research on social interventions that are qualitative in nature may provide additional insight and research-based recommendations that will assist educators, students, and parents in identifying and minimizing other key factors associated with school refusal and poor achievement in the middle grades.

APPENDIX A—CAPSTONE PARTICIPANTS'
ATTENDANCE AND ACHIEVEMENT DATA

Capstone Participants' Attendance and Achievement Data

Student #	Term 1 GPA	Term 4 GPA	Term 1 Abs	Term 4 Abs
1	0.40	0.71	8	5
2	2.00	2.79	14	12
3	1.00	1.60	7	5
4	3.00	2.70	0	2
5	2.17	2.57	4	3
6	1.67	1.57	4	3
7	2.00	2.21	2	1
8	0.80	1.14	2	1
9	1.40	2.72	2	3
10	Long-term suspension			
11	0.40	0.71	2	5
12	Transferred to another Knox County middle school			
13	1.40	1.75	5	10
14	1.20	1.53	8	13
15	Transferred to a middle school in another county			
16	0.00	0.64	10	21
17	1.67	1.50	3	9
18	1.67	1.86	2	2
19	1.00	0.79	8	20
20	1.33	1.29	0	11

APPENDIX B—PAIRED SAMPLES TEST

		Paired Differences		
		Mean	Std. Deviation	Std. Error Mean
Pair 1	Social_Term_1_GPA - Social_Term_4_GPA	-.39667	.47778	.15926
Pair 2	Social_Term_1_Abs - Social_Term_4_Abs	.889	1.537	.512
Pair 3	Academic_Term_1_GPA - Academic_Term_4_GPA	-.17500	.29345	.10375
Pair 4	Academic_Term_1_Abs - Academic_Term_4_Abs	-6.625	4.307	1.523

		Paired Differences		
		95% Confidence Interval of the Difference		
		Lower	Upper	t
Pair 1	Social_Term_1_GPA - Social_Term_4_GPA	-.76392	-.02941	-2.491
Pair 2	Social_Term_1_Abs - Social_Term_4_Abs	-.292	2.070	1.735
Pair 3	Academic_Term_1_GPA - Academic_Term_4_GPA	-.42033	.07033	-1.687
Pair 4	Academic_Term_1_Abs - Academic_Term_4_Abs	-10.226	-3.024	-4.350

APPENDIX C—PAIRED SAMPLES TEST

		df	Sig. (2-tailed)
Pair 1	Social_Term_1_GPA - Social_Term_4_GPA	8	.037
Pair 2	Social_Term_1_Abs - Social_Term_4_Abs	8	.121
Pair 3	Academic_Term_1_GPA - Academic_Term_4_GPA	7	.136
Pair 4	Academic_Term_1_Abs - Academic_Term_4_Abs	7	.003

REFERENCES

Alexander, K., Entwisle, D., & Horsey, C. (1997). From first grade forward: Early foundations of high school dropouts. *Sociology of Education, 70,* 87-107.

Anderson, A., Christenson, S., Sinclair, M., & Lehr, C. (2004). Check & connect: The importance of relationships for promoting engagement with school. *Journal of School Psychology, 42*(2), 95-113.

Campbell, C., & Brigman, G. (2005). Closing the achievement gap: A structure approach to group counseling. *The Journal for Specialists in Group Work, 30*(1), 67-82.

Carnegie Council of Adolescent Development. (1989). *Turning points: Preparing American youth for the 21st century.* New York, NY: Carnegie Corporation of New York.

Dube, S., & Orpinas, P. (2009). Understanding excessive school absenteeism as school refusal behavior. *Children & Schools, 31*(2), 87-95.

Fuchs, L., Fuchs, D., & Compton, D. (2010). Rethinking response to intervention at middle and high school. *School Psychology Review, 39*(1), 22-28.

Graham, L., Bellert, A., Thomas, J., & Pegg, J. (2007). QuickSmart: A basic academic skills intervention for middle school students with learning difficulties. *Journal of Learning Disabilities, 40*(5), 410-419.

Hall-Lande, J., Eisenberg, M., Christenson, S., & Neumark-Sztainer, D. (2007). Social isolation, psychological health, and protective factors in adolescence. *Adolescence, 42*(166), 266-286.

Hartnett, S. (2007). Does peer group identity influence absenteeism in high school students? *The High School Journal, 91*(2), 35-44.

Neild, R., Balfanz, R., & Herzog, L. (2007). Preventing student disengagement and keeping students on the graduation path in urban middle grades schools: Early identification and effective interventions. *Educational Psychologist, 42*(4), 223-235.

Picucci, A., Brownson, A., Kahlert, R., & Sobel, A. (2004). Middle school concept helps high-poverty schools become high performing schools. *Middle School Journal, 36*(1), 4-11.

Poynton, T., Carlson, M., Hopper, J., & Carey, J. (2006). Evaluation of an innovative approach to improving middle school students' academic achievement. *Professional School Counseling, 9*(3), 190-196.

Rosenfeld, L., Richman, J., & Bowen, G. (2000). Social support networks and school outcomes: The centrality of the teacher. *Child and Adolescent Social Work Journal, 17*(3), 205-226.

Zinth, J. (2009). Middle grades. The progress of education reform. *Education Commission of the States, 10*(4), 1-6.

CHAPTER 10

A CLOSER LOOK AT WRITING IN THE THIRD GRADE

Tiffany McLean

Writing is essential to a young learner's growth and development; however, writing achievement has declined in recent years. Students writing achievement has come under increased scrutiny as more than 70% of U.S. fourth through eighth, and 12th-graders do not write on a proficient level (Collopy, 2008). This decline also puts pressure on teachers and schools to revamp and explore options to improve writing in their classrooms and buildings. The No Child Left Behind Act was passed in 2001 and has been the driving force behind educational policy over the past 10 years. The Act requires states to develop assessments to provide evidence of accountability with the results of these assessments being linked directly to federal funds and Adequate Yearly Progress (AYP) which measures whether students are making adequate achievement gains and affect local school district budgets and performance (Dappen, Isernhagen, & Anderson, 2008). The Tennessee Comprehensive Assessment Program writing test that is given in fifth-grade is one of such tests which are factored directly into AYP.

This study will explore Six Traits writing as a means to increase student understanding of writing and writing terms that are directly linked

Great Leaders Equal Great Schools:
Alliances and Discourse for Educational Reform, pp. 173–188
Copyright © 2012 by Information Age Publishing
All rights of reproduction in any form reserved.

to characteristics of strong writing as measured by a score of six on the TCAP writing assessment. It is the schools hope that exposing students to such terms in the third-grade will increase students' ability to write as they progress into the fourth and fifth-grades. According to the Tennessee Department of Education (TDOE) website, a score of six on the fifth-grade TCAP writing assessment represents a writing sample that is well organized coherently developed, clearly explains or illustrates key ideas, demonstrates syntactic variety, clearly displays facility in the use of language, and is generally free from errors in structure. All of these elements are directly aligned with the Six Trait Model which provides a writing tool for both teachers and students. The Six Trait Model addresses writing along six dimensions or traits which are Ideas, Organization, Voice, Word Choice, Sentence Fluency, and Conventions (Spandel, 2005). An explanation of each trait is listed (Isernhagen & Kozisek, 2000). If teachers are not communicating across the grade levels about students' writing ability, the trajectory of student learning is directly affected. This was evident in the fifth-grade students writing scores which decreased from 84% proficient in 2009 to 78% proficient in 2010. This is a clear illustration of the urgency surrounding issues of improving writing instruction school wide.

Table 10.1.   The Six Traits Writing Model

Description	Trait
Ideas	Ideas are the heart of the message, the content of the piece, the main theme, together with all the details that enrich and develop the theme.
Organization	Organization is the internal structure of a piece of writing, the thread of central meaning, the pattern that holds everything together.
Voice	Voice is the writer coming through the words, the sense that a real person is speaking to us and cares about the message.
Word choice	Word Choice is the use of rich, colorful, precise language that communicates not just in a functional way, but in a way that moves and enlightens the reader.
Sentence fluency	Sentence fluency is the rhythm and flow of the language, the sound of word patterns, the way in which the writing plays to the ear.
Conventions	Conventions are the mechanical correctness of the piece such as grammar, spelling, paragraphing, capitalization, and punctuation.

While the school studied uses a pacing guide to model how to teach writing, there is not a set writing curriculum in place. Furthermore, the pacing guide serves primarily as a timeline for a teachers to ensure that they teach specific skills at specific times. The teachers follow the pacing guides, but are not required to teach the writing skills in the same way. The pacing guide specifies the genre that the teacher should focus on, but it gives them the liberty to teach the genre in the manner of which they choose. The result is a lack of consistency in how writing skills are taught throughout the school and from grade to grade. The teachers do not use a common language for writing and the students' exposure to writing varies from classroom to classroom. The case study that is at the heart of this chapter explores the implementation of the Six Traits Writing Model as an intervention to improve student writing and teacher writing strategies in the third-grade at Gibbs Elementary by the end of the 2011 school year.

The study seeks to answer the following two questions:

1. How does the Six Traits Writing Model Influence teachers and their teaching strategies for writing?
2. Will implementing Six Traits Writing as a writing intervention improve student writing?

The study explores the use of Six Trait Writing in one school setting and within one grade level which causes it to be less generalizable. The school is situated in a rural area with limited diversity within the classroom, and the study explored in six third-grade classrooms with one teacher per classroom. Additionally, the data in the study is self-reported. Some delimitations to the study include the teachers training over each of the traits. Prior to the study each of the teachers participated in 1 day of training over the Six Traits Writing Model. This is the sole training that they received prior to participating in the study. This study contributes to educational research in two key areas. It examines the effectiveness of strategies that propose to improve student writing skills, and teachers' teaching. Additionally, the results of the study will be used to inform future practice in how writing is taught in the school.

REVIEW OF LITERATURE

The Six Traits based approach to writing was developed in the mid-1980s in response to teachers' needs for an assessment tool that was closely linked to effective writing instruction (Bellamy & Kozlow, 2004).The model addresses writing along six dimensions or traits which are ideas, organization, voice, word choice, sentence fluency, and conventions (Spandel, 2005).

Only six traits were identified opposed to naming many more because these traits are easily measured and teachers and students are more able to focus on specific areas of instruction and improvement (Porath, 2010). Providing only six traits gives teachers a set of specific strategies to focus on and encourage them to develop specific skills to improve student writing. The use of this model provides a guide for our teachers to follow and gives students a common language to use when talking about writing.

The Six Traits Writing Model is often cited as an example of best practices in writing instruction and has been widely adopted to improve writing instruction and improve students' writing ability (Collopy, 2008). The Six Traits Writing Rubric was designed to help teachers teach writing more effectively and to encourage students to revise their writing with more focus in conjunction with creating a consistent language and assessment regarding writing (Spandel, 2005). However, Mabry (1999) along with Anderson and associates (2008) would argue that the model promotes reliability in performance assessments by standardizing scoring and writing and believe that rubrics are not accurate measures of how well students can write. Porath (2010) would also agree and say that teachers should only use the model as a support for teaching and talking about writing so that the curriculum does not become too narrowed and the writing does not become too formulaic (Porath, 2010). However, Porath (2010) goes a little further to extend her point by highlighting the original intent of the Six Trait rubric which was to create consistent language when discussing writing, because using the same terminology from year to year is crucial for building a deeper understanding of writing. It provides a model that is easy to follow and directly aligns with the states expectations of writers. Appendices A illustrate the correlation between the Six Traits rubric and the Knox County Writing Rubric for Grades 3, 4 and 5.

With the advent of state testing, benchmarks, and standards, elementary school teachers are pressured to prepare students with proper writing skills (Jasmine & Weiner, 2007). Additionally, few teachers have been trained to teach writing or exposed to effective writing strategies (Reed, 2006). The six trait model provides a guide that leads more toward process writing. The teaching of writing has changed over the years. In the past, writing was not taught; it was assigned and corrected and teachers emphasized the final product of writing, not the process that produced it (Jasmine & Weiner). The Six Traits changes this approach. The Six Trait Model creates a language for teachers to use with students in order to focus more on the process and can provide a starting point for teachers to initiate conversations about writing with their students (Porath, 2010). These conversations that evolve from using the model could also open up opportunities for teachers to collaborate with one another and could result in the development of a variety of strategies based on the traits that could lead to improved student writing. A deeper understanding of writing for students along with additional support for teachers is what the school is seeking and the traits model is capable of providing both. One study showed that students who were in classrooms that implemented six traits felt they had made progress in their writing abilities both in their eyes and in the eyes of their educators (Isernhagen & Kozisek, 2000). If in fact the Six Trait Model defines what we value in writing, then teaching students the traits teaches them, by definition, what good writing is, and teaching them what good writing is the goal that we aim to meet (Arter & Spandel, 1994).

ABOUT GIBBS ELEMENTARY SCHOOL AND THE METHODS OF RESEARCH USED

I followed a 12-week intervention program that focused on Six Traits Writing at Gibbs Elementary School. The study aimed to answer two questions with the focus of one of the questions being on the third-grade teachers and with the other focusing on the students. Over the course of 12 weeks, the students were taught two lessons over each of the six traits by their classroom teachers and then received two minilessons in addition to the lessons which were taught once a week over the 12 weeks by a designated person who was not their teacher. The teachers each selected two students who scored in the developing range which is a 3 or 4 according to the Tennessee Writing Assessment Coaching Rubric for Grades 3, 4, and 5 to track their progress throughout the study. (This rubric can be found in Appendix A). Each of the teachers were interviewed at the conclusion of the 12 week intervention. The study aimed to answer two questions: (1) How does the Six Traits Writing Model Influence teachers and their teaching strategies for writing? (2) Will implementing Six Traits Writing as a writing intervention improve student writing? The Six Traits Model served as the guide for all of the lessons that were developed through the collaboration of teachers and the researcher.

Gibbs Elementary is located in a small close-knit community in Corryton, TN, that claims less than 10,000 residents. The school and the community are rich in history and strong relationships. The school demonstrates a strong commitment to creating a nurturing and safe learning environment for all students. This commitment is represented in the smiling faces of the teachers and the genuine concern that they express for the wellbeing of their students. There are a total of 46 certified teachers on the teaching staff with 37 of these teachers being regular education classroom teachers, four being Prekindergarten teachers, and four Comprehensive Development teachers. Additionally, the grade levels are broken down as 7 first grade teachers, 7 second grade teachers, 6 third-grade teachers, 5 fourth-grade teachers, and 5 fifth-grade teachers. One principal and two assistant principals function as the administration.

The principal at Gibbs sets high expectations for the staff and they rise to the occasion because of that expectation. Student achievement is a top priority at Gibbs. The principal and staff review and reflect upon data on a daily basis and use it to guide their instruction. Each of the grade levels are divided into professional learning communities (PLC) that meet weekly and discuss math, reading, or writing. There are also many occasions where the Curriculum and Instruction facilitator sits in on these PLC meetings to discuss student concerns that may arise. It is within the PLC setting that the third-grade teachers will be developing plans for teaching the Six Trait Writing.

There are roughly 830 students in the building with approximately 40% of these children on free and reduced priced lunch. Of the school population, 98% of the students are White, less than 1% is African American, less than 1% is Hispanic, and less than 1% Asian. This study focuses on the third-grade which consists of six classroom teachers and approximately 123 students. Looking at the third-grade, 100% of the teachers are White and 99% of the students are White with less than 2% of the students being African American, Hispanic, or Asian.

The population studied consisted of 6 third-grade classrooms with one teacher per classroom. There are approximately 123 students dispersed among the six classrooms. This study will examine the interviews of all 6 third-grade teachers and sample 2 students from each of the classrooms and examine their writing. All of the third-grade students receive additional instruction that focuses on the Six Traits writing in the form of 30 minute minilessons that serve to supplement the lessons taught by their teachers.

DATA COLLECTION TECHNIQUES

Twelve weeks were devoted to the collection of student writing samples. Then, teachers were asked to complete an interview which focused on questions regarding their writing teaching strategies as well as their students' development as writers. Each of the six teachers chose two students who scored in the developing range based on the Tennessee Writing Assessment Coaching Rubric for Grades 3, 4, and 5 and submitted his or her writing to be examined for the purposes of the study. Each of these students completed a writing prompt prior to receiving the six traits intervention which was scored by a teacher. The same students completed a writing prompt at the end of the 12-week period which was then scored by the same teacher. The rubric scores the students on a one to six point scale with 1 meaning needs improvement and a six being exemplary. The teacher interviews were coded and examined for common themes from the design. The student's pre and post writing samples were examined to see if the students showed significant improvement following the intervention.

A BIT OF CONTEXT: PROCEDURES RELATED TO STUDENT INSTRUCTION

Teachers met once a week to plan lessons and focus on one trait to focus on for a 2-week period which is taught using a teaching strategy that teaches the skills of one of the traits. They do a 2-week rotation for each of the six traits. They complete lessons for the focus trait throughout the designated 2-week period. They also choose two students from their classroom who have scores of three which means that he or she is in the developing range of writing according to the Knox County rubric. Minilessons are then taught to each of the classrooms once a week for 12 weeks. These minilessons are planned and taught by two people outside of the classroom; they are aligned with the teachers' designated trait for the 2-week period

PROFESSIONAL LEARNING COMMUNITIES

The third-grade teachers meet in PLC once a week. During these meetings they focused on one content area and brought student data from tests or student work samples that were analyzed during the PLC. The teachers use the PLC time to plan the large group lessons for each of the six traits. They focus on one trait at a time and spend their PLC collaborating strategies for teaching the trait 1 week before it is introduced. Studies show that while there is little evidence that one-time, sit-and-get workshops change teachers' practice, studies show ongoing, collaborative efforts are effective in doing so (Reed, 2006). The teachers will continue to collaborate all throughout the year in order to encourage a higher likelihood of changing their writing practice.

SIX TRAITS TEACHER INSTRUCTION

Following the PLC meetings, the teachers each teach a writing trait for a 2-week time period. Together they plan the lessons and teach them to their students on the same days. The students have multiple opportunities to practice the trait during the 2-week time period.

SIX TRAITS MINILESSONS

The minilessons are taught once a week during their morning for each of the six classes block so that the students do not miss any instructional time. The lessons supplement the trait that the teacher is teaching during the 2-week time period and provide additional support to the students. The lessons aim to help the students move toward proficiency in their grade level writing.

WHAT THE DATA SHOWED

Teachers were highly reflective as they answered the interview questions, so there was a wealth of information that streamed from their responses. There were several ideas that emerged from the research; however, there were three major themes that were the most common. First the teachers acknowledged that writing is a process. Second they realized that students respond better to writing when they can identify with it, and third the traits gave both teachers and students more direction. The first discovery from the data illustrated that writing is a process and takes time. Four out of six teachers addressed this thought in their interview. They each made statements that addressed the understanding that writing takes time and requires an understanding of necessary steps in order to effectively improve their students writing.

MAKING WRITING PERSONAL TO STUDENTS

The teachers also realized that students responded better to writing when they made their writing assignments more personal and attached them to their interests. The interviews revealed that four out of six teachers recognized the importance of this thought. Because of this new understanding, the teachers began to have conversations about how to incorporate the student's personal interests into their writing from the very beginning of the school year. Now we will listen to some comments of the teachers about their understandings of the benefits of making writing personal.

Teacher A: Their writing got better when it was something that they chose and thought about.... I started making it more personal to them.... It helps them become better writers and will make them better writers later on.

Teacher C: We were solely focused on writing and there was someone new coming in and doing the minilessons, so they were very enthusiastic and excited about writing.

Teacher C: I started using things that are close to them to draw them in. There was more of a desire to write when things are close to them. They take more ownership in it.

Teacher E: I saw a change in their enjoyment in writing. Everybody wanted to write and everybody wanted to be creative. That was the biggest change I saw. They began to develop their ideas better, and they were more interested in it.

DIRECTION AND FOCUS

Four out of six teachers noted that the Six Traits Model provided them with more direction in how to teach writing. When thinking through this finding, I think that it is important to point out that this theme is very similar to the teachers realization that writing is a process; however, the first thought demonstrates a new understanding about writing yet the new thought is a tool that the teachers can use. They commented that the Six Traits Model provided them with an outline to use with their students, so in turn it provided direction for both teachers and students. The following notations from the teachers further elaborate on the effects of the Six Traits Model and how it improves teacher's abilities to teach writing.

Teacher A: It gives them more direction and gives me more direction in my teaching.

Teacher D: It helped students see or focus ... kind of a guide ... and to see why they did something specific.

Teacher E: It gave me direction and focus.

Teacher F: I think having a more outlined focus as a teacher, made it easier to teach writing. Well for me it did because I like for things to be a little more structured and you just having the Six Traits, you know, more or less an outline for it made me have more direct teaching approaches.

BUT WILL SIX TRAITS WORK?

To understand is implementing the Six Traits Writing Model would help student writing improve I examined the pre and post writing samples from the students and analyzed the responses from the teacher interviews. The pre and post writing samples reflected improvements in the student's writing. The writing samples revealed that of the pre and post writing scores that were collected and scored, 67% of the students increased their writing scores. Thirty-three percent of these students writing scores remained the same which means their scores neither increased nor decreased. There were no decreases reflected in the students writing scores.

The teacher's interviews served to further answer research question number two. The interviews provided additional information and insight into the students' progress and writing improvement. They provided specific examples and teacher insight into the effects that the traits had on student writing. From the data collected in the interviews, three themes about student writing improvement emerged. First, the teachers noticed an increase in their students' abilities to develop ideas. Second they began to see a change in the students' desire and excitement about writing, and third the students became more confident about their writing.

INCREASE IN ABILITY TO DEVELOP IDEAS

The first finding indicated an increase in the students' abilities to develop ideas. "Ideas" as a category is one of the six elements of the traits approach and the trait that was referred to most frequently by the teachers in the interviews. Three out of six teachers addressed the student's new development and understanding in their interview. Each of these teachers referred to the change in their students' abilities to stay on topic and develop their ideas in their writing. Now here are some comments from the teachers about their new understanding.

Teacher A: The main change that I saw in my students was their ability to stay on topic and develop their ideas. They really started staying on topic and not jumping from one idea to a new one, and that is something that I saw more of before we started this process.

Teacher D: They began to develop their ideas better once we started, and they were so much more interested in it.

Teacher E: It became easier for them to come up with ideas. When they got stuck, I would refer back to the lessons and they worked hard to stick to and work on one idea.

INCREASE IN STUDENT CONFIDENCE

The teachers also noted that there was an increase in the students' confidence when writing. There was a shift in the way their students viewed and approached writing. This was evidenced in three out of six interviews where teachers commented on their students' shift in confidence. The following remarks from the teachers give further indicate student's increase in confidence when writing.

Teacher B: They also have a strong desire when they write something for me to read it. It's like they are so proud of what they have written that they can't wait for me to read it ... and I think that just in general putting such a focus on writing and using the Traits made writing more important to them.

Teacher E: I look at my students' confidence in writing and I see a change. Since starting the traits they are more willing to write. They are more confident in their writing.

Teacher F: I think they were more confident in their writing. Umm ... I think as a whole I could see a change, and I think that even as the teacher's confidence grows, so does the students.

INCREASE IN EXCITEMENT

The final finding reflected an increase in their students' excitement' about writing. One of the teachers reported that writing was more like a chore before they started working with the Six Traits, but the interviews reflect a shift from this frame of thinking. The teacher's comments are evidence that the students perceptions about writing improved. This theme was the most common; it revealed that four out of six teachers saw an increase in both their students' excitement and enthusiasm about writing. Now we will listen to some comments of the teachers about their students' excitement about writing.

Teacher F: They are so much more enthusiastic about righting. They kind of get excited about it, and the writing doesn't feel like such a chore to them anymore.

Teacher C: The students were very excited about writing. They wanted to write.... I think that it really made a difference for my borderline writers.

Teacher B: I saw a change in their desire and excitement about their writing.

Teacher D: I saw a change in their enjoyment in writing. Everybody wanted to write and everybody wanted to be creative.

The teachers also addressed additional ways in which the Six Traits Model helped their students' writing improve. They made additional statements to support their students' improvement in writing One of the teachers goes on to state, "It helps them become better writers and makes them better writers later on." This statement further validates the effect the Six Traits Model has on improving student writing.

SO WHAT DOES THIS ALL MEAN?

The implementation of the Six Traits intervention resulted in several new understandings for the teachers involved. The findings revealed a new understanding of writing as a process; it provided direction and focus for both teachers and their students; and further highlighted the fact that writing is well received by students when they can take ownership in what they write. Additionally, the pre and post writing samples showed an improvement in writing across the third-grade. It also encouraged students to better develop their ideas, become more confident in their writing, and develop a new excitement about writing.

I started this study by asking the following two questions: (1) How does the Six Traits Writing Model Influence teachers and their teaching strategies for writing? (2) Will implementing Six Traits Writing as a writing intervention improve student writing? Through the research I found that the teachers involved in the study had a new understanding for writing as a process when using the Six Traits Model. Additionally, they found that if they used writing that is personal to them as a part of their teaching strategies, then the students produced better writing samples. The teachers also found that using the model provided them with direction and focus which benefitted both teacher and student. After completing the intervention and evaluating the students writings samples, it was evident that more than 60% of the sample improved their writing scores based on the Tennessee Writing Assessment Coaching Rubric for Grades 3, 4, and 5. What I found in this study is consistent with the literature in this area. The study allowed the teachers to see and understand that writing is a process. In the past the teachers were more focused on the finished process that they report of writing not being taught in the past, but being assigned and corrected. Their research emphasized the final product of writing, not the process that produced it. Jasmine and Weiner (2007) reported that in the past, writing was not taught; it was assigned and corrected and teachers emphasized the final product of writing, not the process that produced it, but Porath (2010) eluded to the strength that the Six Traits bring to the process of writing and explained that the process and can provide a starting point for teachers to initiate conversations about writing with their students. This study further validates their findings.

Both teachers and students benefitted from the Six Traits intervention. The teachers had a better understanding of how to teach writing, in turn their students' writing improved. The Six Trait Model defines what we value in writing and embodies the characteristics of what good writing is so by teaching students the traits; we are giving them a strong writing foundation and teaching them what good writing is, which is the goal that we aim to meet (Arter & Spandel, 1994). Overall, this study benefitted the school's students which were evidenced in their change of attitude as well as in their improvement of their writing scores.

The study was limited in terms of the size and scope; however, the benefits for the school's third-graders were tremendous. It served the needs of the students and the school. The teachers are already discussing ways of which the Six Traits can be implemented in their classrooms in the next school year. In order to aid them in this mission, I compiled several lessons in binders that the teachers can follow to implement the traits in their classrooms. The Six Traits can be implemented across all of the grade levels, so these lessons will be available to all grade levels in the fall, so it is my hope that the teachers in other grade levels will take time to identify and implement the traits in their classrooms.

In sum, I felt that the 12 week intervention was a success. The grade level learned valuable lessons about writing including an understanding of the writing process and obtained a new knowledge of the importance of focus and direction while teaching this process. The teachers realized that writing is a process and discovered that is easier to teach when the topic is personal to the students. They also developed a better understanding of writing as a process. Additionally, the study helped the third-grade students' writing as well as their attitude about writing improve. The students learned to better develop their ideas, became more confident in their writing, and were excited and enthusiastic about writing.

This study gave me a great amount of insight into how teachers approach teaching writing and into ways of which the Six Traits can help teachers as well as students grow and develop. It also further evidences the benefits of the Six Traits Model. The study gave the teachers a toolkit to refer back to and improved their comfort and confidence in writing while encouraging the students to be more open to writing.

APPENDIX A—TENNESSEE WRITING ASSESSMENT, GRADES 3-4-5: NARRATIVE, 6-PT. COACHING RUBRIC

Criteria	2 In the Starting Blocks Emerging	3 Into the First Turn Developing	4 In the Final Stretch Competent	5 Wow! In the Passing Zone Commendable	6 Breaking the Tape Exemplary	Total
Story parts: Organizing your ideas	Missing several parts or most of story is very weak	Missing one part of the story or one part is very weak	Has a beginning, middle, and end	Well organized	Outstanding organization	Score Key
Details: Explaining your IDEAS	Hardly any details	Missing some important details	Uses details to explain the story	Many details explain action	Outstanding details clearly explain action	$24=6$ $23=6$ $22=5$ $21=5$ $20=5$
Word choice and sentence variety	Poor word choices and weak sentences	Uses simple describing words and sentences	Has some descriptive and action words, some sentence variety	Uses figurative language and has sentence variety	Exceptional word choice and sentence variety	$19=5$ $18=4$ $17=4$ $16=4$
Editing	Very poor editing	Has many Editing errors	Has some editing errors	Very few editing errors	Generally free from errors	$15=4$ $14=3$ $13=3$ $12=3$ $11=3$ $10=2$ $9=2$ $8=2$

APPENDIX B—INTERVIEW PROTOCOL

Hello Ms. _____,

The interview is the final piece to conclude our research study over the Six Traits Writing model. Each teacher will be asked the exact same questions, and every interview will be conducted in the same manner. I will ask a question and you will be given an opportunity to respond. This interview will be recorded; however, all responses will only be used for the purposes of this research study. The interview will take approximately 10 to 15 minutes. Do you have any questions before we begin?

Interview Questions

1. How did you implement Six Traits Writing in your classroom?
2. Did you see any changes in your student's efforts to achieve in writing following the Six Traits lessons and minilessons that were taught during the intervention? If so, what changes did you see?
3. Did implementing Six Traits writing effect your perception of teaching writing? If so, what were the effects?
4. Did the Six Traits model encourage you to use different teaching strategies? If so, what strategies were encouraged?

REFERENCES

Arter, J., & Spandel, V. (1994). *The impact of training students to be self assessors of writing.* Portland, OR: Northwest Regional Educational Laboratory.

Bellamy, P., & Kozlow, M. (2004). *Experimental study on the impact of 6+1 trait writing model on student achievement in writing.* Portland, OR: Northwest Regional Educational Laboratory.

Collopy, R. M. (2008). Professional development and student growth in writing. *Journal of Research in Childhood Education, 23*(2), 163-178.

Dappen, L., Isernhagen, J., & Anderson, S. (2008). A statewide writing assessment model: Student proficiency and future implications, *Assessing Writing, 13*(3), 45-50.

Isernhagen, J., & Kozisek, J. (2000). Improving student's perceptions as writers. *Journal of School Improvement, 1*(2), 3-4.

Jasmine, J., & Weiner, W. (2007). The effects of writing workshop on abilities of first grade students to become confident and independent writers. *Early Childhood Quarterly, 35*(2), 131-139.

Mabry, L. (1999). Writing to the rubric: Lingering effects of traditional standardized testing. *Phi Delta Kappan, 9*(9), 673-679.

Porath, S. (2010). 6 traits writing rubric: Things that make us smart can also make us dumb. *Wisconsin English Journal, 52*(2), 54-57.

Reed, D. (2006). Time's up: How to stop running out of time for writing across the curriculum. *Journal for Staff Development, 27*(3), 36-42.

Spandel, V. (2005). *Creative writers through six trait writing assessment and instruction.* Boston, MA: Pearson Education.

CHAPTER 11

COMPREHENSIVE APPROACHES TO BEHAVIORAL DISORDERS

Terry L. Nieporte

An effect of No Child Left Behind legislation has been an alignment with academic standards and assessment. However, behavioral standards have not been defined from state to state or even from school to school within a district. Sailor, Stowe, Turnbull, and Kleinhammer-Tramill (2007) stated that "if standards-based educational reform efforts and systems alignment are to have the intended impact on schools, social-behavioral standards must become a part of reform efforts, and effective strategies for ensuring that result must be identified" (p. 368). In a 2004 national survey (Public Agenda, 2004), 76% of middle and high school teachers indicated that if student discipline problems were less prevalent they would be more effective in their teaching.

Additionally, while schools may use an office referral system to track disciplinary issues, the use of these data to address behavioral issues has traditionally been to remove the student from the classroom through exclusionary measures such as in-school or out-of-school suspension or expulsion (Gregory & Ripski, 2008). This loss of classroom attendance along with the disruptive behavior when in the classroom setting can impact the academic achievement of these students (Arcia, 2006; Sailor et

Great Leaders Equal Great Schools:
Alliances and Discourse for Educational Reform, pp. 189–210
Copyright © 2012 by Information Age Publishing

al., 2007). According to Sailor and colleagues (2007), "this is so because many of the students referred out of class will have less exposure to instruction in an academic context but be nevertheless required to participate in the general assessments" (p. 370).

When at-risk students are involved, the negative impact due to disciplinary issues on academic success may be even larger (Noguera, 2003). School districts have employed a variety of techniques to address the issue of students with multiple disciplinary referrals as a means to increase these students' social and academic success. Researchers (Cohen, Kincaid, & Childs, 2007; Sailor et al., 2007) have typically investigated the impact of specific strategies of a particular program to decrease discipline referrals and to increase the academic growth for students who previously had been negatively impacted by their own behavioral choices. However, an investigation into a more comprehensive approach to discipline issues using a variety of strategies and a combination of several plans may yield a more positive gain for the students. A comprehensive discipline plan will include the components of a discipline tracking system, a schoolwide positive behavior support program, and a multidiscipline intervention team focusing upon the students with needs due to inappropriate behavior.

The purpose of the research in this chapter was to explore the effectiveness of a comprehensive approach to address disciplinary issues of students with frequent office referrals. Interest for this study originated when disciplinary and academic data from the 2006-2010 school years were collected and analyzed in September 2010. Based on the data collected it appeared that the school was less successful addressing the academic needs of the at-risk students with multiple behavioral issues than the students with few office discipline referrals. Because the administration and the leadership team felt that disciplinary issues were impacting student achievement, a comprehensive discipline plan was devised that combined several components of previous discipline initiatives with a new discipline tracking system to create a schoolwide discipline plan.

A comprehensive discipline plan comprised of the combination of a discipline tracking system, positive behavior support plan, and professional intervention team will positively impact the school's disciplinary issues by decreasing the number of exclusionary actions by the school such as suspensions in general and for at-risk students. The research will be a mixed methods design with quantitative data on the number of suspensions and the number of at-risk students. This data study will examine the number of suspensions to determine if the comprehensive discipline plan has resulted in a decrease in the number of suspensions and at-risk students. Qualitative data will also be collected through teacher and student interviews asking for their perceptions as to the consistency and effectiveness of the comprehensive discipline plan. These interviews will be analyzed for recurring themes and perceptions concerning the effectiveness of the comprehensive discipline plan.

RESEARCH QUESTIONS

To help determine the effectiveness of the comprehensive discipline plan, this mixed methods case study addressed two questions:

1. Does a comprehensive discipline plan significantly decrease the number of suspensions for the school?
2. How do students and staff perceive the effectiveness of a comprehensive discipline plan?

A delimitation of this work was the restriction of previous discipline data due to the discrepancy between school years 2006-2008 and school years 2008-2010. While additional years could provide a more in-depth look at school trends, a change in administrators resulted in different expectations and discipline procedures. Due to the use of several initiatives to combat discipline issues, the study did not address if one approach had a more significant impact than another. It was also difficult to determine the effects of various programs with Mitchell, Bradshaw, & Leaf (2010) even suggesting that the effects of programs may "vary by contextual factors at the classroom and school level" (p. 278). However, for the purpose of this study the effect of several plans combined to combat discipline referrals and academic achievement was deemed more relevant than the effectiveness of individual plans.

Research is available on several discipline intervention programs. However, information and research are not as available on multiprogram approaches. This gap in the research can be lessened by the results of this study. If a more comprehensive approach addressing behavior issues can positively impact disciplinary issues, then educators and administrators may want to investigate a combination of strategies to help their at-risk students become successful. Greenberg and colleagues (2003) suggested that for schools to be successful educating their students to be "knowledgeable, responsible, socially skilled, healthy, caring, and contributing citizens (p. 466) there needs to be "comprehensiveness and greater coordination in planning and implementation" (p. 471) of programs.

Another merit of this study was the focus on the at-risk students whose needs are not met by the universal or group supports in Schoolwide Positive Behavioral Support (SWPBS). The at-risk students in this research were more likely to be in the 5% needing intensive individualized intervention and support as recommended in SWPBS. This study will help address the effectiveness of a comprehensive discipline plan for the students most in need of individualized help.

High stakes testing and student achievement merit the focus of educators today. However, discipline issues can negatively influence the quality of classroom instruction. Not only can students with inappropriate behavior harm classroom instruction for the entire class, but also the student with behavioral issues may be impacted academically if the result is loss of class time for the misbehaving student. Typically, students with disciplinary referrals are removed from the classroom environment and placed in in-school or out-of-school suspensions resulting in lost instructional opportunities. At-risk students, such as minorities and males, may be even more adversely affected academically if discipline consequences limit their access to an education. Students cannot learn as expected if they are not in school. Different initiatives are available to decrease the number of discipline problems and thereby increase the time available for teaching. However, a plan to incorporate different approaches to resolve discipline issues may employ a variety of strategies to differentiate for a range of student difficulties, thus being more effective than any one plan alone.

TERMS

Although terms have been defined throughout the introduction to this research, included in this section is a collection of common terms for the clarification of the reader.

At-risk student: At-risk students will be defined as those students with three or more office discipline referrals in 1 month.

Comprehensive Discipline Plan: A comprehensive discipline plan will include the components of a discipline tracking system, a schoolwide positive behavioral intervention support program, and a multidiscipline professional intervention team focusing upon the students with needs due to academics and/or behavior.

Discipline Log: The Discipline Log is a schoolwide, in-house, systematic computerized approach to classroom management issues to be utilized by teachers and other school staff following specified misbehaviors by students with set consequences for the student.

ODR: An office discipline referral system tracks discipline and consequences as administered by school administrators and entered into a districtwide computer program.

PIT: A Professional Intervention Team is comprised of multidiscipline personnel, such as school counselor, social worker, administrator, psychologist, teachers, and administrators, focusing upon the students with needs due to academics and behavior.

Problem Behavior: behavior by a student that hinders learning

School Exclusion: removal or exclusion of students from the classroom or school through disciplinary actions usually involving suspension (in-school and out-of school) or expulsion

SWPBS: Schoolwide Positive Behavior Support is sometimes referred to as Positive Behavior Support (PBS) or Schoolwide Positive Behavior Intervention Support (SWPBIS). According to the OSEP Technical Assistance Center on Positive Behavioral Interventions and Support website, Schoolwide Positive Behavioral Support "is a decision making framework that guides selection, integration, and implementation of the best evidence-based academic and behavioral practices for improving important academic and behavior outcomes for all students" (U.S. Department of Education, Technical Assistance Center on PBIS, 2009).

When reviewing literature for this research several avenues of study were examined. Since the comprehensive discipline plan has a range of components, the review of literature will also delve into various areas of research, namely disciplinary data tracking, SWPBS, and interdisciplinary approaches. However, even before these investigations can be considered, one question needs to be asked. Why do we care? This can best be answered by looking at students most at risk for receiving disciplinary actions and the outcomes of their actions. The children most likely to receive disciplinary actions in school are those students whose needs are not being met (Noguera, 2003), particularly the students who are behind academically (Arcia, 2006; Martin, Martin, Gibson, & Wilkins, 2007), or suffer from abuse or neglect (Singer, 1996). A common practice for students with disciplinary issues is to remove or to exclude them from the classroom or from the school through a type of suspension or expulsion (Gregory, & Ripski, 2008; Noguera, 2003; Sailor et al., 2007). Is this removal successful in terms of the affected students' social behaviors or academic achievement? The answer has to be no (Noguera, 2003; Sailor et al., 2007; Skiba, & Peterson, 2003). Suspended students are more likely to be retained (Civil Rights Project, 2000), experience frustration and isolation in school (Lovey, Docking, & Evans, 1994), have low academic achievement (Arcia, 2006), and be given future suspensions (Skiba & Noam, 2002). They are also more likely to drop out of school, to participate in the juvenile justice system, and to be imprisoned later in life (Baker et al., 2001; Civil Rights Project, 2000). Skiba and Peterson (2003) concur when they state "far from improving student behavior or ensuring school safety, disciplinary exclusion appears to be associated with a host of negative outcomes for both students and the school climate" (p. 69).

DISCIPLINE DATA TRACKING

There are several ways to track disciplinary issues with students. "An essential part of schoolwide PBS efforts is the consistent use of data to inform and guide the intervention" (p. 187) with office discipline referrals being one method to track the reasons for the referrals and the times and location of inappropriate student behavior (Warren, Bohanon-Edmonson, & Turnbull, 2006). As Irvin, Horner, and Ingram (2006) noted in their research

> Many types of ODR-related information, such as student name, referring teacher, time of day, and nature/location of problem behavior, are potentially useful for facilitating decision-making regarding schoolwide and/or individual student behavior. Because ODR measures are a source of data that most schools routinely collect in some manner, most school building staffs already have much of the essential information necessary for such decision-making. (p. 10)

The Irvin and colleagues (2006) research indicated that ODR measures are regularly used in schools for database decision-making and that its use is regarded as effective and efficient. However, office discipline referrals may result in school discipline which "seems to involve the use of punishment, most often school exclusion, to enforce student conformance with established standards, as expressed by school discipline codes" (Skiba, & Peterson, 2003, p. 66). Decreasing the ODR rate is connected with increased academic performance (Lassen, Steele, & Sailor, 2006) with the ODR rate decreasing with the implementation of SWPBS (Morrissey, Bohanon, & Fenning, 2010, Warren et al., 2006), even in urban, inner-city schools (Warren et al., 2006).

POSITIVE BEHAVIOR SUPPORTS

The United States' Department of Education through the Office of Special Education Programs created SWPBS to give schools information and technical assistance to assist in the identifying, adapting, and sustaining of schoolwide disciplinary practices (U.S. Department of Education, 2009). Sailor et al. (2007) believe that SWPBS is a viable option to help all students meet state standards. The premise by Sailor and colleagues (2007) is based on the theory that if

> sizable numbers of students are experiencing reduced time in academic instruction because of exclusionary responses to problem behaviors, then efforts to teach positive behaviors in the context of academic instruction should yield positive academic results simply by increasing time in instruction. (p. 373)

Warren and colleagues (2006) agreed when stating,

> it is reasonable to expect that decreased behavior problems will correspond with increased academic achievement; with fewer students losing instruction time due to office referrals and suspensions, and with less class time being sacrificed in responding to behavioral issues, opportunities for instruction and learning should be increased. (p. 196)

SWPBS has three levels of interventions and strategies referred to as Level 1, universal support, Level 2, group support, and Level 3, individual support (Sailor et al., 2007). Sailor and colleagues goes on to explain that

> the three components-universal, group, and individual support-operate on three continua. First, they operate on a continuum of *scope*. Universal support is provided to all students, group supports are applied to targeted groups of students in specific problem contexts (e.g., hallways, lunchroom, gym), and individual support employs functional behavioral assessments to target supports to the needs of individual students. Second, as the scope of the interventions narrows from universal to individual, the supports become more *individualized* to the student's needs. Even universal support is tailored to the needs of the school, as each school is to some extent unique, has its own culture, and experiences different issues with respect to student, teacher, and administrator behavior. Finally, SWPBS provides support on a continuum of *intensity*, or the quantity and strength of the services targeted to the individual, group, or entire school. Universal supports are the least intense; group supports are more intense; and individual supports are the most intense. Simply put, this three-tiered system provides support to all students based on their level of need. (p. 371)

This system helps ensure consistent expectations throughout the school ranging from general supports for all students to interventions for groups of students to intensive interventions for individual students (Bohanon, Fenning, & Carney, 2006). According to findings by Akey (2006), "students who believed that the rules of conduct in their school were clear and fairly administered were more likely to feel engaged and academically successful the next year (p. 27). However, Carr (2008) cautioned, "There is currently no scientific basis for concluding that the universal (primary prevention) component of SWPBS is applicable to all students (p. 267).

MULTIDISCIPLINARY APPROACHES

As interventions are considered for student misbehavior, various members of the school community may have input into the student support systems. Koehler (2006) noted "professionals and parents need effective systems of teamwork for planning restorative outcomes with troubled children and youth" (p. 155). Gregory and Ripski (2008) suggested that school psychologists increase their consultative role "to enhance teachers' capacity to build positive and supportive relationships with students" (p. 349), while SWPBS incorporates a multidisciplinary team approach possibly consisting of school staff, administrators, and other stakeholders (Warren et al., 2006; Sailor, et al., 2007). This multidisciplinary approach is particularly important in the final level of support in SWPBS referred to as tertiary or comprehensive.

Methods

In this study a comprehensive discipline plan comprised of the combination of a discipline tracking system, positive behavior support plan, and professional intervention team was implemented. The research was a mixed methods study using quantitative data from office discipline referrals for suspensions rates and at-risk students and qualitative data from interviews with staff and students. The data was sequential with the quantitative data being collected before the qualitative data.

The research was a mixed method study with the data collected sequentially. The quantitative data was collected first, followed by the collection of qualitative data. The data was sequential due to the interview questions for the teachers having references to the results of the quantitative data. The qualitative data was more central to the study; therefore the sequence of the collection of the data and its importance to the study can be illustrated as quan QUAL.

ODR data from October 2010 was collected and analyzed for the number of suspensions, while students with three or more ODR were identified and classified as at-risk. This same type of data was collected for the month of March. After this data was analyzed, teacher and student interviews were conducted.

Data

The school studied in this research is a magnet performing arts academy in a countywide school district with a student population comprised of 81% African American, 18% White, and 1% Hispanic with 123 sixth-graders, 110 seventh-graders, and 122 eighth-graders for a total of 355 students. It is the only predominately African American urban middle school in the district with 89% of the students receiving free or reduced-price lunch under the National School Lunch program. The school is a Title I school based upon its number of free and reduced-price lunch students and is a Project Grad school. These characteristics of mainly African American adolescents with a high percentage having low-socioeconomic status are common in urban, comprehensive schools (Martin et al., 2007). Students in these schools have lower academic achievement and graduation rates (Baker, 2005) and a higher rate of school failure, school exclusion through suspensions and expulsions, identification as needing special education services, and school violence (Ferguson, 2003).

Although a small middle school by the district standards, this middle magnet performing arts academy is unique. The school is the only middle magnet school in the school district. There are 21 sixth-grade magnet transfer students, 17 seventh-grade magnet transfers, and 17 eighth-grade transfers with 16.12% of the school population being comprised of magnet transfer students. When comparing the percentage of White students by grade level, the sixth-grade is 7.32% White, while the seventh-grade is only 5.92% White and the eighth-grade is 4.51% White.

Funding from Title I was allocated for additional teachers lowering the teacher to student ratio to about 15:1 with even smaller class sizes in math and language arts. Due to the urban classification the district also allocated additional administrators for a total of 3 administrators. During the year of the study an additional assistant principal worked at the school as part of a Leadership Academy initiative between the district and local university to identify and train new administrators.

The school day runs from 8:00 a.m. to 3:00 p.m. because of the dictates of a transportation system busing in children from surrounding areas to the inner city elementary, middle, and high magnet programs. It is the only middle school operating on this time schedule. All students enrolled are eligible for the performing arts classes as long as they qualify academically by not being placed in any academic intervention programs. Honor classes are offered, but magnet students are not necessarily grouped together academically. Although students are encouraged to perform at a high level academically, many students struggle in school. Language! is an intervention program implemented in the school to help struggling students with deficiencies in reading proficiency. These students engage in 110 minutes of Language!, reading, and language arts instruction.

Approximately 60% of all the students are enrolled in this intervention program. Those students enrolled in Language! are no longer eligible for performing arts classes during the regular school day due to time constraints. The intervention program is creating a chasm between the students able to participate in the performing arts and those who cannot. One solution has been to try an after school academy with academic and performing arts courses offered along with free transportation.

The culture is predominately African American. According to 2000 census data (see Table 11.1), the surrounding community has a higher African American contingent and is poorer than the average in the United States.

The demographics of the community include a 53% to 47% female to male ratio. The female to male ratio is higher than in the metropolitan area with 51.7% female and 48.3% male and the general United States population, which has 50.9% female and 49.1% male. This could be due to the higher than average number of single households with a female as head of the household. The population is 56.6% White and 41.2% African American with metropolitan area being 88.1% White and 8.6% African American and the U.S. average of 75.1% White and 12.3% African American. There are few other ethnic groups within the community.

The school's community has a population with 74.4% completing high school and 16.7% with a bachelor's degree. In the U.S. 80.4% have a high school diploma and 24.4% have a bachelor's degree. The metropolitan area has an even higher graduation rate with 82.5% of the population graduating from high school and 29% holding a bachelor's degree. The

Table 11.1.   2000 Census Data

U.S. Census	School	District/County	State
Female to male ratio	53:47	52:48	51:49
Ethnicity	56.6% White 41.2% African American	88.1% White 8.6% African American	75.1% White 12.3% African American
Schooling	74.4% Graduated high school 16.7% Bachelor's degree	82.5% Graduated high school 29% Bachelor's degree	80.4% Graduated high school 24.4% Bachelor's degree
Residents in workforce/disabled	58.1% Workforce 26.7% Disabled	64.4% Workforce 20.2% Disabled	63.9% Workforce 19.3% Disabled
Poverty level	15.1% Families 19.3% Individuals	8.4% Families 12.6% Individuals	9.2% Families 12.3% Individuals
Median value of single family home	$73,000	$98,500	$119,600

percentage of residents in the workforce is 58.1% with 26.7% of the residents having a disability. The metropolitan area is similar to the U.S. average with 64.4% of the people in the workforce and 20.2% being disabled, while in the U.S. 63.9% are in the workforce with 19.3% having a disability. With the economy in a downturn the last few years, an assumption would be that the unemployment rate is higher than in 2000. The poverty level of the community includes 15.1% of the families and 19.3% of individuals classified below the poverty line as compared with 9.2% of the families and 12.3% of the individuals in the United States. The difference between the U.S. and the metropolitan area is similar with only 8.4% of families and 12.6 of individuals below the poverty line. The median value of a single-family home is $73,000 as compared to $98,500 in the metropolitan area and $119,600 for the United States.

Although the parents are generally very supportive of the school, the students experience much change in their home lives with guardianship changing from parent to parent or to other relatives. Also, the students experience high mobility with 40% of the students moving at least once during the year. To help provide services to families that may not have access, the magnet school is home to a school/community-based clinic providing quality medical care for the entire child. This service is possible through the support and collaboration between the school district and a nearby university college of nursing. The clinic provides services to Head Start and the school district students from three to 18 years of age. Students may receive care at the clinic ranging from sports physicals, screenings, and immunizations to physical exams. There are no charges for any services provided at the clinic.

SAMPLE

The teacher interviews were a purposeful sample. The three teachers identified for the interview were chosen on the following criteria. The teacher with the most entries, the median number of entries, and the least entries on the discipline tracking system were interviewed. If more than one teacher had been identified at each of these levels, the teachers at that level would be assigned a number and the number chosen randomly. The rationale for this assignment of interviews was to assure a cross section of teachers using the discipline tracking system.

The students to be interviewed were assigned to one of three groups. One group consisted of students with no in-school or out-of-school suspensions in either month studied. The second group was comprised of students with one to two suspensions in either of the months studied. The third group was students who had three or more suspensions in either month. The students were chosen randomly by assigning each student in the respective groups a number and then using a random number generator to select one student from each group respectively.

Quantitative data included the number of suspensions based upon information in the district's student information system, known as STAR. Due to differences in the number of days per month the suspensions were tallied for the same number of days. For example if 1 month in the study had 22 school days and the second month in the study had 23 school days, then the suspensions for the first 22 school days will be studied in the second month. To account for differences in enrollment, the only students involved in the study were those who were enrolled in the school for both time periods. Students as a percentage of the total school population were identified in three groups. The first group was students without any suspensions for either time period. The second group was students with one or two suspensions in either or both time periods. The third group was those students with three or more suspensions in either time period.

To avoid bias in the teacher interviews, a third party from a different school was to conduct the teacher interviews. It was felt that teachers might not feel as free to speak if an administrator or school personnel conducted the interviews. The researcher conducted student interviews. Many students at the school deal with issues of trust. The researcher did not believe the students would be as honest and open with a stranger.

Questions in the interview dealt with consistency, fidelity to the program, and challenges with the comprehensive discipline plan. Notes were taken during the interviews and the interviews were recorded. Recordings were transcribed. The interviews were examined to identify common themes and perceptions. Two other researchers not involved with this research studied the interviews to verify the common themes and perceptions.

The quantitative findings answered the research question: Does a comprehensive discipline plan significantly decrease the number of suspensions for the school? Students enrolled in the school in November 2010 and March 2011 were identified. Any students not enrolled both of those months at the school were eliminated from the study for a total of 323 students in the study. Then the total number of days in school for each month was determined with each month having the same number of days in school. Suspension rates were calculated as the number of suspensions for each month divided by the number of students enrolled. The suspension rate for November was 80/323 or .248 and the suspension rate for March was 83/323 or .257. The number of suspensions increased by 3 from 80 in November to 83 in March and the difference in suspension rates was analyzed to determine if the rate was significant.

The November suspension rate was used as the base rate or null number with which to compare the March suspension rate to see if the March rate was significantly different from the November rate. The lower and upper limits of a 95% confidence interval for a proportion were calculated according to two methods outlined by Newcombe (1998). The methods were derived from a procedure for confidence intervals described by Wilson (1927) in which the first method used the Wilson procedure and the second method used the Wilson procedure with a correction for continuity. The 95% confidence interval around the sample proportion (i.e., the rate of .257 from March) extended from .212 to .307 in the 95% confidence interval with no continuity correction and from .211 to .309 in the 95% confidence interval including the continuity correction. Because the null value of .248 was inside the 95% confidence interval in both methods, it can be concluded that the suspension rate in March did not differ significantly from the base rate of suspensions calculated in November. Therefore, the research question can be answered that the comprehensive discipline plan did not significantly decrease the number of suspensions in the school.

TEACHER INTERVIEWS

Three teachers were purposefully selected based upon whether they had the most, the median, or the least number of infractions in the discipline tracking system. Originally, a third party was to conduct the interviews. However, all three teachers expressed the desire to speak with the researcher. They believed the researcher would be unbiased and felt more freedom in speaking with someone they knew. Since all three teachers agreed on this issue, the researcher conducted the interviews.

Teacher A had the most entries for student infractions (155). She was an eighth-grade teacher with 8 years of teaching in an urban setting, but in her first year at the school. Teacher B had the median number of entries (58). She was a sixth-grade teacher with 3 years of teaching with two of those in an urban setting, but also in her first year at the school. Teacher C had the least number of entries (1) with 15 years of teaching with 8 years in an urban setting and in her eighth year at the school. The teachers shared some commonalities. All of them had some experience in urban settings with high rates of students eligible for free or reduced-price lunch, although the amount of experience varied with teachers A and C having 8 years experience and teacher B having 2 years experience. Teachers A and B were in their first year at the present school, while teacher C was in her eighth year at the school.

The most relevant difference in the teachers for this study was in the participation in the comprehensive discipline plan. Teacher C with the most total experience and the most years in the school had opted out of the school's discipline program. When asked which were the most effective components of the comprehensive discipline plan, she responded, "In all honesty I don't use any of the components." She listed several reasons for not using the plan.

> I don't use the discipline log. I think those are the items the classroom teacher should use as part of her classroom management … and it takes time to go to the computer to log on and record those infractions. If you don't record them then, then you are keeping notes around to record it. It's just keeping track of it and delaying punishment and can set a negative tone in the classroom. The positive behavior comes through when I think I do it verbally, should be built in how you manage your classroom when they (the students) do a good job.… I don't use the "Caught Doing the Right Thing" tickets and stamps (part of the SWPBS incentives). When a student does the right thing it is immediate and I recognize it immediately.

Teacher C thought of her classroom as her home saying the students "are my children and I am the parent, in loco parentis. This is my home and I am the parent." She believed in immediate positive and negative feedback and only wrote Office Discipline Referrals for such matters as class cuts.

Teacher Theme #1: Discipline Tracking System was the Most Effective Component of the Comprehensive Discipline Plan

Teachers A and B both used all components of the comprehensive discipline plan including the discipline tracking system and SWPBS. They both thought the most effective component of the comprehensive discipline plan was the discipline tracking system, albeit for different reasons. (Note that the discipline log was the school name for the discipline tracking system and Time for Time was an after school detention. There were five steps in the discipline log with the fifth step being an ODR. Steps one through five would repeat with each multiple of five being an ODR.)

Teacher A thought the tracking system had clear student consequences for each step in the system. She said,

> I think the discipline log was the most effective when it was monitored all the time because there were very clear steps in the discipline log for the students. It was consistent for if you received 5 (infractions), you had an office

referral. If you received 1 (infraction) it was a warning and a call to parents, so the students knew exactly what step they were on and what the consequence was.... I made sure students knew exactly what the eighth-grade discipline was, on the wall, and they understood the consequences of their actions.... I have noticed that students will say to me, "I've reached the sixth step on the discipline log and I don't want to go back to ISS or Time for Time," so now they know what each step is and the consequences.

Teacher B liked that she could investigate particular students and patterns in their behavior. She concluded that as a teacher,

The tracking of kids reassures me that these things are happening in a variety of settings and allows me to look and talk with others to say these things are happening elsewhere across a variety of settings. What plan can we set up? What information, is it another student he or she is with all the time? We can identify triggers or causes of behavior and trends in behavior.

Teacher B continued by saying her students were more aware of consequences with all the staff using the same language throughout the school. She commented,

I have been more vocal about consequences, if you choose to do that you will go in the discipline log. I think I have made my kids more aware of consequences as a whole since everybody is using the same thing; there is the same language throughout.

Teacher Theme #2: SWPBS was the Least Effective Component of the Comprehensive Discipline Plan

Both teachers A and B thought the Schoolwide Positive Behavior Support was the least effective component of the comprehensive discipline plan. None of the teachers followed the plan with fidelity and did not use the rewards or common expectations regularly. They recommended that more attention be spent on SWPBS. Teacher A said,

I believe the least effective component was the PBS (SWPBS) aspect because number one, I do not think it was consistent and it was not practiced by every teacher. I would recommend that we look more at Positive Behavior that we figure out a way that each teacher buys into a consistent behavior plan.... That is what I would improve; I would improve the positive piece because I think that has a greater effect on the children than the negative.

Teacher B agreed and indicated that SWPBS was not implemented consistently. She said,

I don't think the positive behavior support has gotten as much support or the same backing as the discipline log. I don't find that people are using positive behavior the way we are using negative behavior. Perhaps it is so hard to see cause when I am looking at a class of 18 and 17 are misbehaving, it's very hard to approach the positive behavior.

Teacher Theme #3: The Comprehensive Discipline Plan was not Implemented With Fidelity, or With the Full Support of the Administration

Consistency and fidelity in implementation was a common theme throughout the interviews. The teachers also felt that the administration did not fully support the implementation of the plan. Teacher A described a time period when she felt the administrators were out of the building more than usual and its effect on the discipline log by saying,

> When all the pieces were put together all the time it (the discipline tracking system) worked well, but because through nobody's fault we had administrators not here, I believe there was a time period when the overall plan was not in place, and so there was a time period when it was not consistent. The students knew this. For example when I would get in my classroom and say in the classroom you have reached the third step in the classroom management and next time you will be placed in the discipline log, students would say to me, "So what, nothing is going to happen to me." Now that everyone (administrators) is able to be here at school and not overwhelmed with discipline issues, consistency has returned.

Teacher B mentioned her own lack of consistency in the plan, but also thought that lack of support from the administration was even more of an issue.

> As far as the positive behavior support goes, I think it is not very consistent and I myself have not been consistent. I haven't been good about Caught Doing the Right Thing tickets (incentives for positive behavior) and I don't think I have seen anybody else using them. I haven't seen kids with them and they haven't talked about them. I talk to students and don't see them using them.

Teacher B continued to address the lack of administrative support particularly in sixth-grade. She attributed this to the sixth-grade classes being housed in a separate building form the rest of the school. She responded,

> Our discipline hasn't change because people's personal styles haven't changed. There is no consistency in administration being here (in the sixth-

grade building), so there is no driving force from administrators in this building saying you have to change.... Just because we use the discipline log doesn't mean discipline is consistent. I think it was put into place to make discipline more consistent, but I don't think it is. I think the biggest struggle with discipline comes from a lack of support from the administration.... As for the discipline log, sometimes; I don't want to follow it through on my half because it is work I don't have time for. I think, "Was this issue big enough to merit this consequence to the student?" I know it was earned over time, but sometimes I felt it isn't necessary for my time. Sometimes it feels like a consequence for me too.

Teacher C agreed with the need for consistency and fidelity to implementation when she said, "We try to standardize as far as trying to keep track of discipline better, but it depends on the fidelity of the teachers. Some log every time, while others may or may not log it (discipline issues)."

STUDENT INTERVIEW

Three students were randomly selected for interviews from three groups. The student selected from the group with zero suspensions in both November and March was an eighth-grade girl. She was designated as student 1. The student selected from the group with one to two suspensions in either or both time periods was a seventh-grade girl and was designated as student 2. The student selected from the group with three or more suspensions in either time period was a sixth-grade boy designated as student 3. The researcher interviewed all three students. The students equated the school comprehensive discipline plan with the discipline tracking system. Whenever they were questioned about the discipline policy, they would only discuss the discipline tracking system or being suspended.

The responses among the three students varied depending on the number of suspensions they had received throughout the year. Student 3 with the most suspensions had a tendency to blame others for his actions with several specific examples of being unfairly accused for misbehavior. For example he said,

I don't like it (discipline tracking system, known as the discipline log) because when the kids don't do anything the teachers make up lies and put people in the discipline log and make stuff up. I was in the library and Ms. _____ put me in and called my momma and then put me in the discipline log.

He also mentioned how others would get in trouble, but try to blame someone else. The child with no suspensions also felt unfairly blamed at times. However, her complaint was that while she had been put in the discipline tracking system for talking, other students had also been talking, but not "caught."

The students were also confused at times about disciplinary procedures. Student 1 thought when students were in a fight, the only one suspended was the one who started the fight. She felt that when both students fought, they should get suspended for the same amount of days. The actual policy in the school was to suspend both students for the same amount of days if both fought, no matter who started the fight. However, suspension times increased if the student had been in more than one fight. Student 1 thought that teachers gave the students in-school suspensions for misbehavior, when the policy was that only administrators could assign any suspensions.

Student Theme #1: The Discipline Log was Considered Equitable and had an Impact on Student Behavior

Two of the students thought the discipline tracking system was fair because it had set consequences. As student 2 stated, "I think it is fair because most students might not do the same thing, but most students deserve the same consequences.... The discipline log changes our behavior because so many times we can get in the discipline log before we go to ISS. Student 3 concurred,

> Teachers will act the same for the same behavior.... Teachers try to put people in the discipline log and that makes students try to be good, they call your momma and put you in ISS or OSS.... After teachers tell us to do something, we need to do something.

Student 1 also agreed the consequences actually had an impact. Student 1 stated, You don't want to miss activities, so it makes us scared to do stuff cause you think it can make you miss out on activities."

Student Theme #2: Although the Plan was Equitable, the Implementation was Inconsistent.

The biggest complaint the students had concerned consistency among the teachers. Students 1 and 2 mentioned specific examples when a student would exhibit certain behaviors in one classroom and be entered in the discipline tracking system, but that same student or same behavior exhibited in another classroom would not warrant an entry. As student 1 offered, "if I did one thing in one class and the same thing in another, it wouldn't be the same discipline ... every teacher reacts differently." Student 2 explained,

> If students misbehave in different teachers' classes, some teachers might not say anything about it, but another teacher might say I'm putting you in the discipline log ... are all students treated the same, not really ... in one of my classes someone got smart with one of the teachers and he got put in the discipline log and sent to another teacher, another student got smart with the same teacher in the same class and the teacher just said, "you need to be more respectful and that wasn't very nice."

However, Student 3 with the most suspensions (and thought teachers made things up about him) said, "Teachers will act the same for the same behavior." He mentioned an example about a student, who got in trouble for certain misbehavior and was entered in the discipline log,

> When I was in first period this girl got in trouble in because she said the teacher was putting people in the discipline log for no reason, then she said the teachers got on her nerves ... in third period she did the same thing and she got in trouble ... the teacher treated her the same by putting her in the discipline log again.

Student Theme #3: Using Best Practices in the Classroom Would Help Discipline

The students had a variety of suggestions to improve discipline in the school. The commonality was to use best practices in the classroom. Student 2 suggested more engaging lessons by "making class fun instead of boring so we don't have to sit and talk to another student for fun." Student 1 thought principals needed to be more visible by sitting "in classes with the kids more often and see how they act."

Teachers and students had mixed feelings about the comprehensive discipline plan. All thought certain components were desirable, such as predesigned consequences. The complaints seemed to deal with implementation. Consistency in implementation and fidelity to the program were suggestions for improvement.

Both data bring the same conclusion that discipline is a complex issue that at times may not have a definitive solution. The quantitative data did not indicate any significant differences after a comprehensive discipline plan was implemented. The qualitative data also had inconclusive results.

Although there was consensus on several issues for the teachers and the students, there were also disagreements. Both groups had components they liked about the plan and components they thought were inconsistent or needed improvement. The consensus seemed to be that the plan was good, but the implementation was inconsistent.

IMPLICATIONS FOR PRACTICE

Whenever change initiatives are introduced to a school, professional development must be given for the staff to understand and implement the changes. This professional development cannot stop after the school year begins, but must continue throughout the school year. Teachers need assistance in implementing the plan. Dialogue between partners and practitioners of the plan must be facilitated throughout the year, as corrections to the plan become apparent. This feedback needs to continue as some members master the components of the plan faster than others. Some teachers may also accept the need for change more readily than others.

Another implication is the awareness that having a multifaceted program is complex. While adding more components can be worthwhile, chances for misunderstandings, errors, and mistakes increase. This complexity also may slow the implementation. Since implementation can already take several years, continuous awareness and adjustments are critical. A worthwhile change imitative should not be abandoned just because it takes longer to implement than originally planned.

REFERENCES

Akey, T. M. (2006). *School context, student attitudes and behavior, and academic achievement: An exploratory analysis.* New York, NY: Manpower Demonstration Research Corporation.

Arcia, E. (2006). Achievement and enrollment status of suspended students: Outcomes in a large, multicultural school district. *Education and Urban Society, 38,* 359-369.

Baker, P. (2005). The impact of cultural biases on African American students' education: A review of research literature regarding race-based schooling. *Education and Urban Society, 37*(3), 243-256.

Baker, J. A., Derrer, R. D., Davis, S. M., Dinklage-Travis, H. E., Linder, D. S., & Nicholson, M. D. (2001). The flip side of the coin: Understanding the school's contribution to dropout and completion. *School Psychology Quarterly, 16,* 406-426.

Bohanon, H., Fenning, P., & Carney, K. L. (2006). Schoolwide application of positive behavior support in an urban high school: A case study. *Journal of Positive Behavior Interventions, 8*(3), 131-145.

Carr, E. G. (2008). SWPBS: The greatest good for the greatest number, or the needs of the majority trump the needs of the minority? *Research and Practice for Persons with Severe Disabilities, 33/34*(4/1), 267-269.

Civil Rights Project. (2000, June 15-16). *Opportunities suspended: The devastating consequences of zero tolerance and school discipline policies.* Report from a National Summit on Zero Tolerance, Washington, DC.

Cohen, R., Kincaid, D., & Childs, K. E. (2007). Measuring school-wide positive behavior support implementation: Development and validation of the benchmarks of quality. *Journal of Positive Behavior Interventions, 9*(4), 203-213.

Ferguson, R. (2003). Teachers' perceptions and expectations and the Black White test score gap. *Urban Education, 38(4),* 460-507.

Greenberg, M. T., Weissberg, R. P., O'Brien, M. U., Zins, J. E., Fredicks, L., Resnik, H., & Elias, M. J. (2003). Enhancing school-based prevention and youth development through coordinated social, emotional, and academic learning. *American Psychologist, 58,* 466-474.

Gregory, A., & Ripski, M. B. (2008). Adolescent trust in teachers: Implications for behavior in the high school classroom. *The School Psychology Review, 37*(3), 337-353.

Irvin, L. K., Horner, R. H., & Ingram, K. L. (2006). Using office discipline referral data decision making about student behavior in elementary and middle schools: An empirical evaluation of validity. *Journal of Positive Behavior Interventions, 8*(1), 10-23.

Koehler, N. (2006). Team planning to clear up problems. *Reclaiming Children and Youth: The Journal of Strength-based Interventions, 15*(3), 155-161.

Lassen, S. R., Steele, M. M., & Sailor, W. (2006). The relationship of schoolwide positive behavior support to academic achievement in an urban middle school. *Psychology in the Schools, 43*(6), 701-712.

Lovey, J., Docking, J., & Evans, R. (1994). Excluded from school: Bins or bridges? *International Journal of Adolescence and Youth, 4,* 329-333.

Martin, D. B., Martin, M., Gibson, S. S., & Wilkins, J. (2007). Increasing prosocial behavior and academic achievement among adolescent African American males. *Adolescence, 42,* 689-698.

Mitchell, M. M., Bradshaw, C. P., & Leaf, P. J. (2010). Student and teacher perceptions of school climate: A multilevel exploration of patterns of discrepancy. *The Journal of School Health, 80*(6), 271-279.

Morrissey, K. L., Bohanon, H. M., & Fenning, P. J. (2010). Positive behavior support: Teaching and acknowledging expected behaviors in an urban high school. *Teaching Exceptional Children, 42*(5), 26-35.

Newcombe, R. G. (1998). Two-sided confidence intervals for the single proportion: Comparison of seven methods. *Statistics in Medicine, 17,* 857-872.

Noguera, P. A. (2003). Schools, prisons, and social implications of punishment: Rethinking disciplinary practices. *Theory into Practice, 42*(4), 341-350.

Public Agenda. (2004). *Teaching interrupted: Do discipline policies in today's public schools foster the common good?* New York, NY: Author.

Safran, S. P. (2006). Using the effective behavior supports survey to guide development of schoolwide positive behavior support. *Journal of Positive Behavior Interventions, 8*(1), 3-9

Sailor, W., Stowe, M. J., Turnbull III, H. R., & Kleinhammer-Tramill, P. J. (2007). A case for adding a social-behavioral standard to standards-based education with schoolwide positive behavior support as its basis. *Remedial and Special Education, 28*(6), 366-376.

Singer, S. (1996). *Recriminalizing delinquency.* Cambridge, England: Cambridge University Press.

Skiba, R. J., & Noam, G. G. (Eds.). (2002). *Zero tolerance: Can suspension and expulsion keep schools safe?* San Francisco, CA: Jossey-Bass.

Skiba, R. J., & Peterson, R. (2003). Teaching the social curriculum: School discipline as instruction. *Preventing School Failure, 47*(2), 66-73.

U.S. Census. (2000). Retrieved from http://www.census.gov/

U.S. Department of Education, Office of Special Education Programs, National Technical Assistance Center on Positive Behavioral Interventions and Supports. (2009). Retrieved from www.pbis.org

Warren, J. S., Bohanon-Edmonson, H. M., & Turnbull, A. P. (2006). School-wide positive behavior support: Addressing behavior problems that impede student learning. *Educational Psychology Review, 18*(2), 187-198.

Wilson, E. B. (1927). Probable inference, the law of succession, and statistical inference. *Journal of the American Statistical Association, 22*, 209-212.

CHAPTER 12

FOSTERING INSTRUCTIONAL PRACTICES THAT LAST

Ryan J. Siebe

Instructional practices or "how teachers do what they do" have always interested me. I know for sure that they are at the heart of what makes schools excellent. The First to the Top initiative created a prime opportunity for our school community to utilize Battelle strategies in the classroom. Consequently, I had the chance to develop and present a professional development session for faculty centered on the Battelle strategies. However, just because I presented the information to faculty members, it did not guarantee transformed classrooms with unified practices. I wanted to know the potency of a staff development session in terms of how it translated into everyday practice in the classroom. I used a pared samples t test to analyze observations of classroom teachers in actions before and after the Battelle workshop.

It is difficult to keep in mind academic research and apply it to the everyday work of schools. It surprised me that there was only one strategy that clearly translated into teachers' classroom practices: The simplest one I offered during the professional development session. I have reflected on why this occurred. I think there are several reasons that could be the answer:

Great Leaders Equal Great Schools:
Alliances and Discourse for Educational Reform, pp. 211–226
Copyright © 2012 by Information Age Publishing
All rights of reproduction in any form reserved.

It is either because my professional development skills need to improve, the culture of faculty accountability needs to improve, or there should be more than one session dedicated to working with faculty on using these strategies. Addressing all three of these implications is now part of my own plan for keeping faculty engaged and focused in extending our schools' repertoire of teaching strategies.

I used a sample t test for something that was relative to the "real world" of my job. The experience taught me that there are ways to connect research to practice in my day-to-day work.

Focused coaching and collaboration was another set of skills that became very important once I began to inform practitioners what I learned from the t-test results. Above all, listening and observation were the keys to understanding the dynamics of why faculty gravitated to one particular practice.

Recent years have been rife with change in the world of education. Through the implementation of national standards beginning with the establishment of National Assessment of Educational Progress (NAEP) in 1970 through the Nation at Risk report, to the more notorious implementation of The No Child Left Behind (NCLB) act under the Bush Administration, there has been an ongoing push to have increased accountability in education. The default of this accountability has been through testing. Testing and test results provided accountability that was quantifiable and tangible. However, there is an ongoing debate questioning whether increased accountability is a good thing. According to Snyder and Willow (2009), in 2007-2008 only 44% of teachers surveyed reported that state or federal standards had a positive impact on their satisfaction as teachers. Even if the push for standards did create greater success, clearly teachers did not all perceive this focus as positive on their well-being. Reeves (2005) however, believes that though there may be some changes to the implementation of NCLB in the future, the four basic ideas of standards, accountability, testing, and choice are here are permanent fixtures.

Implementation of new practices in schools is often hampered. Reasons for poor implementation can vary and may include apathy, lack of understanding, poor or no professional development, and/or negative perceptions of new initiatives implemented due to increased accountability. Ultimately, teachers may be justified in their resistant stance and are not totally to blame for their concerns or possible lack of thoroughness. Another consideration is proper teacher training. According to The Digest of Educational Statistics (2009), nearly 47% of teachers surveyed have only a bachelor's or associates degree as their highest attained educational level. Compounding this problem is the possibility that school administration may not be providing the necessary training to develop teachers. Only 45.6% of teachers surveyed reported that their principals talked to them frequently about their instructional practices. General educational practices would dictate regular formative instructional practices in such a situation to both assure student mastery and guide instruction. It is realistic that a teacher might have never been trained in any method of formative assessment.

Although there may be myriad reasons why lack of implementation exists, the reality is that many classrooms are not utilizing the highest impact practices. This project undertakes the issue of implementation. I attempted to determine exactly what effect professional development might have on teaching practices.

In the modern high stakes atmosphere of education, researchers and teachers seek new methods of instruction beyond what conventional methods. However, these practices are usually not taught to teachers during their normal training. In many cases, teachers may be entering the classroom with a minimal amount of training. It is also possible that teachers in modern schools will not receive the appropriate support from their school administration. Under such variegated circumstances, the needs for common practices that work become clearer. Educators must implement strategies that are research-based and effective. Most importantly, administrators need to know exactly what method to implement such strategies in order to assure the greatest benefits within classrooms (Dufour, 2000).

My hope of this study was to quantify the extent to which an administrator might expect implementation of research-based strategies shared and taught primarily through professional development sessions within the school. As such, the strategies that will be implemented are adopted from *Battelle For Kids* (2011), Formative instructional Practices. These strategies have been identified to be utilized in the Race to the Top legislative initiative enacted in 2010.

Battelle (2011) has already identified seven basic high-impact strategies. They include:

- providing a clear and understandable vision of the learning target or intended learning;
- sharing examples and models of strong and weak work;
- providing regular descriptive feedback;
- teaching students to self-assess and set learning goals;
- designing lessons to focus on one aspect of quality at a time;
- teaching students focused revision; and
- engaging students in self-reflection.

I hoped to have an indicator of the amount of implementation that might be expected at a comprehensive high school in Tennessee given standard Professional Development practices of an approximately 1-hour instructional session to teachers on how to use the aforementioned strategies. After reviewing the literature, it was suggested that the most effective method of professional development was not a 1-hour instructional session with little feedback. Both common sense and research revealed that a program of professional development allowing for reflection and iteration would be more appropriate. However, school protocols do not always align with best practices. It is often appropriate to commence an initiative as soon as possible realizing that in the end, the initiative may require several years of professional development for it reach its maximum effectiveness. However, in many cases, what may have been intended as a series of professional development opportunities on the subject matter can be cut short by unforeseen circumstances. In other cases, the pressures of multiple initiatives or the lack of resources (i.e., money or time) may limit professional development on a given subject to only a cursory introduction. I acknowledge that these circumstances are less than ideal, but as a reality within education, the impact of such an introduction is quite important to ascertain. Thus, I hoped to know to what extent these cursory kick-off events have an effect on teacher implementation. I had two basic questions:

1. Does limited staff development on specific formative instructional practices increase the use of those practices in the classroom?
2. To what extent if any can administrators affect the instructional practices of classroom teachers using only a 1-hour introduction to the specific techniques?

I expect that actions of school-level administrators to support better instruction may go unrewarded. Because professional development practices may be less than ideal, those practices will yield no benefits. As such, I formulated the following hypotheses:

Hypothesis RQ$_1$: Limited staff development on specific formative instructional practices will not increase the use of those practices in the classroom.

Hypothesis RQ$_2$: Administrators cannot make a measurable impact on teacher practices even through a 1-hour professional development session.

The limitations of my inquiry lie in the methods of observation that were utilized to collect data. The head principal and I collected data on the use of the Battelle Formative Instructional practices through random 15 minute walkthrough observations. The Head Principal and I documented specifically the times that teachers used the seven Battelle formative instructional strategies or their derivatives that were linked to specific behaviors denoted on the observation tool. Considering the method of data collection and the observers' positions of authority over the teachers, there a danger of a false effect from the professional development in that teachers were more likely to utilize these formative assessment techniques when they knew that administrators were in their classrooms performing observations or evaluations. Other possible limitations in such a situation were that implementation was not mandatory, but instead voluntary. Teachers that were being observed were not specifically facing a mandate to implement the Battelle strategies and face no discipline if they did not implement the strategies. Thus, I must acknowledge that those who were indifferent to the initiative may have been less likely to utilize the new instructional practices.

Additionally, this exercise was delimited to a random sampling of less than 50 classrooms in both the pre- and postphase. This delimitation was implemented in order to take a sampling without making data collection too overwhelming a task. I only joined the administrative staff of the study school weeks before I began the study. As such, my presence in the classroom could increase the angst that teachers' may feel when an administrator enters the classroom as there had been little time to establish rapport. I made no attempt to account for teacher anxiety as a variable to observed behavior.

Formative assessments have already been demonstrated to have a positive effect on formal test results. Additionally, there have been previous studies about teacher attitudes toward professional development. These studies documented that in many cases, teacher attitudes about staff development deteriorated over time, which, in turn impeded implementation (Torff & Sessions, 2009). However, I tried to look at implementation of staff development initiatives in the classroom. I acknowledged that the best practice for changing teacher behaviors was ongoing professional development. The reality for school administrators however is that such programming may be impossible due to a lack of resources. Even when a plan for ongoing professional development on a unified theme is a possibility, the initial implementation or introduction to the initiative should yield some results. I tried to quantify what impact might be expected.

REVIEW OF LITERATURE

The field of education has had an increasing focus on norms, standards, and national benchmarks. Zhao (2009) believes that NCLB and the ideas that it implements: standards, benchmarking, and accountability have increasing momentum since the act's inception.

Williams (2011) found that a broad array of professional development had a distinct impact on teacher practices. Through both quantitative and qualitative data, the researcher found that teacher learning does in fact affect teacher practices. He, Prater, and Steed (2011) again found that teacher practices could be affected through professional development. However, in their study, the authors undertook training 22 teachers for 46 hours of professional development. Such intensive undertakings are rarely if ever practical in the modern public high school.

Byrnes (2009) identified six traits of effective professional development based on her literature review. These traits are as follows:

1. guided by research on teaching and learning, with a strong foundation in content and teaching methods;
2. integrated with and corresponding to state and district goals while clearly focusing on specific results;
3. planned in response to teacher needs and utilizing a collaborative effort to assure results;
4. generally, based within a single school, and assuring specific time to collaborate;
5. consistent in nature and providing opportunities for further growth; and
6. judged on the outcomes of student results and teacher results rather than qualitative input. (p. 20)

Michael Fullan (2006) took umbrage with Byrnes point four. Fullan said that undertakings of professional development and professional learning, in particular if schools are to develop Professional Learning Communities (PLC) that are self-directed and organic, must be system-wide, not just within a school. However, as individual schools develop their professional learning, they will focus on problems, research, and solutions that are appropriate to their circumstances.

According to Torff and Sessions (2009), the effect and outcome of professional development (i.e., the "buy-in") may be affected by teachers' orientation toward specific subject matter. Conversely, elementary teachers that are asked to teach many subjects may be more amenable to professional development. Buczynski and Hansen (2010) deduced, there may be

the need for professional development programmes [*sic.*] to document actual gains of teacher content knowledge over a more diverse means: a waiting period before the posttest assessment of content knowledge, a measure of correct content usage in the classroom, and some process of determining the teachers' ability to translate their own content knowledge into appropriate concept understanding for students. (p. 600)

The role principals in facilitating and/or leading professional development are clearly an important aspect of the professional development process. Most principals "stressed open and honest communication in any of the practices and the need to give attention to individual's ideas" (Drago-Severson, 2007, p. 74).

In the studies of Engerstrom and Danielson (2006), "Teachers placed a high value on collegiality and viewed the opportunity to engage in professional dialogue with their building-level peers as their preferred way of learning" (p. 172). Teachers, in fact, appeared more greatly motivated by their collegiality than any other single factor present in the study. Gimbel, Lopes, and Greer (2011) affirms the assertion that the importance of a mentoring relationship between the teacher and principal is perhaps the greatest factor in teacher growth. This finding, in conjunction with the beliefs of Dufour (2004), who believes that there is a distinct argument for increasing professional development opportunities, clearly indicates that there should be increased opportunities for professional development within the school rather than in venues that appear divorced from the culture and rapport that already exist within the school. Dufour (2000) elaborates on the idea that schools need to provide professional development within the context of school culture by calling on system-level administration to provide the resources of time and money so that schools might facilitate such professional development opportunities.

Avalos, (2011) in a review of "Teaching and Teacher Education" containing articles spanning the years 2000-2010, finds that there is evidence of teacher professional development having an impact on student achievement. She states that such findings are generally a reason to be hopeful although there is little research to suggest that such impacts are in fact sustainable over the long run.

Richter, Kunter, Klusman, Ludtke, and Baumert (2011) found that teachers' interest in improvement of instructional strategies is not necessarily static across the board. In fact, the authors documented an increased use of professional literature dependent on two factors. Primarily an increase of teaching experience leads to greater attempts at professional growth. Secondarily, an increase in professional duties might also influence teachers' attempts at professional growth.

Opfer and Pedder (2010), found five specific trends around continuous professional development (CPD) in England:

1. There is a lack of effective CPD in terms of levels of classroom con-textualized practice, collaboration with colleagues, and research-informed professional learning.
2. There is a lack of effective CPD practice in terms of both the form and duration of CPD activities.
3. There is little indication that current CPD is seen as having an impact on raising standards.
4. Teachers identify a wide range of benefits of CPD.
5. School leaders report that school-based ... CPD ... provides more value for money than CPD that takes place outside the schools (p. 419).

The review of literature has revealed that certain trends are usually best when conducting professional development. Schools will see greater impact and value for their money if professional development is specific to the school and based within. A pattern of extended professional development that focuses on a specific practice would also be beneficial. The review of literature has even revealed specific types of teachers who would be most amenable to implementing the practices covered in professional development.

METHODS

My research was designed to examine within the specific sample teacher population of Bearden High School, the relationship between participation in limited professional development on Battelle Formative Instructional Practices, and the implementation of those practices in classroom teaching. The literature review revealed several themes that facilitate successful professional development. Byrnes states the themes as follows (2009):

1. guided by research on teaching and learning, with a strong foundation in content and teaching methods;
2. integrated with and corresponding to state and district goals while clearly focusing on specific results;
3. planned in response to teacher needs and utilizing a collaborative effort to assure results;
4. generally, based within a single school, and assuring specific time to collaborate;
5. consistent in nature and providing opportunities for further growth; and

6. judged on the outcomes of student results and teacher results rather than qualitative input. (p. 20)

My study undertook professional development while fulfilling only the first four themes. This undertaking is an acknowledgement to the realities of schools that sometimes only part of a professional development program is available. As such, the essential process will be one preobservation, a professional development session, and one postobservation.

I wanted to ascertain the administration's ability to affect teacher practices with only a 1-hour professional development session. There are two questions and corresponding hypotheses related to this research design:

1. Does limited staff development on specific formative instructional practices increase the use of those practices in the classroom?
2. To what extent if any can administrators affect the instructional practices of classroom teachers using only a 1-hour introduction to the specific techniques?

Based on a review of the literature, hypotheses were developed related to the research questions.

Null Hypothesis RQ1:   Limited staff development on specific formative instructional practices will not increase the use of those practices in the classroom.

Null Hypothesis RQ$_2$:   Administrators cannot make a measurable impact on teacher practices through a 1-hour professional development session.

Population

The research population is comprised of ninth through twelfth-grade teachers at a public high school in the South-Eastern United States. Teachers in all grade levels and all general subject areas participated in the study. For the purpose of this study, one school and 20 teachers from within the school were identified as participants in the sample population. The school chosen as the study site is accredited by the Southern Association of Colleges and Schools.

The entire staff of the school participated in one of four 1-hour professional development sessions that took place during planning periods. These training sessions were known within the school as "Staff Academy."

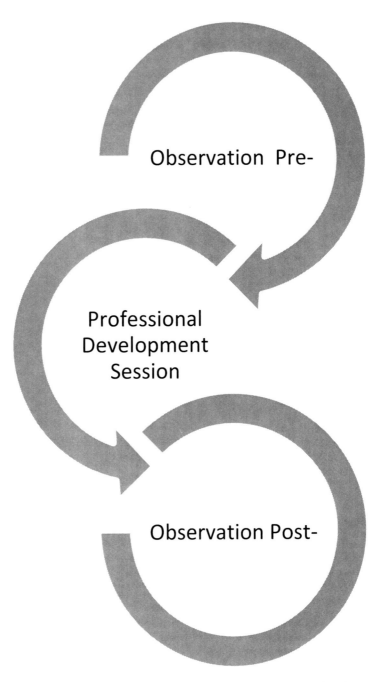

Figure 12.1.   The placement of professional development within the classroom observation cycle.

The teachers that were observed as part of the sample populations included the following subjects: art, ecology, U.S. history, English, French, Spanish, auto-mechanics, latin, chemistry, journalism, world history, biology, algebra, and geometry.

The demographics of the school are as follows. There are nearly 2,000 students enrolled in the school that served as the test site. Approximately 20% of students in the test site are on free or reduced lunch, indicating low socioeconomic status. The student body is comprised of 17% minority population.

The staff at the test school consists of 98 certified employees. Approximately 55% of the staff holds postgraduate degrees. One hundred percent of the staff is considered "Highly Qualified" by Tennessee state standards.

The school itself offers 184 sections of core classes taught by "Highly Qualified" teachers. The school is unique in several aspects. The test site has exceeded state goals for graduation rates from school years '07-'09 with a graduation rate consistently over the 93% goal. Additionally, the research site of nearly 2,000 students had only 145 suspensions in 2009. This number is significantly below the rate of suspension of other schools within the district.

Finally, the sample site is significantly above the state average in both achievement and academic growth. According to the Tennessee State Report Card, the test site school received "A" ratings in all achievement categories and "Above" ratings in all growth categories for school year 2009-2010.

Procedures

The sample consisted of twenty classrooms covering the aforementioned subject areas. The sample group went through the same professional development as the entire staff. Twenty classrooms were selected with consideration given to covering an array of subject areas. However, no classes were selected with prior knowledge of teacher practices. Although the sample was not random, one might still deduce that the practices observed were representative of what might be occurring across the school.

The head principal of the school and I reviewed the indicators of each strategy in order to calibrate observations and assure we both were looking for the same thing. During the ten minute "walk-through observation" any evidence suggesting that any of the strategies were used or would be used was considered evidence of the strategy.

During the first round of observations, the teachers were not aware that the observers were looking to see any specific strategies. In fact, the head principal already utilized walk-throughs to assess teaching within the school.

The second round of evaluations happened following the 1-hour professional development sessions on formative assessment. No specific mandate was given to teachers outside of not being held accountable for utilizing the Formative Instructional Practices.

The observations are in fact a quantitative method. The observer's only duty is to record evidence that any of the formative assessment strategies are, will be, or have been used within the class period that is being observed. There is no judgment involved, merely the recording of the implementation of the strategies.

The classrooms were observed in a manner that facilitated a paired t test to ascertain the reliability of the data collected. The design of the study was thus solely quantitative. An increase in number of strategies used per classrooms observed provided a quantitative measure of both research questions.

I wanted to compare the effect of a 1-hour professional development session on the actual teacher practices in the classroom. Seven Battelle Formative Instructional Practices were identified as high-impact strategies that are aligned with the "First to the Top" initiative. The effect of the 1-hour professional development session was studied, in order to ascertain if professional development that is not systematic and sustained can still have an impact on teacher practices.

A paired-samples t test was conducted to compare the implementation of Battelle's Formative Instructional Practices prior to professional development and following professional development. There was not a significant difference in the scores pre ($M = .55$, $SD = .76$) and post ($M = .70$, $SD = .79$) conditions; $t(19) = 0.42$, $p = 2.09$. This result suggests that limited professional development had no significant impact on teacher practices.

Additionally, the t test clearly demonstrated that there was no significance in total implemented strategies in sample classrooms either pre or post.

Thus, I failed to reject the aforementioned null hypothesis. There was not enough information to assure a significant effect within the study. Of course, the failure to reject the null hypotheses does the leave the risk of a type II error.

Table 12.1 demonstrates the exact number of implemented strategies per classroom as found in the study.

In spite of the failure of the professional development sessions to have a significant impact, there was one notable exception to the overall study that should be mentioned here. Specifically, I looked at implementation of specific strategies and whether or not they increased or decreased.

**Table 12.1. Formative Instructional
Practices Observed in Sample Classrooms**

Classroom	Pre	Post
1	0	1
2	0	0
3	1	0
4	0	2
5	0	0
6	2	2
7	0	0
8	0	0
9	0	1
10	0	1
11	1	1
12	2	2
13	0	1
14	0	0
15	0	0
16	1	1
17	0	0
18	2	0
19	1	1
20	1	1
Mean	0.55	0.7
SD	0.76	0.73
t-test result	Sig. < .05	.42

There was one notable finding, in spite of the lack of significance found in the t test. The first strategy: Providing a clear and understandable vision of the learning target or intended learning, showed gains of 62.5%. In contrast, the six other strategies within the Battelle Formative Instructional Practices required more complex processes and thus more complex training in order to affect implementation.

DISCUSSION

Professional development that is not systematically implemented and sustained over the long term does not have a significant impact on the practices of teachers in the classroom. Initial introductory professional development sessions, which have no follow up, are ineffective. There was a hint within the data that the simplest strategies may be affected through such a manner, but further research will be necessary to ascertain the validity of such a postulation.

Implications

Schools that have identified high-impact strategies and are tied to specific goals should follow the six basic themes Byrnes (2009) identified for successful professional development. These themes recur throughout nearly all of literature pertaining to the subject of professional development. These themes are:

1. guided by research on teaching and learning, with a strong foundation in content and teaching methods;
2. integrated with and corresponding to state and district goals while clearly focusing on specific results;
3. planned in response to teacher needs and utilizing a collaborative effort to assure results;
4. generally, based within a single school, and assuring specific time to collaborate;
5. consistent in nature and providing opportunities for further growth; and
6. judged on the outcomes of student results and teacher results rather than qualitative input (Byrnes, 2009, p. 20).

Too much is at stake for professional development at the school level to be haphazard and carefree. Schools must take the appropriate steps in planning and sacrifices in time in order to assure that appropriate resources are devoted to quality professional development.

I cannot help but wonder about the significance of the spike in the implementation of the simplest strategy. Is it possible the professional development strategies dealing with the most basic teaching strategy be dealt with appropriately enough in one 1-hour professional development session that it might impact a spike in teacher implementation? The professional development session that covered Battelle's Formative Instructional Practices covered seven strategies in a 1-hour period. Had one strategy only been covered in a more thorough manner, would there have been greater implementation of that strategy? I can't help but believe that this is a distinct possibility.

Without a doubt, the majority of research that exists on professional development concludes that a systematic, long-term approach to professional development is clearly the most appropriate manner for teaching teachers. Yet, circumstances often leave school administrators in situations where they must often sacrifice what the plan for a more practical approach.

My study reinforces the importance of long-term professional development. It was no coincidence that the most intricate teaching practices showed little growth in implementation while the simplest practices showed the greatest gains. The reality of teaching is that it is never simple. Conversely, teaching is complex. As such, training for teachers and the professional development sessions should be of the utmost importance for school administration.

REFERENCES

Avalos, B. (2011, January). Teacher professional development in "teaching and teacher eduction" over ten years. *Teacher and Teacher Education: An International Journal of Research and Studies, 27*(1), 10-20.

Battelle For Kids. (2011). Tennessee: First to the top. Retrieved from http: //portal.battelleforkids.org/tennessee/Services/FormativeInstrucion.html? sflang=en

Buczynski, S., & Hansen (2010). Impact of professional development on teacher practice: Uncovering connections. *Teaching and Teacher Education: An International Journal of Research and Studies, 26*(3), 599-607.

Byrnes, K. A. (2009). *Investigating teacher attitudes about action research as a professional development tool.* Retrieved from ProQuest Dissertations & Theses. (Publication No 3383882).

Drago-Severson, E. (2007). Helping teachers learn: Principals as professional development leaders. *Teachers College Record, 109*(1), 70-125.

Dufour, R. (2000, Summer). Superintendents can provide time. *Journal of Staff Development, 21*(3), 29.

Dufour, R. (2004, Spring). The best staff development is in the workplace, not in the workshop. *Journal of Staff Development, 25*(2), 63-64.

Engerstrom, M. E., & Danielson, L. M. (2006). Teachers' perceptions of an on-site staff development model. *The Clearing House, 79*(4), 170-173.

Fullan, M. (2006). Leading professional learning. *School Administrator, 63*(10), 10-14.

Gimbel, P. E., Lopes, L., & Nolan Greer, E. (2011, Winter). Perceptions of the role of the school principal in teacher professional growth. *AASA Journal of Scholarship & Practice, 7*(4), 19-31.

He, Y., Prater, K., & Steed, T. (2011, February). Moving beyond "just good teaching:" ESL professional development for all teachers. *Professional Development in Education, 37*(1), 7-18.

Opfer, V. D., & Pedder, D. (2010). Benefits, status and effectiveness of continuous professional development for teachers in England. *Curriculum Journal, 21*(4), 413-31.

Reeves, D. (2005, March). Constructive alternative in a destructive debate. *Principal Leadership, 5*(5), 38-43.

Richter, D., Kunter, M., Klusman, U., Ludtke, O., & Baumert, J. (2011, January). Professional development across the teaching career: Teachers' uptake of formal and informal learning opportunities. *Teaching and Teacher Education: An International Journal of Research and Studies, 27*(1), 116-26.

Snyder, T. D., & Dillow, S. A. (2009). Digest of education statistics. *National Center for Education Statistics* (NCES 2010013). Washington, DC: U.S. Government Printing Office.

Torff, B., & Sessions. (2009). Teachers' attitudes about professional development in high-SES and low-SES communities. *Learning Inquiry, 3*(2), 23-33.

Williams, R. (2011, February). The contribution of gaining an academic qualification to teachers' professional development. *Journal of Education for Teaching: International Research and Pedagogy, 37*(1), 37-49.

Zhao, Y. (2009). *Catching up of leading the way: American education in the age of globalization.* Alexandria, VA: Association for Supervision and Curriculum Development.

CHAPTER 13

THE JEANIE IN A BOTTLE

How Writers' Workshops Create Middle School Success Stories

Shay Mercer Siler

Reading and writing are reciprocal skills that build a student's skill base in literacy. I had studied the workshop model intimately for three summers (2004, 2005, 2006) with Lucy Calkins and her staff developers at Columbia University in New York and I utilized my training in the workshop model as an elementary curriculum coordinator and assistant principal. I wanted to study the true impact that the workshop model had on student achievement and teacher perceptions in writing. I experienced both successes and difficulties as I began my project and throughout the data collection stages. I found it difficult to provide staff development on Writers Workshop for the teachers during the same time of the project. This was because teachers were gaining an awareness and foundational knowledge in the workshop approach at the same time I was analyzing the impact it had on student achievement. Reflecting on this awareness, I would provide complete training on the workshop model prior to implementing the full project and data collection.

Great Leaders Equal Great Schools:
Alliances and Discourse for Educational Reform, pp. 227–239
Copyright © 2012 by Information Age Publishing
All rights of reproduction in any form reserved.

I experienced the feeling of success during conversations with teachers and their new desire and motivation to teach writing which reflected in their students' motivation for writing. Teachers who had initially been intimidated by writing were developing a comfort in writing with and in front of their students.

As I look toward the future working with additional teachers in the area of writing, I will keep the knowledge and awareness gained from this project at the forefront of my planning allowing it to help craft my strategic plan for increasing student achievement in writing.

I used a mixed methods approach in my project to allow me to analyze the scores obtained through student writing and information gained through teacher interviews on teacher perceptions in teaching writing. I was able to use my knowledge of the workshop model to train teachers and to provide model lessons in the identified classrooms. As a former curriculum coordinator, I used my knowledge of working with adult learners to ease teachers' possible discomfort of learning something new and making it a comfortable experience.

INTRODUCTION

The topic of effective writing instruction has been discussed among educators, researchers and educational professionals for decades now. Donald Graves was known as the "writing researcher" who identified a holistic approach to writing as the most effective way to engage students in the area of writing. Graves focused his research on revealing that writing "is a natural human need for expression and a way to develop and hone critical thinking skills" (Slover, 2005, p. 1). According to Slover (2005), Graves stated "children want to write ... they want to write the first day they attend school" (p. 1).

Writing instruction in elementary schools typically consists of teachers assigning writing activities such as short answer responses, completing open-ended worksheets, or writing in response to literature or reading assignments. Many teachers report that writing is their least favorite subject to teach in school. "Researchers from Vanderbilt University surveyed a nationwide sample of 300 fourth, fifth and sixth-grade teachers about their writing instruction practice and two-thirds of the teachers felt their college coursework left them ill-prepared to teach writing to their students" (Gilbert & Graham, 2010, p. 1). Teachers need more than one set of skills to teach writing, and unfortunately, often rely on the textbook version of writing instruction. Textbook writing, often found in basal readers, requires students to practice isolated grammatical skills and mechanics embedded in a given story starter or prompt. The crucial aspect of students being able to express themselves in the written word is neglected for the prescriptive writing features desired from the given task. Effective writing skills are a critical skill set for elementary students because they have been linked to powerful learning strategies. According to Bangert-Drowns, Hurley and Wilkinson (2004), "writing requires the active organization of personal understandings ... and promotes better retention and understanding of subject matter content" (p. 29).

THE PROBLEM

Since the 1970s, there has been continuous research in the area of writing instruction in our schools. Following the No Child Left Behind (NCLB) mandate in 2001, writing has been one of the primary areas of instruction nationwide in the standardized assessments included in the accountability factor for schools. Students in the state of Tennessee are assessed in writing on the Tennessee Comprehensive Assessment Program (TCAP) assessment administered in annually in the month of February.

A variety of instructional methods are utilized across the nation in teaching writing to students at the elementary school level. A very popular framework for writing instruction in the last 25 years has been that of the Writer's Workshop model. Writer's Workshop was initially proposed by Donald Graves, but in the last few years has been led by Lucy Calkins out of Columbia University's Teachers College.

Teachers at Carter Elementary School had utilized a prompt-based approach to writing instruction for approximately the past 5 years. Teachers presented a prompt of the teacher's choice to students during their identified writing block, and students employed the strategies taught to them to respond to the prompt. In the past, the most common approach to writing instruction was for teachers to give students a topic and a specified amount of time to complete the assignment. Students turned in a finished product that was graded on mechanics (i.e., spelling, grammar, & punctuation) and the mastery of the selected genre. The National Assessment of Education Progress found that no more than half of U.S. students are able to write adequate responses to informative, persuasive or narrative writing tasks (Lucas, 1993). In May 2010, kindergarten through fifth-grade teachers at Carter Elementary School identified writing as an area in which they would like more staff development with a specific purpose of moving into more process writing. Teachers desired staff development on writing instruction that would lead their children to be more engaged and independent writers with focused and deliberate mini lessons on writing skills and strategies. The purpose of this chapter is to highlight a study that focused on whether Writer's Workshop increases student achievement in writing and to identify teachers' perceptions regarding writing instruction when utilizing a workshop model. The project utilized the data from the fourth-grade writing assessments and surveys of teacher perceptions in the effectiveness of the workshop model. For the purpose of this project, two research questions were developed below:

1. Does the Writer's Workshop model increase student achievement in writing as evidenced by an increase in students' writing scores over the course of the 2010-2011 school year?
2. How do teachers' perceive the benefits/changes in their writing instruction after implementing the workshop model?

The significance of this project was to identify a framework or model of instruction for writing for teachers at the elementary level. The writing scores in fourth-grade at Carter Elementary school showed a decline in student achievement during the 2009-2010 school year in 75% (3 out of 4) of the fourth-grade classrooms, and the teachers expressed through anonymous surveys that they would like to explore different approaches to writing instruction than what had been implemented in the past few years. The project focused on fourth-grade students and the implementation of the Writer's Workshop framework in the fourth-grade writing instruction.

While there are multiple curriculum resources and programs for teaching writing, the purpose of this project was to identify the effectiveness and relationship between the implementation of the Writer's Workshop model and student achievement in writing. The project also identified teacher perceptions in the implementation of the model and identified specific areas within the model that are most associated with the student achievement.

REVIEW OF LITERATURE

Educators have wrestled with writing instruction for decades now as far as identifying one particular method of instruction that is most successful in ensuring student achievement in writing. According to Calkins, "in the past, writing was not taught; it was assigned and corrected. Teachers emphasized the final product of writing, not the process it produced" (Jasmine & Weiner, 2007, p. 132) "The process writing approach, first developed by Graves in 1983, focused on instruction, which allowed teachers to help students brainstorm ideas, solicit feedback, revise their work, then edit and proofread the final product before publishing" (Jasmine & Weiner, 2007, p. 132). Writing programs that encourage students to use their voice, rather than emphasizing mechanics and conventions, tend to increase students' awareness that writing is meaningful and individual (Thompson, 2011).

Writing has seen a shift in emphasis from product writing to process writing over the last 40 years. During the 1980s, writing instruction focused primarily on product-centered writing products where the teacher stressed mechanics and grammar. Currently, the accepted instruction in writing is the five-step approach along with the traditional journal writing, brainstorming, conferences and multiple drafts (Smith, 2000). The scaffolding should allow students to take a more active role in their learning of writing, building on students' knowledge of writing, following a natural sequence of thought that enables students to learn useful approaches to writing, collaborating and conferencing with students (Smith, 2000). Because students are being assessed in the area of writing at the national level, it is imperative that teachers devote instructional time to the topic of writing. According to Peterson (2003):

> a report by the National Academy of Education's Commission on Reading that supports the view that teachers not prepared to teach writing aren't teaching it … in one recent study in grades one, three and five, only 15% of the school day was spent in any kind of writing activity. (p. 1)

The Workshop model allows teachers to focus on their own writing, learning side-by-side with their students, and modeling to their students that writing is often times getting comfortable with the thoughts and words put on paper. Looking deeper into the structure of the writing program within a classroom, one must consider the amount of time that is dedicated to writing instruction. Peterson (2003) stated that "many American schools are not giving students time to write. National studies and assessments of writing over the past 3 decades have shown that students spend too little time writing" (p. 3). The Workshop model allows for students to have independent time to create their own writing pieces while also receiving guided instruction and feedback from which to learn and incorporate later into their writing.

Teachers have typically taught writing by teaching grammatical skills and mechanics in isolation and then requiring students to respond to a given prompt incorporating their own voice and appropriate usage of grammar/mechanics. Halbrook (1999) states that this approach to writing instruction is a "blueprint for mediocrity" (p. 8). He also states that "this drill and practice approach is a disservice to students...it has limited value in preparing adults for the writing demands of higher education" (Halbrook, 1999, p. 9).

A critical component of writing knowledge as educators is that there is a distinct difference between a novice writer and an expert writer. Research cited by Gillespie (1999) concluded that novice writers such as elementary students, "may lose their train of thought because they have to attend to more mechanical concerns such as letter formation, handwriting and spelling" (p. 20). Expert writers are able to devote more time and energy to revising and editing larger chunks of texts as opposed to novice writers. Novice writers have not yet to develop a sense of confidence in their writing skills and abilities as they are still in the process of receiving inundated amounts of instruction and feedback.

According to the National Council of Teachers of English (NCTE), studies report that time has indeed decreased for writing instruction. While the NCTE cannot identify one single effective approach to writing instruction it does concur that a holistic approach to writing is most effective (National Council of Teachers of English, 2008).

METHODOLOGY

The design for this project was a mixed method approach with a focus on the data collection and analysis of writing assessments and teacher interviews focusing on the teachers' perceptions of instruction utilizing the workshop model. The purpose for this project was to identify growth or lack thereof in student writing achievement when students were instructed in Writer's Workshop. Students were assessed with a pre- and postassessment that validated the instruction and learning in order to determine whether the framework model of instruction had an impact on student achievement. A secondary purpose for this project was to identify teachers' perceptions of their writing instruction after implementing the Workshop model. Teachers were asked interview questions pertaining to their perceived strengths/challenges/changes in their instructional format after implementing the model.

The design for this project was a mixed methods approach with a focus on writing assessment data collection and teacher interviews focusing on the teachers' perceptions of instruction utilizing the workshop model. The quantitative component of this project relied on the students' achievement scores in writing as the data directly related to students' growth in writing from October to February. The same narrative prompt was used in both assessments. Students received a numerical score from 0- 6 on their writing assessments. The students' scores were analyzed in two ways: (a) in terms of individual student growth from October to February, and (b) in terms of classroom growth in writing from October to February. Individual student growth was recorded, and classroom growth was recorded in terms of means and standard deviation. The qualitative component of this research relied on teacher interviews. The fourth-grade teachers were asked a set of interview questions that allowed the researcher to identify statistical information including means and standard deviation.

CARTER ELEMENTARY SCHOOL

Carter Elementary School is a public school in the Knox County School system. It is a Kindergarten through fifth-grade school, and it is located in the rural, eastern section of Knox County, Tennessee. The student enrollment at Carter Elementary school was 510 students, and 57% of the total enrollment qualified for the free or reduced-price lunch program. There were 69 kindergarten students, 82 first-graders, 71 second-graders, 85 third-graders, 90 fourth-graders, and 89 fifth-graders. The student population was 41% male and 59% female. The English as a Second Language program (ESL) served approximately 1% of the student population (less than 10 students). The greatest diversity was found when looking at socioeconomic status.

I used convenience sampling in choosing this site because it was where I worked as assistant principal. The Writer's Workshop model was not being utilized at this school so it was an ideal location for my project. Additionally, writing was an area where the results of teacher surveys showed a need for growth in regards to exploring alternatives in writing instruction. There were ten teachers involved in the workshop model; however, for the purpose of this project only the four fourth-grade teachers were represented. I ensured confidentiality by identifying teachers as Teacher 1, Teacher 2, Teacher 3 and Teacher 4. The number of students engaged in the Writer's Workshop model of writing instruction was approximately 210 students. This was slightly less than half of the student population, but the quantitative data represented the 90 fourth-graders. Students were identified as Student 1, Student 2, Student 3 through Student 90.

STAFF DEMOGRAPHICS

Mrs. Julie Thompson served as principal, and I served as assistant principal during the project. Mrs. Thompson had served as principal at Carter Elementary School for 8 years now, and I had served at Carter Elementary School for 2 years. The number of staff had grown slightly each year as the student population grew in numbers. There were four kindergarten teachers, five first-grade teachers, five second-grade teachers, four third-grade teachers, four fourth-grade teachers and four fifth-grade teachers. There was one resource teacher, speech teacher and speech assistant. There were five teaching assistants and one teaching assistant who also served as the personal accountability class teacher as needed. The site had one art teacher, one physical education teacher, one music teacher and one librarian. The site had a part-time school nurse, a part-time guidance counselor, part-time psychologist and part-time occupational therapist. There was a full-time curriculum & instructional facilitator for the second year being funded by the stimulus Title One funds. The degree certification of the staff varies in that 40% held a bachelor's degree, 52% held a master's degree, 7% held a masters plus degree, and 1% held an educational specialist degree. The teaching staff had a wide variety of years' experience. The experience level of the staff varied with 29% having 5 years' or less experience, 25% having six to 10 years experience, 25% having 10 to 20 years experience and 21% having 21 or more years' experience.

The staff at Carter Elementary School had been engaged in Professional Learning Communities for the past 5 years. In 2009, they partnered with the National Staff Development Council and the Learning School Alliance. They entered their second year as a member of the Learning School Alliance in 2010-2011, and they were very proud to represent the state of Tennessee as one of only two schools in the entire state who participated in the Learning School Alliance. Carter Elementary School was the only school in Knox County in the Learning School Alliance, and this past July they were asked by the National Staff Development Council to present their work in Writing PLC at the national summer conference held in Seattle, Washington. They were very humbled and honored to have presented their work and represented the Knox County Schools system, the state of Tennessee, the students and staff and the wonderful community in which they serve. They were proud to have been asked to present again next summer in Anaheim, California. They were diligent in focusing their strategies and goals toward continuous improvement and purposeful teaching and engaged learning.

DATA COLLECTION AND ANALYSIS

This project compared and analyzed pre- and posttest writing assessments completed by fourth-grade students. Participants were instructed in writing utilizing the writers' workshop framework, and my focus was on whether or not there was an increase in student achievement. Students in each of the four fourth-grade classes completed the assessments, and their writing was scored immediately following each test administration.

The same prompt, a personal narrative, was utilized at each administration of the assessment to ensure fidelity in the data collection and assessment of student growth in writing. Teachers were interviewed at the end of the school year on their perceptions of the writing model as they reflected on their teaching practices utilizing the Workshop model. Fourth-grade teachers were asked a series of questions regarding their implementation of instruction, analysis of student achievement and perceptions of writing utilizing the Writers' Workshop model for instruction.

Assessments were administered in the months of October and February. Student growth in writing was analyzed from the pretest and posttest utilizing a *paired-samples t* test to report the descriptive statistics. The assessment was a personal narrative prompt and was utilized in both October and February. The data analysis included comparing students within the same classroom and a comparison in assessment results among the four classrooms. The differentiating statistics of each classroom was documented in the final research report (i.e., socioeconomic status of children within classrooms, Free/Reduced lunch, male versus female enrollments, TCAP achievement scores among classrooms, and Discovery Ed scores among classrooms).

Teacher interviews were recorded and analyzed for similar teacher perceptions. Teacher perceptions of utilizing the workshop model were recorded and compared among the various teachers' responses. The analysis was completed by reviewing the notes and the transcripts to identify common themes in teacher perceptions. The researcher identified areas of similarities and differences among the teacher interview responses and areas of differing perceptions and responses.

FINDINGS

The quantitative data consists of the pre- and posttest writing assessment scores for fourth-grade students ($n = 90$). The pre- and postassessment data used a *paired samples t* test. The scoring rubric used by the fourth-grade teachers was provided by the state for the fifth-grade Tennessee Comprehensive Achievement Program (TCAP) writing assessments. The final score was an aggregate of Grammar, Conventions, and Context. The score range was from 1 to 6 with a score of 1 being the lowest score attainable and a score of 6 being the highest score attainable. The pretest mean was equal to 3.5 with a standard deviation of 0.962. The total scoring Proficient or Above was 57%. The posttest mean was equal to 4.0 with a standard deviation of 0.963. The total scoring Proficient or Above was 60%. The paired samples *t*-test results showed a statistically significant difference ($p < .05$).

Qualitative Data analysis from the interview protocol utilized to acquire data about the teacher's perceptions in writing instruction after implementing the Writer's Workshop model. Teachers were interviewed individually and their responses recorded on audiotape as well as notes taken during the interview process. The findings focused on the following areas: what areas were most helpful and least helpful, what would the teacher do differently with the workshop model next year, what would the teacher change about their daily writing instruction, what areas of professional development are desired for the future and did the teachers observe more student engagement in writing?

AREAS MOST AND LEAST HELPFUL

When asked what areas teachers felt were most helpful during the year of implementing the Workshop model, three out of the four responded that the model lessons I provided were helpful. Teacher 1 commented that "the model lessons were of great value because I thought it would look differently than how it was actually modeled." All four teachers responded that the mentor text support was most helpful. Mentor text is a piece of literature used by an author to teach a strategy. Teacher 2 responded "the mentor texts gave me ideas on what children's books I could use to teach grammar skills."

Three out of four teachers responded that conferencing was least helpful. Teacher 4 responded that "it is still new for me, and I don't have enough background knowledge or experience to do it effectively." The three teachers reported that they would desire more staff development pertaining to this topic in the future. Teacher 2 responded that she felt the usage of writer's notebooks as least helpful since she did not have much knowledge on how to implement the notebook in class.

REVISIONS FOR NEXT YEAR

The four teachers all gave different responses to this interview question. Teachers 1 and 3 responded that they would like to be able to spend more time in staff development with all the suggested items from question 1. For example, Teacher 1 responded "I would like to be able to have all the training during the summer so that I may start the year with all upfront and begin the year implementing the full workshop model." Teacher 3 responded that she "wanted to spend more time with each component gaining more knowledge for instruction."

A common response from three of the four teachers was the desire to have more time in their daily schedule devoted to writing instruction. Teacher 2 responded that she "would like to find a way to incorporate more cross-curriculum writing during the week to further support the writing skills of students." Teacher 3 responded that she would "like for children to have more flexibility in their writing so that I am better able to fully implement a Workshop model."

All four teachers responded that they would desire more staff development in conferencing with students. Teacher 4 suggested incorporating videos and classroom observations of teachers conferencing with students in the staff development sessions.

STUDENT ENGAGEMENT

All four teachers reported seeing more student engagement this year in writing. Teacher 4 reported "we did more mini lessons and used mentor texts to support our writing in the classroom." Teacher 3 reported that she "did more writing as the classroom teacher than ever before ... felt writing scores were better this year because students were more engaged on a daily basis." Teacher 1 responded that it was the "first year utilizing a writer's notebook concept and I felt that it positively impacted student writing and achievement in writing."

In sum, this mixed methods project was designed to study whether the Writer's Workshop model would impact student achievement in writing. According to the quantitative data analysis, there was a statistically significant difference between the students' pre- and posttest scores. These results suggest that the model positively influenced student achievement in writing for the fourth-grade students. The qualitative data suggested that teachers believed that their students were more engaged in writing this year compared to previous years. Additionally, with more opportunities for staff development in the various areas of the Writer's Workshop model, teachers may be better equipped with the various areas of the model, which would further positively impact student achievement in writing.

My project focused on the implementation of Writer's Workshop, a process writing approach employed in fourth-grade classrooms. The researcher was guided by the following two questions: (1) Does the Writer's Workshop model increase student achievement in writing as evidenced by an increase in students' writing scores over the course of the 2010-2011 school year? (2) How do teachers' perceive the benefits/changes in their writing instruction after implementing the workshop model? The quantitative and qualitative data supports the assumption that the Writer's Workshop approach to writing instruction impacts student achievement in writing.

In the literature review, I identified several recurring themes. These themes included: teacher training, modeling writing, time, and student choice in writing. Throughout the project, these themes presented themselves repeatedly in conversations with classroom teachers supporting the assumption that these themes are relevant and precursory to an effective writing program for instruction in the elementary classroom.

According to the National Council of Teachers of English (2004):

> developing writers require(s) support. This support can best come through carefully defined writing instruction oriented toward acquiring new strategies and skills. Certainly, writers can benefit from teachers who simply support and give them time to write. However, instruction matters. Teachers of writing should be well versed in composition theory and research, and they should know methods for turning that theory into practice. When writing teachers first walk into classrooms, they should already know and practice good composition. However, much as in doctoring, learning to teach well is a lifetime process, and lifetime professional development is the key to successful practice. Students deserve no less. (p. 1)

Teacher preparation programs need to prepare our young teachers by providing focused instruction on writing just as they do on reading, math, psychology and classroom management. According to the Vanderbilt study previously mentioned, "the findings indicate that teacher education programs need to provide better preparation to teach writing and teacher should devote more class time to writing instruction" (Gilbert & Graham, 2010, p. 1). Novice teachers should be prepared to write as a model for young children in the elementary setting allowing young writers to see drafts and revisions in daily writing. Teachers should provide numerous opportunities for writing in the classroom and across subject matter for a variety of purposes and audiences. These supporting features allow classroom teachers to implement a Writing Workshop model with fidelity. Students must have ample time and opportunities to write. The goal of writing should elicit authentic emotions related to their experiences and interests rather than simply writing a response to a prompt given by the teacher. Allowing students to have choices in their writing allows students to be more engaged, on task, and encouraged to support life-long writers at an early age.

Elementary classroom teachers should encourage young writers to write about their lives, experiences, and interests each day while modeling authentic writing of their own. Teachers should ensure that students are given ample opportunities and time each day for writing. The Writer's Workshop model provides a holistic structure for students to engage in self-selected writing topics instead of teacher-generated topics as well as allowing students to have choices in their writing which results in more engaged student compositions. Donald Murray, stated that "our discipline … has increased its research into significant but peripheral issues, decreased its efforts to understand through research how writing is made and how writing is taught. We are a profession with a black hole in the center. We do not yet know how effective writing is made, and all theory and practice should grow from that understanding" (Ballenger, 2008, p. 297). If we teach students to love writing and give them tools to express themselves confidently through their words, good writing scores are a natural by-product" (Thompson, 2011, p. 58). Thompson (2011) also makes the argument that "perhaps when instructing students in writing, we shouldn't be teachers. We should be guides, facilitators, and cowriters. By stepping out of the teacher role and giving students control, we ensure that individuality, creativity and student voices are heard" (p. 61). While the Workshop model may not be the answer to every teachers' instructional dilemma toward writing, it does offer evidence to produce more engaged writers in the elementary classroom setting.

REFERENCES

Ballenger, B. (2008). Donald Murray and the pedagogy of surprise. *College English, 70*(3), 296-303.

Bangert-Drowns, R. L., Hurley, M. M., & Wilkinson, B. (2004). The effects of school-based writing-to-learn interventions on academic achievement: A meta-analysis. *Review of Educational Research, 74*(1), 29-58.

Halbrook, A. (1999). Formulaic writing: Blueprint for mediocrity. *GED Items, 3*, 8-9.

Gilbert, J., & Graham, S. (2010). Survey reveals problems with writing instruction in elementary schools. *The Elementary School Journal, 110*(4), 1-10.

Gillespie, M. K. (1990). Using research on writing. Retrieved from http://www.ncsdl.net

Jasmine, J., & Weiner, W. (2007). The effects of writing workshop on abilities of first grade students to become confident and independent writers. *Early Childhood Education Journal, 35*(2), 131-139.

Lucas, J. (1993, January). Teaching writing: emphasis swings to process, writing as tools for learning. *Curriculum Update*, 1-5.

Peterson, A. (2003). Because writing matters: A book that shares what we know. *The Quarterly, 25*(1), 1-5.

Slover, K. S. (2005). The write way. *The University of New Hampshire Magazine, 20*, 1-4.

Smith, C. B. (2000). Writing instruction: Changing views over the years. Retrieved from http:// www.ericdigest.org/2001

Thompson, C. L. (2011). A dose of writing reality: Helping students become better writers. *Kappan Magazine, 92*(7), 57-61.

CHAPTER 14

DO THIS, NOT THAT!

Inside Data Analysis and the Instructional Decisions of Math Teachers

Jamie Snyder

As a literacy coach for 6 years prior to my professional transition into administration, I consistently worked alongside teachers collaboratively looking at different types of data to make decisions about instruction or instructional groupings for students. During this time, I noticed that numerous teachers were extremely uncomfortable when presented with their own data and asked to analyze it concerning gains and losses. My observations were reinforced when I moved into administration and thus inspired the rationale behind this project, which researched why teachers make the decisions they do about data.

During this study, I was honored to work with seven teachers who were very honest with their thoughts as well as intrigued in learning more about their craft and practice as a classroom teacher. From this study, teachers were given time to reflect and analyze the process they take when making instructional decisions for students and focus on an area of growth and development for themselves. Additionally, this project was a

Great Leaders Equal Great Schools:
Alliances and Discourse for Educational Reform, pp. 241–258
Copyright © 2012 by Information Age Publishing
All rights of reproduction in any form reserved.

growth experience for me as a researcher, an administrator, a curriculum coach and most importantly as a teacher. With this knowledge, I can better guide and encourage teachers to look at data differently and help increase their professional growth and knowledge as a teacher. Some of the difficulties recognized from this study include the limited amount of time available for research as well as minimal observations recorded to be included in the study.

My experience as a classroom teacher grounded me in the practice of creating and using lesson plans. Similarly, my experience as a reading coach fostering my teacher colleagues' implementation of data in their daily lesson plans provided background skills that were invaluable to this study. Being a practitioner allowed me to understand the research project from two lenses, one as the researcher and the other as a teacher. I was able to translate what the teachers were saying through their interviews and relate those concepts to my observations of their practices in their classrooms and on their lesson plans.

Since the inception of the No Child Left Behind Act (NCLB), schools have been challenged to ensure that they are academically competitive with not only schools that are demographically similar and in the same district, but also with schools in the same state and nationally. School leaders have been inundated with numerous new sources of student data forcing them to come to grips with data analysis for predicting end-of-year outcomes and to drive areas of professional development, school expenditures and even personnel decisions in order to achieve school goals. Standards and accountability continue to be the primary policy lever for improving student achievement in our schools (Ingram, Louis, & Schroeder, 2004). Years prior to NCLB, principals had end-of-year state test data to chart students who were classified into advanced, proficient and basic categories, as well as the overall status of grade levels and the school. For the most part, these data were rarely used to make informed decisions about curriculum, instruction or planning for the direction of the school, the following year. Throughout the NCLB period, external data and accountability systems have been assumed to lead to positive change in the day-to-day interaction between teachers and students (Ingram et al., 2004). For this interaction to occur successfully, teachers must know how to interpret data, make instructional decisions about the data and apply the results to inform their instructional practices.

The Reading First initiative brought data-based instructional decision making to the forefront of reading instruction. Until recently, math instruction had not received comparable attention yet scores were equally disconcerting. In the recent report, "Comparative Indicators Education in the United States and Other G-8 Countries: 2009" Miller, Malley, and Burns (2009) outlined the comparative indicators of mathematics performance across various international educational systems. In the United States, 77% of fourth-grade students reach the "Intermediate" international benchmark for math. This is the third lowest among the seven countries reported. Further, 40% of fourth-grade students reach the "High" international benchmark for math. This is the third highest among the seven countries reported. The United States ranks somewhere in the middle across all of the fourth-grade indicators (Miller et al., 2009). Nationally, 84% of fourth-grade students score at or above "Basic" level and 39% score at or above the "Proficient" level using the National Assessment of Educational Progress (NAEP).

In Tennessee, math scores at the elementary level have hovered around 75% of students scoring at or above the "Basic" benchmark and around 30% scoring at or above the "Proficient" benchmark. On a national level, the average score in Tennessee was lower than 43 states and comparable to five states. Tennessee's math scores were only significantly higher than three states. Tennessee's math scores have remained well below the national average for at least the past 2 decades (Miller et al., 2009).

In 2010, the U.S. Department of Education sponsored a competitive assistance program called Race to the Top for state education agencies to outline and implement programs for improving student achievement. In Tennessee's application, the state altered the proficiency levels in all subject areas and the Tennessee Comprehensive Assessment Program (TCAP). This revision has impacted the outcomes for all school districts across the state. Tennessee's decision to increase the rigor of proficiency has increased levels of concern and awareness among all school districts across the state. In Knox County, Tennessee, the Knox County School system saw a parallel decrease with state outcome data in the area of math. The county reported 91% of students in third through eighth-grades proficient and/or advanced in 2009 and 42% in 2010, the same decrease seen in proficiency levels across the state. With new proficiency cut scores in place, the county saw a heavy increase of 58% of third through eighth-grade math students below basic on the TCAP assessment. Compared to the previous year, the county was only 9% below proficiency in the area of math.

Since the state of Tennessee revamped proficiency scores on the TCAP assessment, school leaders, principals, teachers and instructional coaches were challenged to make an adjustment in instruction and other relevant areas. Parents, students and community stakeholders were also forced to evaluate individual test data and become informed as to how and why these instructional adjustments be made in the schools to increase student proficiency. Particularly when looking at math scores, teachers have been challenged to find new strategies and techniques to deliver research-based instruction to students. The challenge they face is two-fold. One challenge is to differentiate their instruction with students who have different levels of need and secondly, teachers must connect curriculum gaps that have become apparent after standards were changed at the state and county level.

The problem, is that we have students who are on the edge of proficiency and teachers who are having to make quick decisions based on current data to adjust curriculum and instructional practices for students in the classroom. This problem has raised questions in regards to the actual practice of making informed instructional decisions for student, such as, what kinds of data teachers use to inform their math planning, how the planning phase informs actual teaching and are decisions made during planning getting translated into their espoused theory of practice in the classroom?

The purpose of this qualitative case study was to examine what types of information teachers use to inform instruction for students who are less than proficient in math, how teachers use this information to inform their math planning and how does their planning inform actual instruction occurring in the classroom. This study examined how closely teachers' espoused instructional decisions informed their actual instructional practices. Following the purpose of the study, I have three research questions that will be addressed in this study. RQ1: What types of information do teachers use to inform instruction of students who are less than proficient in math? RQ2: How closely do teachers use student data to inform their math planning? RQ3: How does teacher planning inform their actual teaching of math? A limitation of this study was the one observation being done on each teacher to collect evidence of what teachers were actually teaching. While reviewing the literature for this study, I found most researchers had conducted their studies at the secondary level where teachers have more content knowledge about the subject matter they teach. Another limitation of this study was the lack of statistical generalizability due to the qualitative design. I delimited this study by conducting it the elementary level in terms of teachers at the elementary level having less specific content knowledge and more course responsibilities than secondary teachers. In addition, elementary teachers may have a less formed espoused theory and consequently would not be able to voice that during an interview. Additionally, there are only seven teachers being examined for this study which presents a delimitation when analyzing results.

Decision making and research around making decisions has been documented for many years, but only since the inception of NCLB has this process been studied in regards to how teachers are making decisions about student data. As I researched making decisions about student data, I found that there was a lack of information on the subject matter. Exploring the process that teachers go through when deciding on what instruction will occur in their classrooms as it relates to current sources of data is needed. My research sought to help fill the void of decision making literature.

REVIEW OF THE LITERATURE

The field of data-driven decision making is relatively new, and findings are predominantly based on studies conducted in the United States (Schildkamp & Kuiper, 2010). One reason for this limited amount of research is that data-driven decision making is receiving increased attention due to accountability, especially with the passing of the NCLB Act of 2001. Alongside this notion of increased attention from NCLB is the rising interest in a nationalized curriculum as well as the idea of compensation for teachers who demonstrate positive student results in growth and achievement. Four main areas of emphasis consistently appear in prior research about making decisions using data and how these would be applicable in a school setting. These four areas, when viewed through the lens of Argyris and Schon's (1974) theoretical framework regarding theories-in-practice and espoused theories will inform this study as it relates to teachers making decisions using data.

Peterson and Comeaux (1987) indicated that expert and novice teachers differ when making decisions using data. The differences involved integration of knowledge, student behavior and interaction among three stages of decision making (Westerman, 1991). For the expert teacher, the three stages of decision making include preactive, interactive, and postactive which were highly related. Preactive decision making is described as the planning and allowance of the wide range of possibilities that occur during teaching. Examples of preactive teaching would be types of information teacher's use such as knowledge of curriculum, subject matter, and student interest to arrive at their goals (Westerman, 1991). Interactive decision making is the actual teaching which is driven by the goals and planning set during the preactive stage. Postactive decision making would include interviews and reflection of how the lesson went and did it line up according to the two previous planned stages. The experts modified their preactive decisions in response to student reactions while moving lessons forward to attain their goals. They often accomplished this by using well-practiced classroom strategies or routines (Westerman, 1991). Westerman (1991) described how expert teachers view decision making as a dynamic process that is not linear in nature. Shavelson (1973) characterized decision making as the basic teaching skill and went on to describe that decision making is involved in every aspect of a teacher's professional life.

Because data based decision making is relatively new, many teachers find themselves grappling with mountains of data. In particular, novice teachers lack the knowledge or skills of what or how to implement the results into the classroom to change instruction for students. There is an idyllic picture about the use of assessment data to improve instruction by making better informed instructional decisions (Even & Wallach, 2004). In contrast to this picture, it is argued that this may be much more complicated in practice (Even & Wallach, 2004). For novice teachers, the three stages of decision making were more linearly related: planning, teaching and then evaluating. The three stages of decision making did not connect to each other in a dynamic way, as they did for the experts. Novices commented on not knowing enough about the topic to discuss it freely as well as not knowing what to do if a comment was made in the classroom that was not covered in the curriculum. This remark demonstrates a lack of both content and pedagogical knowledge (Westerman, 1991). Westerman's (1991) research further suggested that novice teachers increase their awareness of teaching strategies to use in planning and conducting lessons to help students. Novice teachers differ in the cognitive complexity of their schemas for classroom situations. Using data to make informed instructional decisions is a complicated process that requires teachers to build upon the toolbox of strategies they already have as well as continue to learn new strategies and techniques to change instruction for students when needed.

In this context, the use of "expert" and "novice" teachers is not intended to portray expert as older more experienced teachers in the building versus novice as new, younger and less experienced teachers. Rather, to teach successfully, teachers must develop both pedagogical and content knowledge together and then figure out how these two forms of knowledge interact with teaching (Berlinger, 1986). One of the challenges teachers face when making decisions about data is that they rely on their own personal knowledge of the curriculum and their feelings toward the subject matter based on their own history (Morgan & Watson, 2002). This challenge is carried over when teachers meet to review data and begin to make sense of the information in front of them. Often preconceived or biased beliefs about the way teachers feel may be in existence long before they encounter the actual data presented about the students in their classrooms. In these situations, data-informed decision making can be derailed. Having a strong pedagogical and content knowledge is not enough to become an expert (Balinger, 1986). Conversely, teachers must look at the data and make decisions with the mindset of what is best for the students in their classrooms and not allow their personal beliefs and attitudes to skew the results. The conclusion is that teachers at different developmental stages perceive and process problems in different ways

(Westerman, 1991). "Although contemporary rhetoric implies that a shared understanding exists about what it means to use assessment data to improve instruction, *examples offered suggest considerable ambiguity*" (Shepard, 2001, p. 1093, emphasis added).

Professional development, peer collaboration and leadership are all resources to help the novice teacher gain the tools needed to develop into the expert teacher. Teaching is a complex and cognitively demanding activity. A teacher's thinking and decision making organize and direct a teacher's behavior and form the context for both teaching and learning (Medley, 1981). For teachers to be able to make and organize their decisions to advance student learning, they must rely on school leaders whose vision must be communicated and shared with all stakeholders of the school. The school leader should create a climate, a shared vision and norms for data use with a focus on continuous inquiry, learning and improvement based on data rather than a focus on using data to blame [e.g., data should be discussed openly without the fear of repercussions] (Schildkamp & Kuiper, 2010). The assumption is that teachers will try harder and become more effective in meeting goals for student performance when the goals are clear, information on the degree of success is available, and when there are real incentives to meet the goals (Ingram al., 2004). School leaders indicated they used data to shape professional development activities for teachers, including helping teachers to create differentiated instruction activities or learning about school or district wide standards and goals (Breiter & Light, 2006; Brunner et al., 2005). These activities designed for teacher's growth and development will allow them to foster their pedagogical knowledge of the importance of using data to make instructional decisions for students. Sutherland (2004) stated school leaders have to encourage and support data use, be enthusiastic about it, and convey this excitement to the staff.

While novice teachers may need professional development aimed at the basic levels of learning about data-decision making, expert teachers should have acquired the basic levels. Instead, expert teachers need to be adding more nuanced information to their knowledge bank and even presenting strategies that were successful in the classroom to help novice teachers. This type of differentiated professional development within the school can provide novice teachers with rich and meaningful learning while at the same time extending the knowledge and leadership skills of expert teachers within the school. Professional development can contribute to improving teacher knowledge and disposition so they can improve their ability to make sense of assessment data. In the absence of high quality professional development, little attention is given to devising ways to use the rich information acquired about students to make instructional decisions and advance student's learning. The use of assessment data to make instructional decisions is treated as unproblematic, as if there is a simple connection between understanding what students know and applying this knowledge to aid instruction. This view, however, is dangerous because it assumes that effective integration of assessment data with instruction is simple and would occur naturally. Even and Wallach (2004) contended however, that moving teachers to the next level of learning to use assessment data for instructional decision-making is not a simple task, but nonetheless essential. It is naïve to assume that school staff simply masters data collecting, analyzing and using skills straightaway without providing profound professional development and external support (Schildkamp & Kuiper, 2010).

Collaboration among staff members, teacher to teacher, teacher to coach, and teacher to administrator are important pieces toward developing novice teachers into expert teachers. The time has come to take the current body of knowledge on data use (or non use) further by focusing not only on the use of data within schools, but also on how to support school staff in the use of data (Schildkamp & Kuiper, 2010). Many schools use professional learning communities (PLC's) to collaborate with one another about current data and the decisions being made to adjust instructional strategies for all students. During these meetings, teachers begin to analyze current data and start the decision making process of adjusting instruction to meet the needs of the students. The collaboration between colleagues in PLC meetings can be rich and informative for all teachers, regardless of level. Ina study conducted by Young (2006), evidence was found that using data collaboratively helped teachers to support conversations with parents, students, fellow teachers, and administrators.

As stated in the research, a supportive school leader, such as the principal, is an important factor. Schools that were effectively using data had supportive and enthusiastic school leaders, who stressed the importance of using data (Schildkamp & Kuiper, 2010). Smylie (1992) showed that teachers are more willing to participate in decision making if they perceive their relationship with the school leaders as open, collaborative, facilitative, and supportive. Lastly, further results suggest that teacher collaboration may also foster data use within schools (Schildkamp & Kuiper, 2010). School staff members have to become data literate and need strong school leadership, effective professional development, and interactive collaboration to engage ineffective data-driven decision making.

When making decisions about data, whether expert or novice, teachers must understand that data informed instruction is a process and is cyclical in nature. Data evaluation is a continual process and is always being examined and studied to gain insight into the advancement of students. Decision making is a dynamic reciprocal process that is based on cause and effect. Whether you are using data, intuition or extraneous variables to make decisions, there is always an evaluation afterwards. Effective teachers are constantly reshaping, reforming and revising their instruction to make a better decision for students. Huffman and Kalnin's (2003) research on the inquiry process allowed teachers to take data and put the data through an information process cycle. The inquiry cycle consisted of finding a focus for the inquiry, collecting data, analyzing data, identifying a problem, planning for action, monitoring results and evaluating the outcome (Huffman & Kalnin, 2003). After teachers were taught this process, it appears to have helped the teachers get beyond their own classroom walls and begin to discuss and debate issues within their classrooms and the school (Huffman & Kalnin, 2003). Another important finding that emerged from Huffman and Kalnin's (2003) work was the way in which teachers made the inquiry process their own. This allowed teachers to retain the initial excitement of the process and integrated that into the classroom. Young (2006) found that teachers used assessment data for instructional purposes, to move students between groups midyear, and to create and review intervention strategies for individuals (Schlidkamp & Kuiper, 2010). Again, it is up to the school leader to create and foster an environment in which data can be used to help teachers make informed decisions about students.

Data can also lead to unintended responses if the school is using it in undesirable ways. For example, selecting only easy-to-use data to inform instruction rather than detailed and more complicated data results in "strategic use," which means schools ignore opportunities to improve by choosing the easier data (Schlidkamp & Kuiper, 2010). Booher-Jennings (2005) described a school that abused data for "educational triage" purposes. Educational triage practices included teachers dividing students into three groups: safe cases, suitable cases for treatment, and hopeless cases. They focused solely on teaching the so-called bubble kids (those on the threshold of passing the test), targeted resources to the accountables (those included in the school's accountability rating), and decreased the size of the accountability subset by referring students to special education (Booher-Jennings, 2005). The inappropriateness of the educational triage practice is the taking away of services and instruction from all groups except the ones that count on the state outcome tests, or Adequate Yearly Progress (AYP).

Ultimately, teachers and school staff have to become data literate; they need to have certain expertise to engage in effective data-informed decision making. Leaders need to create a climate where teachers are comfortable working with data. Viewing data proactively rather than punitively will foster teachers and leaders to utilize data responsibly. Teachers and school leaders must become "data wise" and raise the goals they have for students.

Argyris and Schon's (1974) provided the basis for theories of action in which I will construct my research on data-based decision making. The researchers asserted that people have mental maps with regards to how to act in situations. These actions include the way they plan, implement and review their behaviors. A theory of action has two contrasting theories. These distinctions are made between those theories that are implicit in what we do as practitioners, and those on which we call to speak of our actions to others (Smith, 2001). The former can be described as theories-in-use; they govern actual behavior and tend to be tactic structures. Theories-in-use contain assumptions about self, others and environment (Argyris & Schon, 1974). The words we use to convey what we do or what we would like others to think we do can then be called espoused theory (Smith, 2001). In this study, I want to examine the relationship between teachers' theories-in-use and their espoused theories as it relates to making decisions about data. I hypothesize that the expert teacher's espoused theory closely resembles the theory they put into use when making decisions about data and how to change instruction in the classroom. Further, I posit that the novice teacher verbalizes their espoused theories during PLC's, grade level meetings and other meeting in regards to data, but the theory that is put into use is different from the one they espouse.

METHODS

This qualitative case study will compare elementary math teachers and their theories-in-use and espoused theories. My goal is to be able to identify a difference between teachers who use their espoused theory as their actual theory-in-use. The teachers who instruct in this practice should have a more organized and structural plan that would lead to better instruction which leads to better student assessments.

I conducted a qualitative study for my research. I hoped to gain a deeper insight into the processes that elementary math teachers use to inform their instruction. By using a qualitative method, I anticipated uncovering a relationship between teacher's theories-in-use and their espoused theories when making data-based decisions.

This study will be a single site qualitative case study designed to explore the relationships between teachers' espoused theories and their theories-in-use. Figure 14.1 describes the framework of the study.

SITE DESCRIPTION

It was conducted at Ritta Elementary School which is located in the Southeastern United States. The current enrollment of Ritta Elementary

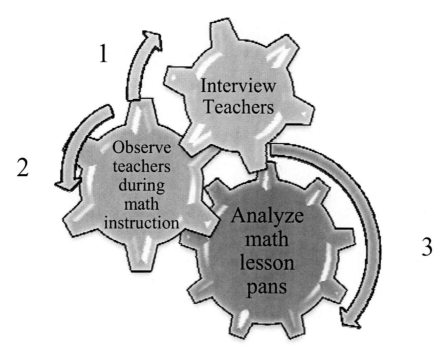

Figure 14.1.   Teachers espoused theories verses theories in use organizing framework.

School is 551 students. The student body is mainly Caucasian along with African American, Asian American, Hispanic and Pacific Islander. Ritta has three students that qualify for ESL services, which is < 1% of the student population. Ritta has 60 students that qualify for special education services, which is 11% of the student population. Ritta Elementary is staffed by a group of experienced and dedicated educators. The school has a principal and an assistant principal in addition to 26 certified classroom teachers to educate students in grades PK-5. Of the 26 classroom teachers, 100% are highly qualified according to the guidelines set by NCLB. The Parent Teacher Organization (PTO) at Ritta is a very valuable resource to teachers, students and the administration. They volunteer on a daily basis in classrooms as well as support the goals of the school financially with a donation at the beginning of each year. The median age in the community is 38.3. The population per household is 2.46. There are 1,599 total housing units with a median family income of $41,266. According to the U.S. Census for the Ritta community, 45% of the students live in homes with an average income of $50,000 and above. Of those parents/guardians, 28.7% work in management positions, 17.9%

work in professional positions, and 14.5% work in service occupations. In examining parent/guardian education, over 60% of parents/guardians have received their high school diploma or GED, and 30% have received some type of higher education. Four fourth-grade teachers and three fifth-grade teachers at Ritta Elementary School participated in this study. The age of the teachers varied from 25 to 55 and years of experience ranged from 4 to 20 years in the classroom. I protected the confidentiality of teacher's responses by assigning each math teacher a number during the data analysis.

I used interview questions, analyzed lesson plans and observed teachers to collect espoused theories regarding their usage of data and the decisions they make for instructing students. I used the Knox County Schools walk-through observation tool to gather observation data of teacher's theories-in-use to determine if their espoused theory matched the espoused theory verbalized from previous interviews and examination of lesson plans. I interviewed seven teachers, four from fourth-grade and three from fifth-grade to obtain data for this study.

I conducted a content analysis of the interviews to see if any consistent themes or trends emerged in teacher responses. I analyzed lesson plans that were collected on the day of the observation to see if teachers planned their math instruction using data. Lastly, I conducted a content analysis of the observations to see if any consistent themes or trends emerged regarding teachers' theories-in-action.

Results from the first research question of the study found consistent themes that emerged from teachers' responses elicited through the interview process: (1) formative and summative data, (2) instructional materials, and (3) test results and processes. When asked what kinds of data were available to teachers for math instruction, most teachers responded by describing state and district tests that were somewhat structured sources of information. For example, Teacher 1 responded to this question by saying, "We have unit math tests, data from Discovery Ed, and TCAP data." Five of the seven teachers responded with a response including the use of the Discovery Education program which is a formative assessment given three times throughout the year measuring students knowledge in the areas of math, reading/language arts, science and social studies. Examples of this type of response include: Teacher 2: "We have Discovery Ed that is new and helps us this year." Teacher 5: "Data we can use for that is Discovery Ed and Knox County's placement tests as well as other assessments we do in the classroom." Teacher 7: "We have Discovery Ed that's online, TCAP tests, quizzes that I give myself, old scores from TCAP's and daily work." One of the seven teachers (Teacher 3) responded with a question in reference to the word "data" used in question 1 of the interview protocol. For example, she responded, "Assessments? Well, I give quizzes, teacher made quizzes and at the beginning of the year we give a pretest or placement test.... I guess TCAP would count and TCAP from the previous year...." Her response indicated that she was unsure if data meant formal assessments such as TCAP or unit tests or if the question meant any data.

Teachers were asked if they used other sources of information to plan for math instruction and if there was anything unique to the way they planned for math instruction. Four of the 7 teachers said they used the curriculum and pacing guides provided by Knox County Schools. Examples of teacher comments that identified other sources of information used to plan for math include: Teacher 4: Curriculum. "I use the curriculum pacing guide with the SPI's (state performance indicators) and I use the textbook."

Teacher 6: "I make sure I cover the curriculum and hit the SPI's." Teacher 7: "I use the pacing guide to plan as well as look at how they've done if I need to review something." Interestingly, Teacher 1 said, "I get stuff from wherever I can. I also make up my own stuff." When teachers were asked if there was anything specific or unique to the way they planned for math instruction, the responses were random and inconsistent. For example, some of the responses were: Teacher 1: "I try to give the kids lots of practice ... do those problems over and over again." Teacher 3: "I do a lot of hands on activities than maybe some others.... I have to be flexible for my group and modify the work. I can't bombard them with 25 problems on a page." Teacher 5: "A lot of the other teachers are able to do independent practice.... I think teaching the lower ability group is unique. I do learning stations." Teacher 7: "I like to do a lot of computer stuff, active board, note taking and white board activities too." These responses indicated that a variety of other instructional materials were utilized when planning for math instruction, not just formal data and in one instance, whatever they could get their hands on would work.

Teachers also indicated they used unique practices to influence math instruction along with a variety of other instructional strategies.Some of the interview protocol questions probed into the data that were being used to inform math instruction and the result of those questions yielded responses that included using test results to help inform instruction as well as the process that teachers acted on to make the best instructional decisions for their students. For example, when looking at data to inform instruction, teachers discussed how it helped them make decisions about mastery of skills. One teacher (Teacher 5) said, "I look at where they master something or not, when I grade the unit tests and I see if I need to ret each that skill ... not to everyone, but to those who didn't get it."Other similar responses included: Teacher 6: "I look at specific SPI's and if they master percentage correct or incorrect to see if they need to work on it, if the child has mastered the skill, I can pair other students who master with those who struggle." Teacher 1: "Looking for questions they missed and trying to figure out why they missed it. I look for kids who scored high or low or look for kids who scored in the same spot". Five of the seven teachers discussed mastery of skills when looking at data to inform their math instruction.

Grouping of students and student motivation were identified as a process that occurred while analyzing data to inform math instruction. For example, four of the seven teachers interviewed responded by saying they had to pay attention to students' interests when planning for math instruction. Some of the responses included: Teacher 2: "The interest of students. I've never done the higher advanced students, so a road block I have coming to me is students who don't enjoy math and are not interested." Teacher 5: "I consider my kids too, they are all different and don't do things the same way." Teacher 7: "I consider the students and more hands on things, different strategies I can teach if they need something different." Three of the seven teachers discussed using the data to form small groups, intervention groups or flexible groups during math instruction. One teacher (Teacher 2) said, "I plan small groups or individual, one on one that I need to do with a student. Whole group for reteaching or do I just need to figure out a different way to teach that skill."

Teachers reported that using formative and summative data, a variety of instructional materials and consideration of student interests as types of information used to inform math instruction for less proficient students. Teachers reported other information during the interviews, but responses were random and varied from teacher to teacher

In terms of answering research question 2, two themes emerged: (1) connections with data, and (2) lack of understanding. Only two of the seven teachers submitted a lesson plan that named the skill being taught, described how they were going to teach the skill, listed how students would practice the skill and indicated they had reviewed some data source to plan the lesson. Some examples from the lesson plans included: Teacher 6: "Objective—Students will solve 3 word problems involving elapsed time.Instruction—The teacher will go through and explain each problem after students have had about 10 minutes to solve. Data—Games are differentiated based on ability to solve elapsed time problems."Teacher 3: "Objective—Rounding decimals. Instruction—I will model rounding again, sing the rounding song. Data—Look at rounding decimals again since many of them struggled on the skill from Unit 7 test."

The lesson plans submitted from the other three teachers exhibited a lack of understanding in terms of what the purpose of a lesson is as well as defining the difference between a plan and practice given to students.

Teachers were asked to turn in lesson plans on the day of the interviews and they were asked to set up an observation time reflecting the lesson plan they were submitting.

Research Question III Findings

The last research question was "How does teacher planning inform the actual teaching of math?" The seven teachers in the study were observed during math instruction. The Knox County Informal walk-through document for elementary schools was used to collect the observation data. As stated earlier, two teachers (Teacher 2 and Teacher 7) did not submit lesson plans so no connection to planning and instruction can be made. Five teachers did turn in plans or activities and two of the five (Teacher 3 and Teacher 7) made a clear connection from planning to the observation of the lesson being taught. Two more teachers (Teacher 1 and Teacher 4) submitted a lesson plan that did not contain a lot of detail, but did follow through in the observation of the skill addressed in the plan. For example: Teacher 1 did teach a math lesson on addition and subtraction of different measurement units. She integrated geography into her lesson and students were actively involved in a whole group setting. She utilized calculators and maps to teach the lesson as well as involved them in a real life activity of predicting flight times and layovers of travelers going from state to state. Teacher 5 turned in a sample of the practice page students were working on therefore, no real connection can be made from planning to instruction. Overall, two of the seven teachers connected planning to instruction.

Evidence from research question 1 suggests that five out of seven teachers identified data that was used to plan for math instruction for less than proficient students. Findings from research question 2 indicated that two of the seven teachers in the study used data to inform their math planning. Lastly, the same two teachers followed through with the process of using their planning to inform their instruction of students who are less than proficient in math.

I have found several consistencies with the information from the review of literature. Below I discuss how these findings provide practical advice for teachers, coaches, administrators and stakeholders. Four themes that exist in some of the current research around teachers making decisions about data are: (1) expert and novice teachers, (2) pedagogy, (3) professional development, collaboration and leadership, and (4) data use/cyclical process.

Prior research noted how teachers, depending on experience levels, make decisions in phases. The preactive, interactive and postactive decision making phases discussed how expert teachers make decisions based on knowledge of curriculum, subject matter and student interest levels. My study found that teachers did rely on curriculum, pacing guides and other forms of data as well as student interest levels to help them in their planning and instruction of math those students who were less than proficient. Additionally, the research also stated that novice teachers lack of knowledge and skills on how to implement decisions elicited from the data led to teachers not using data effectively when following through with instruction. I also found that many of the teachers I interviewed followed the same pattern of novice teachers.

Figuring out how both pedagogical and content knowledge interact with teaching was an important theme from the review of literature. Professional development as how to see the marriage of these two types of knowledge interacting together would certainly be beneficial to all of the teachers in this study. The literature encourages teachers to make decisions with the mindset of what is best for the students as well as reminding teachers not to allow personal beliefs and attitudes to skew what the data says. Most teachers interviewed mentioned they were aware of the needs of their students. One of the teachers discussed how the data were useful, but her "gut decisions" could tell her the same thing as the data.

Although teachers were not specifically asked about their professional development experiences, some teachers did mention in interviews that they received data sources from leaders in the building such as the instructional coach or the administration. Based on the lack of follow through from the planning process to the implementation stage, I can conclude that there was a lack of professional development as far as how to achieve the maximum results of using data to instruct students in math. The majority of teachers interviewed reported that they used data to plan for math instruction, but ultimately when lesson plans were reviewed and observations were done, only two teachers actually used some form of data to inform their instruction.

The biggest outcome from this study is that teachers verbalized that they used data for grouping and organizing students by mastery or non-mastery of certain skills on formative assessments. They stated throughout the interviews that they routinely made decisions about students based on how they did on formative assessments, daily work, quizzes and tests.

In this study, my goal was to examine the relationship between teachers' theories-in-use and their espoused theories as it relates to making decisions about data. I hypothesized that teachers would espouse their theories about data and how to use data, but not follow through with instructing what they said they would do. Agryris and Schon's (1974) espoused theory and theory-in-action certainly applied to this study. Only two of the seven teachers actually did what they espoused they would do based on interview responses. The other five teachers espoused what they did with data, but did not follow through with this theory during lesson planning or instruction. Therefore, I found my research to be consistent with Argyris and Schon's (1974) theory.

REFERENCES

Argyris, C., & Schon, D. (1974). *Theory in practice: Increasing professional effectiveness.* San Francisco, CA: Jossey-Bass.

Berlinger, D. C. (1986). In pursuit of the expert pedagogue, *Educational Researcher, 15*(7), 5-13.

Booher-Jennings, J. (2005). Below the bubble: "Educational triage" and the Texas accountability system. *American Educational Research Journal, 42*(2), 231-268.

Breiter, A., & Light, D. (2006). Data for school improvement: Factors for designing effective information systems to support decision-making in schools. *Educational Technology & Society, 9*(3), 206-217.

Brunner, C., Fasca, C., Heinze, J., Honey, M., Light, D., … Mandinach, E. (2005). Linking data and learning: The grow network study. *Journal of Education for Students Placed at Risk, 10*(3), 241-267.

Even, R., & Wallach, T. (2004). Between student observation and student assessment: A critical reflection. *Canadian Journal of Science, Mathematics, and Technology Education, 4*(4), 483-495.

Huffman, D., & Kalnin, J. (2003). Collaborative inquiry to make data-based decisions in schools. *Teaching and Teacher Education, 19*(6), 569-580.

Ingram, D., Louis, K. S., & Schroeder, R. G. (2004). Accountability policies and teacher decision making: Barriers to the use of data to improve practice. *Teachers College Record, 106*(6), 1258-1287.

Medley, D. M. (1981). *Teacher competence and teacher effectiveness: A review of process-product research.* Washington, DC: American Association of Colleges for Teacher Education.

Miller, D. C., Sen, A., Malley, L. B., & Burns, S. D. (2009). *Comparative indicators of education in the United States and other G-8 countries: 2009* (NCES 2009-039). Retrieved from http://nces.ed.gov/pubs2009/2009039.pdf

Morgan, C., & Watson, A. (2002). The interpretative nature of teachers' assessment of students' mathematics: Issues for equity. *Journal for Research in Mathematics Education, 33*(2), 78-110.

Peterson, P., & Comeaux, M. (1987). Teachers' schemata for classroom events: The mental scaffolding of teachers' thinking during classroom instruction. *Teaching and Teacher Education, 3,* 319-331.

Schildkamp, K., & Kuiper, W. (2010). Data-informed curriculum reform: Which data, what purposes, and promoting and hindering factors. *Teaching and Teacher Education, 26*(3), 482-496.

Shavelson, R. J. (1973). *The basic teaching skill: Decision making* (Research and Development Memorandum No. 104). Stanford, CA: Stanford University,

Stanford Center for Research and Development in Teaching, School of Education.

Shepard, L. A. (2001). The role of classroom assessment in teaching and learning. In V. Richardson (Ed.), *Handbook of research on teaching* (pp. 1066-1099). Washington, DC: American Educational Research Association.

Smith, M. K. (2001). Chris Argyris: Theories of action, double-loop learning and organizational learning, *The Encyclopedia of Informal Education, 3,* 107.

Smylie, M. A. (1992). Teacher participation in school decision making: Assessing willingness to participate. *Educational Evaluation and Policy Analysis, 14*(1), 53-67.

Sutherland, S. (2004). Creating a culture of data use for continuous improvement: a case study of an Edison project school. *The American Journal of Evaluation, 25*(3), 277-293.

Westerman, D. A. (1991). Expert and novice teacher decision making. *Journal of Teacher Education, 42*(4), 292-305.

Young, V. M. (2006). Teachers' use of data: Loose coupling, agenda setting, and team norms. *American Journal of Education, 112,* 521-548.

CHAPTER 15

THE BEST FIVE

Effective Professional Development Components Utilized by School Leaders in That Really Affect Teacher Practices

Robert Speas

The focus of this chapter was to help school level administrators identify key components that can make professional development move from a box that must be checked to an activity that can change what teachers do everyday in their classrooms. Professional development is often thought of as a four-letter world in the field of education. Anyone who has spent time in the classroom can attest to countless hours wasted in a large room, hearing a lecture from some "out of towner" who has the newest and greatest "fix" that teachers should be using in order to reach their students. While this picture of "professional development" is often seen all over the country, is it hardly one that will result in teachers changing their instructional practices. Growing teachers through effective professional development is one of the most important duties of school leaders, but very few administrators understand how to develop the gifts and talents of their educators. This study seeks to identify five hard and fast rules that

Great Leaders Equal Great Schools:
Alliances and Discourse for Educational Reform, pp. 259–276
Copyright © 2012 by Information Age Publishing
All rights of reproduction in any form reserved.

school leaders can use as a lens to evaluate the professional development in their schools.

The experience of reading the literature on "effective" and "meaningful" professional development provided me with an opportunity to look at professional development from a theoretical vantage. Many times school administrators are rushed to create a training session for teachers amid their other time consuming duties. By taking the 1,000-foot view from above on professional development, I learned a great deal about what we should be doing rather than having another failed "PD" session show another thing we should not be doing.

Timing forced this study to take an odd turn in regards to sequence. The bulk of the professional development activities were already held prior to the review of the literature. It was very difficult trying to create a study focused on effective professional development when I knew that many of the sessions did not meet the criteria for effective professional development.

Gathering staff feedback on professional development activities can be a very simple yet powerful piece of data for school leaders. I was able to collect the staff's input on the quality of professional development using an electronic survey website, *Survey Monkey*. If these pieces of feedback are utilized, future professional development exercises will prove to be more fruitful. The use of *t* tests to compare pre and post data allowed me to determine if real impact to instructional practices was made through professional development activities. Often times we look at data and see the conclusions we want to see that than using more sound statistical principles to make our decisions.

INTRODUCTION

The field of education is faced with a pressing need for quality professional development. Several factors are responsible for this necessity. Recent reform trends in education have dramatically increased expectations in terms of student learning outcomes (Borko, 2004). A shift from a traditional local economy to a global, information-based economy has placed a greater emphasis on equipping a nation with highly educated citizens (Darling-Hammond, 2005). An aging teaching corps, various educational reform movements, increased emphasis on technology, growing diversity in student populations, and developing fields of knowledge are just some of the issues that teachers are attempting to manage (Yates, 2007).

Through raised state standards to increased accountability under the No Child Left Behind Act (NCLB), students are expected to achieve at levels higher than ever before. This era of high stakes testing has brought about an awareness and focus on best teaching practices (Lester, 2003). It is through professional development that teachers are able to renew their curriculum knowledge and pedagogical procedures to reflect on these best practices (Yates, 2007). As standards increase, teachers must meet this challenge by providing students with the best instruction possible. It is up to teachers to meet these challenges with a change in classroom practice. Borko (2004) stated that "changes of this magnitude will require a great deal of learning on the part of teachers" (p. 3). Through professional development, teachers assume the role of life-long learners.

School leaders are charged with the duty of providing teachers with meaningful opportunities for increased growth and development. However, school leaders often lack the appropriate knowledge and understanding of the components of professional development that change teachers' practices and perceptions to be meaningful toward their growth as educators. This study intends to provide school leaders with an understanding of the five components of effective professional development that will lead to a change in teacher instructional practices.

The purpose of the single site, quantitative study that is the focus of this chapter was to explore professional development opportunities for teachers that produce changes in instructional practices, assess the school leaders' perceptions of professional development activities and to determine the teacher's perception of the effectiveness of the professional development.

In order to achieve the purpose of this study, the following research questions were asked:

1. Did providing professional development result in a change in teacher instructional practices?
2. What were school leader perceptions' of the professional development activities with regards to the five components of effective professional development?
3. Did teachers perceive the professional development as beneficial?

This study will be delimited to one urban high school. I will observe and survey only the six teachers from the science department for their change in teacher instructional practices and their perceptions of professional development that was provided to the staff as a whole. Also, the study will be delimited by its location. The school studied was located in Knoxville, Tennessee.

Several factors limited this study, which stemmed from the data collection procedures. The first form of data was classroom observational data collected by administrators. This was conducted through a series of three to five minute "snapshot" observations where instructional strategies implemented by teachers were recorded. Because of the limited time the administrator spends in the classroom, the data from the observations were limited. These data are also limited by a lack of interrater reliability between administrators when they categorize what instructional strategy teachers were implementing. While administrators were trained and practiced in teams to develop interrater reliability, the training was not enough to ensure fidelity among the six administrators. The second form of data was teacher surveys over their perception of professional development. Self-reported data are inherently limited. The third form of data was administrator ratings of professional development activities in regards to the components of effective professional development that lead to changes in teacher instructional practices. These data were self-reported data and were limited in nature.

As education is entering an era of increased standards and higher expectations for student learning outcomes, school leaders are searching for ways to bridge the gaps between current achievement levels and expectations. One of the ways school leaders will seek to close these gaps is to increase the quality of instruction that teachers deliver to students on a daily basis. This study helps to educate school leaders on how to structure professional development that will increase teacher learning so that teacher practice will change leading to improved student outcomes.

REVIEW OF THE LITERATURE

The review of the literature will address the areas of professional development and components that make professional development effective in changing the instructional practices of teachers. It will first address the need and importance of teacher learning and how it relates to increased student learning. Then it will discuss the shortfalls of many existing professional development practices. Finally, five components of effective professional development were identified and discussed.

As NCLB calls for teachers to be accountable for the learning outcomes of all students, Fullan (1996) believes that "you cannot improve student learning for all or most students without improving teacher learning for all or most teachers" (p. 41). One cannot separate student learning from teacher learning, the two are inextricably linked together (Jeanpierre, Oberhauser, & Freeman, 2005). If we expect students to learn more, we must start with increasing the knowledge base and skill sets of our teachers.

Teachers are willing to assume the role of the learner if they feel the learning will improve their teaching (Lester, 2003). Because effective teachers define their success by the level of learning of their students, they will engage in learning in order to equip themselves with the proper tools to educate their students. Teacher learning can serve to increase the knowledge and skills of teachers and contribute to their growth, but ultimately the potential benefits to their students drive teachers toward continuous improvement (Guskey, 1986). Professional development through teacher learning can lead to modifications in classroom practices that improves student learning (Borko, 2004).

While the need for teacher learning is widely accepted, there are no clearly defined best practices for accomplishing this task through professional development. Current professional development standards and practices are inconsistent at best. Borko (2004) acknowledged "the professional development currently available to teachers is woefully inadequate" (p. 3). Sykes (1996) takes this concept a step further by calling the lack of quality of professional development the "most serious unsolved problem for policy and practice in American education today" (p. 465). What teachers experience for professional development equates to a series of "formal and informal, structured and unstructured, planned and serendipitous … opportunities … over the course of their teaching careers" (Yates, 2007, p. 213). The result is a fragmentation of teacher learning with outcomes dependent on the circumstances rather than the processes (Yates, 2007).

Policy makers recognize the shortcomings of professional development and current reform models reflect the need for teachers to enhance knowledge and develop new instructional practices (Borko, 2004). Professional development is a central component in every proposal for improving education (Guskey, 1986). NCLB requires states to provide teachers with "high-quality" professional development; however, it fails to clarify what separates "high-quality" from subpar professional development (Borko, 2004). A significant lack of empirical evidence and data exists concerning what constitutes "high-quality" professional development, specifically between the activities teachers participate in and the enhancement of professional knowledge and skills (Yates, 2007). The research that does exist is often inconsistent and sometimes contradictory (Guskey, 2003).

Through reviewing multiple studies concerning professional development, five components of effective professional development have been identified: focus on content and pedagogy, collaborative in nature, school based, coherence, and time (Borko, 2004; Curry & Killion, 2009; Darling-Hammond, 2005; Garet, Porter, Desimore, Birman, & Yoon, 2001; Guskey, 1986, 2003; Guskey & Yoon, 2009; Jeanpierre et al., 2005; Lester, 2003; Lydon & King, 2009; Newmann, Kings, & Youngs, 2000; Yager, 2005; Yates, 2007). While the studies all contained other elements to professional development, these five components were the most prevalent when analyzed.

FOCUS ON CONTENT AND PEDAGOGY

Professional development focused and aligned with a specific content may be the most important factor when examining whether instructional practices and student outcomes were changed (Jeanpierre et al., 2005). Professional development surrounding content includes content knowledge and skills as well as pedagogy. Teachers need to understand how students best learn and understand specific content if they are to change their classroom instructional practice. While teachers typically have a strong knowledge of content, they often lack an understanding of how to teach using specific content-based pedagogy (Garet et al., 2001). When consulting with teachers after professional development sessions, a direct relationship was discovered between the amount of content focused of development opportunities and the degree that teachers experience an increase in knowledge and skills (Jeanpierre et al., 2005). Professional development based in content specific knowledge is especially beneficial for student conceptual understanding of math and science (Garet et al.). Teachers value professional development that provides "specific, concrete, and practical ideas that directly relate to the day-to-day operations of their classrooms" (Guskey, 1986, p. 6). Increasing the teacher's content knowledge and pedagogical skills is the easiest way to accomplish this task.

Collaborative in Nature

The impact of professional development was deepened when teachers were given the opportunity to experience learning in a collaborative environment. Group interactions allowed teachers to work collegiality and engage in meaningful discussions with one another (Lester, 2003). Guskey (2003) reported that teachers value working together to reflect on practice, exchange ideas, and share strategies. This collaboration can take many different forms including small study groups, careful reflecting, coaching activities, comparing notes about particular lessons, developing lesson plans together, and modeling successful practices (Darling-Hammond, 2005; Garet et al., 2001; Lester, 2003; Lydon & King, 2009).

The nature of these collaborative activities should focus on teachers actively learning (Garet et al., 2001). Darling-Hammond and McLaughlin (1995) agreed by connecting:

Teachers learn by doing, reading and reflecting (just as students do); by collaborating with other teachers; by looking closely at students and their
work; and by sharing what they see.... To understand deeply, teachers must
learn about, see, and experience successful learning-centered and learner-
centered teaching. (p. 598)

While this concept of active learning for teachers seems appropriate,
professional development activities often fail to meet these criteria.
Lieberman (1995) stated:

What everyone appears to want for students—a wide array of learning opportunities that engage students in experiencing, creating, and solving real
world problems, using their own experiences, and working with others—is
for some reason denied to teachers when they are the learners. (p. 591)

The way teachers learn was very similar to the ways that students learn,
much more so than was previously thought (Jeanpierre et al., 2005). As we
encourage our teachers to provide students with collaborative, active
learning environments the professional development we expose them to
should reflect these elements.

SCHOOL BASED

Professional development that is collaborative benefited when the members of the same teaching staff were involved. School-based professional
development allowed teachers who work together to discuss concepts,
skills, and problems that arise. Teachers were more likely to share common assessments and curriculum materials. Teachers from the same
school shared a common instructional context (Garet et al., 2001). As
these teachers were engaging in collaborative discussions around shared
content, the conversations were enriched through debate and reflection.

This enrichment led to levels of greater understanding as teachers
shifted from isolated practitioners to members of an educational community (Yager, 2005). Promoting professional development through collaboration among teachers from the same school led to the strengthening of
school capacity (Newmann et al., 2000). When school and organizational
capacities were increased, student-learning outcomes were likely to
increase as well. Many professional development activities failed due the
lack of building school capacity (Newmann et al., 2000).

COHERENCE

As teachers were overwhelmed with the day-to-day demands, it was
important that leaders provided professional development that had

coherence. With the high number of reforms and innovations in education today, professional development needed to be aligned as such (Guskey, 2003). Rather than a series of misaligned and disconnected activities, professional development was more effective when it formed a coherent pattern with a wide set of opportunities for teacher learning (Garet et al., 2001). Coherence included alignment with state standards and assessments, districtwide initiatives, school policies, and other professional experiences (Garet et al.; Jeanpierre et al., 2005; Newmann et al., 2000).

TIME

In order for sustained changes in instructional practices due to professional development, sufficient amounts of time must be allocated for teachers. Extended amounts of time were needed for professional development to be meaningful and positive (Yates, 2007). Simply devoting time to professional development was not enough. Time must be well organized, thoughtful, purposefully directed, and wisely used (Guskey, 2003; Guskey & Yoon, 2009).

Time was also well invested in collaboratively planning for professional development. When teachers were able to spend time planning development activities it led to increased buy-in and participation (Lester, 2003). Longer time in professional development helped to lead to greater depth of discussions on content and pedagogy. Extended time allowed teachers to trying new strategies, reflecting on the practice, and collaboratively discussing the effects on student outcomes (Garet et al., 2001).

When examining the five components of effective professional development, it became difficult to separate them. There was a tremendous overlap of the components as they served to support and strengthen one another. The best example of how to encapsulate these components into one concept is through examining reform professional development. Curry and Killion (2009) noted that reform-oriented professional development is more effective in changing teacher practice than a traditional approach.

Reform-oriented professional development places an emphasis on creating specific structures that addressed teacher learning. These structures included teacher study groups consisting of teachers from the same school focusing on content through collaborative discussions. These groups were sustained over time and possessed a high level of coherence within other reform initiatives (Curry & Killion, 2009). As school leaders look to structure professional development that will lead to teacher learning and a change in teacher practice, it is suggested that a reform-oriented model be followed.

METHODS

A quasi-experimental design was utilized in which teachers were provided professional development concerning the implementation of specific instructional strategies. Teachers attended four after school sessions and received training regarding the effectiveness of using the specific research-based instructional strategies for improving student achievement. Two sessions involved large, staff-wide information sessions, while two other sessions separated teachers into departmental groups. The staff-wide sessions provided background information while the departmental sessions were more collaborative and content based in nature. Data concerning the teachers uses of these specific instructional strategies were collected prior to these professional development sessions to be used a baseline. A second round of data was collected after the professional development sessions to determine if there was a change in teacher practice as a result of the activities. Collection of the second set of data began the week following the final professional development session. In addition to these data, science teachers were asked to complete a survey to obtain their perceptions of the effectiveness of the professional development in regards to changing their instructional practices.

Austin-East High School has a culturally diverse student population of 680 students. The enrollment profile for the 2009-2010 school year was 89.8% African American, 9.5% White, and 0.7% students of other ethnic origins. The student body consisted of 46.0% male and 54.0% female. Eighty-three percent of the student body qualified for the federally funded free and reduced-price lunch program. The special education population was approximately 14.0% of the student body or 95 students. This number included students who were placed at alternative facilities. To ensure special education students received more intensive instruction in core academic courses, inclusion programs have been incorporated into English, math, and science classes. The school had six administrators, four guidance counselors, 68 teachers, three instructional coaches, four Special Educational aides working under direct supervision of highly qualified teachers, and a media specialist. The administrative team consisted of an executive principal, a curriculum principal, a special education assistant principal, and three SLC assistant principals. The Counseling Department was comprised of four counselors, one per grade level—the ninth-grade counselor worked exclusively with the "Focus" SLC, while the other three worked across both "Impact" and "Discovery" SLCs. The lead counselor oversaw the department, served as test coordinator, and ensured coordination between Project GRAD, an external student support program, and the counseling office.

Ninety-seven percent of the faculty was highly qualified and 100% of the academic core staff, teaching 140 classes, was highly qualified. Fifty-five percent of the faculty hold master's degrees or higher. The teaching staff was comprised of 30 males and 38 females. The faculty was comprised of 40% African American and 59% were White.

Sample

All six teachers from the science department were selected to participate in this study. This included six science teachers: two ecology teachers, two chemistry teachers, and two biological science teachers. All six teachers responded to the survey in addition to being included in classroom walk-throughs. Three forms of data were used in this investigation. The first data source was derived from classroom observations using a "snapshot" method of classroom walkthrough conducted by school administrators. This instrument provided information on what instructional strategies were being utilized by teachers. Two sets of walkthrough data were analyzed: one set prior to professional development, and one set post professional development. The data were compared to see if a significant change in teacher practice had occurred. The second data set was the results of a survey completed by teachers concerning their perception of the effectiveness of the professional development sessions. The results were analyzed using a descriptive method. The mean score for each survey item and standard deviation were calculated. The third form data consisted of a set of rating scales completed by school administrators. The school leaders rated the professional development activities from one to ten in regards to the five components of effective professional development that resulted in a change in the instructional practices of teachers.

INSTRUMENTS

Each of the three types of data was collected using a different instrument. School administrators conducted classroom walkthroughs with a duration of three to five minutes. During this time, administrators logged what (if any) instructional strategy was utilized by the classroom teacher. This information was collected using the *McREL Power Walkthrough*. This electronic checklist allowed users to record one of 25 predetermined instructional strategies the user observed the teacher implementing one of these strategies. The Power Walkthrough also has the ability to log the level of Bloom's Taxonomy utilized by the teacher, instructional technology used by the teacher and students, and evidence of student learning. Once observations were recorded, the user uploaded the information into a large electronic database that was shared by all users. Users with the proper level of authorization created data reports concerning any of the areas measured by the Power Walkthrough. The researcher was able to access the walkthrough data from all administrators at Austin-East High School during this analysis. While this process may seem complex, the Power Walkthrough was little more than a tally sheet used to measure the instructional practices of teachers. The electronic nature of the instrument made it easy to gather and analyze multiple data points.

The school administrators at Austin-East High School completed a rating scale as the third data set for this study. The rating scale asked administrators to rank the professional development sessions from one to ten in regards to each of the five components of effective professional development that led to a change in the instructional practices of teachers. One was considered the lowest score, while ten was considered the highest score. In order to ensure the administrators had an understanding of each of the five components of effective professional development, a brief overview of each component was included in the rating scale. The results of this rating scale were analyzed using a descriptive method. The mean score for each survey item was calculated as well as the standard deviation. This was done to determine an average score for each component of effective professional development.

The third piece of data collected was a survey of six science teachers. The survey was designed to capture the teachers' perceptions of the effectiveness of the professional development sessions. Specifically, the survey measured whether or not teachers felt the professional development would lead to a change in their instructional practices. The survey instrument was created by Yates and Harris and entitled, *Teacher Perceptions of Professional Learning* (Yates, 2007). Six science teachers completed the survey by responding to the eighteen statements in regards to the four professional development sessions concerning instructional strategies. The survey used a four point scale ranging from 1 *strongly disagree*, 2 *disagree*, 3 *agree*, and 4 *strongly agree*. The survey was administered electronically using the web based survey program known as *Survey Monkey*. The survey statements are located in Table 15.3.

FINDINGS

Research Question I

Did providing professional development result in a change in teacher instructional practices? After reviewing administrative walkthrough data using McRel's Power Walkthrough, this question could not be definitely answered. Six different administrators conducted 39 walkthroughs where observations on the instructional strategy used by six science teachers were observed and recorded. Teachers attended four professional development sessions focused on instructional strategies and a second set of 72 walkthroughs were conducted. Following the professional development activities, the six science teachers reviewed the walkthrough results and collectively choose two sets of instructional strategies to begin to use at a greater frequency. These particular sets of instructional strategies, Identifying Similarities and Differences (ISD) and Summarizing and Note Taking (S&NT), were studied when determining if the professional development had an impact on affecting teacher instructional practice. Below is a table showing the data from administrative walkthroughs.

The null hypotheses associated with this research question were:

$Ho1_1$: The professional development sessions did not lead to a change on the instructional practice of teachers in regards to the use of Identifying Similarities and Differences.

$Ho1_2$: The professional development sessions did not lead to a change on the instructional practice of teachers in regards to the use of Summarizing and Note Taking.

**Table 15.1. Power Walkthrough Results—
Pre- and Postprofessional Development**

Item	% Pre PD	% Post PD
Number of Walkthroughs	39	72
Identifying Similarities and Differences		
Teacher 1	0.00	0.00
Teacher 2	0.00	0.08
Teacher 3	0.33	0.00
Teacher 4	0.00	0.07
Teacher 5	0.11	0.17
Teacher 6	0.00	0.17
Summarizing / Note Taking		
Teacher 1	0.00	0.21
Teacher 2	0.00	0.00
Teacher 3	0.33	0.07
Teacher 4	0.29	0.07
Teacher 5	0.00	0.08
Teacher 6	0.00	0.33

In order to determine the validity of these null hypotheses, simple paired two-tailed t tests were calculated. The t test for $Ho1_1$ resulted in a value of 0.92 and a critical value of 2.571 when considering a $p = 0.05$ and $df = 5$. This results in a failure to reject the null hypothesis meaning there was no significant change in teacher instructional practice as a result of the professional development sessions.

The t test for $Ho1_2$ resulted in a value of 0.80 and a critical value of 2.571 when considering a $p = 0.05$ and $df = 5$. This results in a failure to reject the null hypothesis meaning there was no significant change in the instructional practices of teachers after their participation in the professional development sessions. However, it is important to note that the change in values could be the result of a Type II error.

Research Question II

What were school leader perceptions of the professional development activities with regards to the five components of effective professional development? Data collected to answer this research question consisted of a rating scale completed by five of the six administrators involved in the planning and implementation of the professional development sessions. These school leaders were asked to rate the professional development sessions on a scale of zero to ten in regards to each of the five identified components of effective professional development that leads to a change in the instructional practices of teachers—Focus on Content and Pedagogy; Collaborative in Nature; School Based; Coherence; and Time. The mean and standard deviation for each component were calculated and is listed in Table 15.2.

Overall administrators involved in these professional development activities felt that the sessions were strongly correlated in four out of the five components. The components that focused on Coherence and Time were given the highest ratings with both having a mean of 7.40 on a 10

Table 15.2. Mean and Standard Deviation
of Administrative Rating Scale ($n = 5$)

Item	Mean	SD
Focus on content and pedagogy	5.80	1.64
Collaborative in nature	7.20	0.84
School based	7.20	1.79
Coherence	7.40	1.34
Time	7.40	1.14

point scale. School Based and Collaborative in Nature both were rated with a mean value of 7.20. The lowest scoring component was Focus on Content and Pedagogy which scored a mean of 5.80. Overall, the school leaders felt the professional development sessions were adequate but could have been closer aligned to the five components of effective professional development.

Research Question III

Did teachers perceive the professional development as beneficial? This is an especially important question to study in light of the results of research question one that suggested that professional development sessions did not result in a significant change to the instructional practice of teachers. While the data may not reflect changes in teacher instructional practice during the short period which research was conducted, if teachers believed the professional development sessions were beneficial to their teaching, long term impacts on instructional practice may result; thus the time and energy spent on these sessions were of value. Likewise, if teachers did not perceive the professional development as beneficial and the data showed no change in teachers' instructional practices, then the time and energy was wasted.

The survey instrument was created by Yates and Harris and entitled, *Teacher Perceptions of Professional Learning* (Yates, 2007). Six science teachers completed survey by responding to the statements in regards to the four professional development sessions concerning instructional strategies. The survey used a four point scale ranging from 1 *strongly disagree*, 2 *disagree*, 3 *agree*, and 4 *strongly agree*. The survey was administered electronically using the web based survey program known as *Survey Monkey*. The survey results are listed below.

When three questions from the survey were reverse scored, the overall mean for the teacher responses on the survey resulted in a value of 2.93 and a standard deviation of 0.61. Assuming a value of 2.5 is neutral; overall the survey showed that teachers felt the professional development sessions were beneficial.

DISCUSSION

Research Question I

Did providing professional development result in a change in teacher instructional practices? Two null hypotheses were analyzed using a two-tailed *t* test to determine if a significant change in the instructional practice of the six science teachers involved in this study. In both cases, I failed to the reject the null hypothesis because the value of t failed to show a sig-

Table 15.3.   Mean and Standard Deviation of Teacher Perceptions of Professional Learning (*n* = 6)

Item	Mean	SD
• I learned new and different ideas from the PD.	3.00	0.89
• Knowledge gained from the PD will improve my teaching skills.	2.67	0.52
• I look forward to trying new things in my teaching.	3.17	0.41
• The PD increased my knowledge of what can be done in the classroom.	2.83	0.75
• The PD will improve student learning opportunities in the classroom.	2.83	0.41
• The PD provided me with an opportunity to focus on improving student learning outcomes.	2.67	0.52
• The PD renewed my enthusiasm for teaching.	2.50	0.55
• The PD encouraged me to reflect on aspects of my teaching.	3.17	0.75
• I plan to use the knowledge gained from the PD in my work with students.	3.00	0.63
• The PD gave me some useful ideas of how to improve student outcomes.	3.00	0.63
• The PD updated my professional knowledge.	2.67	0.52
• Adequate support is available to teachers at my school to share information gained from PD.	2.83	0.75
• Teachers in my school share ideas, knowledge, and skills gained from attendance at PD.	2.83	0.41
• I think the ideas presented in the PD will be too difficult to put into practice.	2.00	0.63
• The PD was a waste of teacher time.	1.67	0.52
• I did not find the PD useful.	1.67	0.52
• Information presented in PD was directly relevant to teaching and learning in my school.	2.83	0.75
• Information presented in PD was directly applicable to teacher's work in schools.	3.00	0.63

nificant change in the instructional practices of teachers (t (5) = 0.92, $p <$ .05 and t (5) = 0.80, $p < .05$).

While the quantitative data and resulting t tests did not show a significant change in the instructional practices of teachers, it is possible that the professional development did impact teacher instructional practice and was not captured during the data collection. The method of collecting data was flawed due to the sporadic and limited nature of the walkthroughs conducted by administrators. Had the walkthrough method been more regimented both before and after professional development, it is possible that the data would have been more reliable thus allowing for more accurate assumptions for the implications of the professional development sessions. Another factor that would have lead to clearer results would have been a much larger data set due to increased administrative walkthroughs.

Research Question II

What were school leader perceptions of the professional development activities with regards to the five components of effective professional development? Data collected to answer this research question consisted of a rating scale completed by five of the six administrators involved in the planning and implementation of the professional development sessions. These school leaders were asked to rate the professional development sessions on a scale of zero to ten in regards to each of the five identified components of effective professional development that led to changes in the instructional practices of teachers—Focus on Content and Pedagogy; Collaborative in Nature; School Based; Coherence; and Time

Administrators felt the professional development sessions were strongest in regards to Coherence and Time with an average rating of 7.40. School Based and Collaborative in Nature also rated well with an average score of 7.20. The component Focus on Content and Pedagogy scored much lower with a rating of 5.80. This was an unexpected result as the basis of the professional development was Marzano's Instructional Strategies, which dealt directly with pedagogy. However, the bulk of the sessions involved implementing these strategies with the entire faculty. Had the sessions been broken into smaller content groups of teachers and how to best implement a specific strategy in a specific subject matter, this component may have scored higher on the administrative rating scales.

Research Question III

Did teachers perceive the professional development as beneficial? After reviewing the data from Research Question One, this becomes an especially important question to answer. While the resulting data did not show a change in the instructional practices of teachers, the professional development sessions may have proven to be worthwhile if the teachers perceived them as beneficial. Teachers could have made long-term changes to their instructional practices that may not have been captured during administrative walkthroughs. Likewise, if the teachers did not perceive the professional development as beneficial and the data showed no change in teachers' instructional practices, then time and energy was wasted.

The resulting data from the survey, *Teacher Perceptions of Professional Learning* (Yates, 2007), showed that teachers did find value in the professional development sessions. The overall average value for the statements to which teachers responded received a value of

2.93. Assuming that 2.5 is a neutral value, the average value corresponded to teachers "agreeing" with more statements than they disagreed. Interestingly, while the overall opinion was positive, no single statement scored higher than 3.0 which correlated to *Agree*. This means teachers did not *Strongly Agree* to any of the survey items. While teachers viewed the professional development as both positive and beneficial, they did not have a strong opinion that the activities were overly impactful to their practices.

When examining the findings of the three research questions in a holistic manner, it is possible to make assumptions concerning the impact of the professional development sessions on the instructional practices of the six science teachers involved in this study. Considering that the quantitative t test failed to show a significant change in teacher instructional practice, the mixed results of administrative rating scales, and the slightly positive data from teacher perceptions of the professional development sessions, the results suggest that the professional development activities failed to produce a change in teacher instructional practice both in the short-term and long-term. While teachers may have increased their knowledge concerning Marzano's Instructional Strategies, the data collected through this study did not support the postulation that professional development impacted the instructional practices of teachers positively or negatively.

As administrators strive to provide teachers with meaningful professional development, it is important that they have a framework to help guide them through the important planning and implementation of professional development. Providing school leaders with this framework is the greatest impact of this study. The components of effective professional development are Focus on Content and Pedagogy; Collaborative in Nature; School Based; Coherent with other initiatives; and sustained over Time. If administrators and other school leaders are knowledgeable about these components, they are able to continue to increase the knowledge base of their teachers. In turn, a more knowledgeable teacher is able to deliver higher quality instruction to their students. If school leaders wish to see better student outcomes, one possible way to attack this problem is to provide students with better teachers. When school leaders are able to provide teachers with professional development that meets the criteria of these five components, they have an opportunity to increase student outcomes.

REFERENCES

Borko, H. (2004). Professional development and teacher learning: Mapping the terrain. *Educational Researcher, 33*(8), 3-15.

Curry, M., & Killion, J. (2009). Slicing the layers of learning. *Journal of Staff Development, 30*(1), 56-62.

Darling-Hammond, L. (2005). Teaching as a profession: Lessons in teacher preparation and professional development. *Phi Delta Kappan, 87*(3), 237-240.

Darling-Hammond, L., & McLaughlin, M. (1995). Policies that support professional development in an era of reform. *Phi Delta Kappan, 76*(8), 597-604.

Fullan, M. (1996). Turning systemic thinking on its head. *Phi Delta Kappan, 77*(6), 420-423.

Garet, M. S., Porter, A. C., Desimore, L., Birman, B. F., & Yoon, K. S. (2001). What makes professional development effective? Results from a national sample of teachers. *American Educational Research Journal, 38*(4), 915-945.

Guskey, T. (1986). Staff development and the process of teacher change. *Educational Researcher, 15*(5), 5-12.

Guskey, T. R. (2003). What makes professional development effective? *Phi Delta Kappan, 84*(10), 748-50.

Guskey, T., & Yoon, K. S. (2009). What works in professional development? *Phi Delta Kappan, 90*(7), 495-500.

Jeanpierre, B., Oberhauser, K., & Freeman, C. (2005). Characteristics of professional development that effect change in secondary science teachers' classroom practices. *Journal of Research in Science Teaching, 42*(6), 668-690.

Lester, J. H. (2003). Planning effective secondary professional development programs. *American Secondary Education, 32*(1), 49-61.

Lieberman, A. (1995). Practices that support teacher development. *Phi Delta Kappan, 76*(8), 591-596.

Lydon, S., & King, C. (2009). Can a single, short continuing professional development workshop cause change in the classroom? *Professional Development in Education, 35*(1), 63-82.

Newmann, F., Kings, M. B., & Youngs, P. (2000). Professional development that addresses school capacity: Lessons from urban elementary schools. *American Journal of Education, 108*(4), 259-299.

Sykes, G. (1996). Reform of and as professional development. *Phi Delta Kappan, 77*(7), 465-467.

Yager, R. E. (2005). Achieving the staff development model advocated in the national standards. *Science Educator, 14*(1), 16-24.

Yates, M. Y. (2007). Teachers' perceptions of their professional learning activities. *International Education Journal, 8*(2), 213-221.

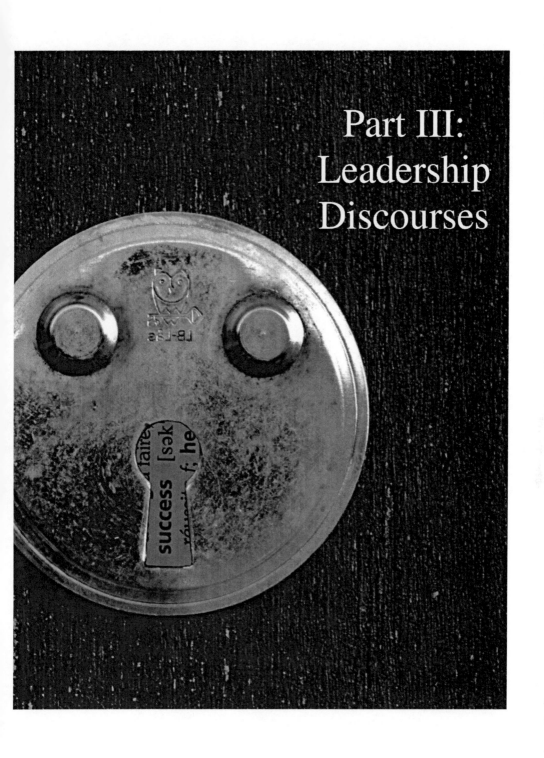

Part III:
Leadership
Discourses

CHAPTER 16

REFLECTIONS FROM ALLIES

A CONVERSATION WITH SENATOR LAMAR ALEXANDER

Currently serving as the 27th Chairman of the Senate Republican Conference, Lamar Alexander is arguably one of the great forces in educational reform in modern United States history. His efforts to improve schools and the quality of educators are well documented in the national arena. He is a graduate of both Vanderbilt University and New York University School of Law. Under President George H. W. Bush, he served as the fifth United States Secretary of Education. From 1979-1987, he was the 45th Governor of Tennessee. Following that service, he was installed as president of the University of Tennessee and served from 1988-1991. He also was a professor at the Harvard University's Kennedy School of Government. Along the way in 1987, Mr. Alexander helped to found Bright Horizons Family Solutions, a company that has now become the largest provider of worksite daycare in the nation. Senator Alexander boasts a legacy as visionary, politician, leader, and reformer.

Two administrators from The Center for Educational Leadership had the opportunity to speak with Senator Alexander about educational reform and his views on school leadership preparation. What follows below is a transcript of the conversation between The Center's Director, Autumn Cyprès (**AC**) the Center's Principal-In-Residence, Betty Sue Sparks (**BSS**), and Senator Alexander (**LA**):

Great Leaders Equal Great Schools:
Alliances and Discourse for Educational Reform, pp. 279–296
Copyright © 2012 by Information Age Publishing
All rights of reproduction in any form reserved.

AC: Among many of your contributions to our nation is that you were one of the first governors to push for school reform.

LA: I was elected governor on the same day that Bill Clinton was elected governor of Arkansas and Dick Riley was elected governor of South Carolina and Bob Graham was elected governor of Florida and William Winter already was governor of Mississippi. All of us were southern governors, and all of us saw the need for raising family incomes in our state and all of us saw the relationships of better schools to better jobs. So we worked together from 1979 through 1987 doing many of the same things. For example, Governor Graham and I, in Tennessee and Florida in 1983 and 1984, worked hard to become the first states to pay teachers more for teaching well, which resulted in our master teacher program or career ladder that 10,000 Tennessee teachers and principals voluntarily joined. It's interesting to me, I must literally run into one or two of those teachers every day that I'm in Tennessee, who tells me how much that program meant to them.

BSS: Senator, I was one of the first career level three principals.

LA: Good for you, which means you stuck your neck out.

BSS: Yes I did, and it was worth it.

LA: Well, it wasn't a perfect program but it was a way to honor teachers and to improve skills. We've done a lot of things that had never been done before, and Tennessee teachers really had to create the career ladder system themselves. But my point was that Tennessee was able to get it done before Florida did. Never the less, Governor Graham flew to Nashville and met with me and with Senator Annabelle Clement O'Brian who was chairman of the Senate Education Committee. He helped to persuade her to support the Master Teacher Program, and she cast the deciding vote to get it out of committee and that helped pass the program. So we really worked together. Then in 1985 and 1986 when I was chairman of the National Governor's Association and Governor Clinton was Vice Chairman, we devoted the entire year to the subject of what we called Time for Results, which was a focus on education and was the first time since the Governor's Association had been formed under president Theodore Roosevelt that all the governors had worked together on a single subject for an entire year. So that was really the beginning of a national interest in how to improve schools. Secretary Bell's A Nation at Risk came in the midst of that, and since then we've had many governors and many legislatures, many groups who've worked to create accountability standards and ways of rewarding outstanding teaching and charter schools and opportunities for more choices of schools. We've had no child left behind to help us see what kind of results we were getting in different schools. So that was the beginning of a wave of interest in better schools.

AC: From you're perspective as the former president of The University of Tennessee, I was wondering how you think we might traverse the gap that seems to exist between the "ivory tower" of academia and "real world" of schools? How do you think we can get schools and universities in a closer place when it comes to improving schools?

LA: Well, that's a very good point. People have always worried that there's a lot of good educational research going on in the United States but somehow it never gets into the classroom as effectively as we would like. And many of the colleges of Education not only were involved with some of the school reform, some of them were outright opposed to it. For example, I had many professors of education at reputable colleges of education tell me there was no way to reward outstanding teaching because you couldn't tell a good teacher from a bad teacher. Which you know is utter nonsense, and now we know that. But it's hard a hard task to undertake. And there is no question it is equally hard to do this in a fair way. But there is a way to do it. There is a third area that we never really focused on in the way we should have: That of school leadership preparation programs. Our Better Schools Program in Tennessee not only rewarded outstanding teaching, it rewarded outstanding school leadership. We had master principals as you mentioned, and we had for a while a principal's academy, which tried to bring in leaders from other walks of life and give principals a chance to learn leadership skills. Today there's a lot more of that going on than when we first tried this idea. And there are private organizations like new leaders for new schools, working in Memphis, which recognizes school leadership is different than classroom teaching, just like coaching's different than being an All-American wide receiver. And they're doing a good job of training school leaders.

I am sure that probably the single best bang for an education dollar's buck would be to spend it on training better principals, because we all know that it's hard to have a good school without a great principal. There are a defined number of principals, and it would be possible actually to select them well and to train them well to be better leaders.

AC: I couldn't agree more, that's the reason I left the principalship. As a principal in Arizona I focused, I noticed that there weren't enough academics who had been in the field who were successful principals. I enjoyed being a principal very much but wanted to give back to the training of them rather than move to a superintendent's position. So I became a professor at Kent State, and I spent a decade studying these exact issues we are talking about. When the opportunity came to serve as the first director of the Center (for Educational Leadership) it was an offer I could not refuse as this model does exactly what you are talking about. We bring in people from disciplines who serve in leadership roles to train our fellows, along side professors of educational administration and school leaders. And we provide an internship that is one of the most intensive in the nation; structured on something we call the medical model. In other words our students serve as interns in much the same way that physicians in training do with long continuous hours. Fellows are placed in full time positions of leadership and a classroom teacher is hired fulltime to relieve Fellows of their duties as classroom teachers. They are in the field every day serving as administrators. I'm thrilled to hear your take on quality leadership preparation this because this absolutely echoes what's reflected in the pages of this book.

LA: Thank you.

AC: Do you mind if we switch gears for a moment and you could talk about what you think the purpose of school is? It's always an interesting question to me because people usually say "Well, the purpose of school is to produce good citizens." And I agree with that, but you know that's kind of an obtuse answer.

LA: Well I'll give you a couple of definitions. I was at an educator's meeting in Rochester, New York, years ago and the president of Notre Dame asked the group of educators, what's the rationale for a public school? And there was this silence all around the room until Albert Shanker, who's head of the American Federation of Teachers spoke up and said that the public school was created for the purpose of teaching reading, writing, arithmetic, and what it means to be an American, to immigrant children with the hope they would go home and teach their parents. Professor Coleman at the University of Chicago said that a school is for the purpose of helping parents do what parents don't do as well. I've always liked both of those definitions because the first one reminds us that there really isn't any justification for a public school unless it has a public purpose. We could have private schools as we once did, and an essential part of a public school is to help children understand what it means to be an American. Which is why I think we ought to begin each day with the Pledge of Allegiance and allow some child to take three minutes and say here's what it means to be an American to understand what's special about our country. We do it in the United States senate; we ought to do it in our schools. I think that Dr. Coleman's description is very profound because it reminds us that some parents are able to do much more than others in educating their children, and that what schools have to do is meet the children where they are. There may be children whose parents are PhD's at Oak Ridge National Laboratory and have devoted a lot of time to the children from the time they were born. Those parents may expect a lot from school for gifted children. Or it may be parents who home school their children and they may not expect much. But the school ought to fit into the lives of whatever the parents are able to do for their children. Or the children may come from a broken home and not have had breakfast before they come to school and the school has to help that child differently. So I like the definition of a school is for the purpose of helping parents do what parent's don't do as well. And the other reason I like that definition is because it puts the first responsibility of education where it ought to be, which is with parents.

AC: Let's extend this line of thought for a minute. Could you include in your perspective of the purpose of school your take on language acquisition?

LA: If you go back to Shanker's definition of teaching reading, writing and arithmetic and what it means to be an American, and in America reading means reading in English. You don't become Americans based on your ancestry or your race; you become Americans based upon learning our common language and learning our common principals. I spoke at a naturalization ceremony in Maryville last week for 165 new citizens from 61 countries and they all had to learn our common language, English, in order to become a citizen. And they had to learn enough about American history to pass a test because to become American you have to know our common language and common principals. So I'm in favor, I believe our public schools especially have a responsibility to teach English as quickly as possible to every child.

AC: I think the more yeasty conversations occur when people start wondering/thinking about the process of delivering English

Language instruction to students whose primary language is not English. Is there anything else you would like to add to your comments that speaks to the purpose of school in society or the role that communities play?

LA: I think in the end that the communities and parents can have schools that are as good as they want them to be. Now that offends some people to say that, because they say we all don't have the same advantages; that some parents and some communities have a harder time than others or have lower income than others, or have some difficulty than others. And former Education Secretary Bill Bennett used to say to me when I would give the example of Maryville schools that look at first blush to be upper middle class. And that every community is not like Maryville. But I contend that Maryville is a pretty good example because when I was growing up it was not a rich community; it was a middle to low-income community. And yet the community at that time decided it wanted superior schools for all the children who went to school there. My father and a group of others ran for the school board and stayed on it for 25 years in order to do that. My mother had her own nursery school and kindergarten and lobbied the school board to have a public kindergarten. So when I saw this past year that Maryville High School won both the state football champion and was named the best public high school it didn't surprise me very much. The principal was interviewed, and he was asked how that happened. And he said, "Well it's kind of a town school. Something happens, everybody just shows up." So the community can decide what the quality of education can be. While the state can help create a framework and the federal government can help a little, I think to try to pretend that Washington or Nashville can make schools better in Maryville or Wartburg or Oak Ridge or Kingsport is the wrong way to think about it.

AC: I also think because Washington policies are so far away from the everydayness of school, that's why a principal is so important. Because its not just that a principal helps their staff embrace accountability, it is the principal who can be the conduit to the community to really make that school the heart of a community.

LA: Right.

AC: Well, I think our agreement that principals are the key to school improvement is probably the perfect place close this interview. Thank you so much for your time.

LA: Thank you so much for your time, and thank you for letting me be a part of your book.

For an additional take on Career ladder and the reform that Lamar Alexander initiated visit: http://www.ascd.org/ASCD/pdf/journals/ed _leadel_198511_furtwengler.pdf

REFLECTIONS ON SCHOOL LEADERSHIP
By Oliver "Buzz" Thomas
President of Great Schools Partnership
and Cochair of the Public School Forum of East Tennessee

Ernest Hemingway was once asked how to write a good book. "Write the truest sentence you know," he said. "Then, write another." The truest sentence I know about education is this: *The community with the best schools wins.* Whether we're talking about per capita income, economic development, family health or even personal happiness, the answer is the same. The community with the best schools wins!

Here's the second truest sentence I know about education. Great schools *require* great principals. That's why the University of Tennessee and the Knox County Schools have partnered to create one of the most promising principal-preparation programs in the county. Based on the highly successful Boston model, this program combines research-based collaborative learning in a small cohort of talented candidates with hands-on experience under the tutelage of some of Knox County's most successful principals.

In short, Knoxville is training principals like most cities train physicians. Only better. In addition to rigorous instruction and hands-on experience, my observation has been that we are developing school leaders who are capable of creating actual "learning communities." These are the places where students and teachers can fearlessly open their minds and hearts to achieve anything. It is within such communities that we are able to see and realize that what we once thought impossible is doable. Here, we can transcend as thinkers, doers and citizens committed to a common cause. Improving both ourselves and the conditions of our society is— after all—at the heart of what schools *should* be doing.

The Irish philosopher John O'Donohue may be getting to the heart of the matter when he speaks of Anam Cara or "soul friend." More than mere mentorship, school leadership preparation depends on the close respectful exchange of intellect, values, and experience. We become soul friends. Mind friends. New school leadership depends on both a total commitment to the sacristy of learning as well as an unwavering courage to embrace accountability.

This is what I see happening at this new leadership academy. I see it in the growth of its students, and I see it in the impact they are having on our schools and our classrooms.

And it gladdens my heart.

NEW SCHOOL LEADERSHIP IN TENNESSEE
Dr. Bob Rider
Dean College of Education, Health, and Human Sciences, The University of Tennessee, Knoxville

First and foremost, leadership is the most critical component to the success of any organization, whether it is in regard to business, industry, nonprofits, or education. Specific to education, school leadership and effective teaching are the two most essential contributors to a successful school and success in the academic achievement of students. Given the significant attention being paid to schools and schooling within today's society, effective school leadership has never been more important. It is in this light that I will endeavor to respond to the following series of questions.

School, or otherwise known as a center of learning, is the centerpiece of any community, whether we are talking about Tennessee or anywhere else in the world. It is that place that brings people together, predominantly teachers, students and family, to provide learning opportunities for today's youth in a way that facilitates understanding and propagates success in life. While I would not intentionally dismiss the importance of other community entities, such as faith based organizations, public service agencies, neighborhood parks and recreation facilities and the like, the school is that place in the community where ideas emanate, learning takes place, and concepts, both intellectual and social, become engrained in the minds and bodies of our children.

Making schools better seems to be the "front page" story on just about every newspaper and education-based website in existence. In my estimation, we can make schools better by overcoming poverty. Research demonstrates that poor White kids do just as poorly in school as poor Black, Hispanic and other under-represented children. The key word in the previous sentence is "poor." We have poor performing schools because we have poor families living in and around the neighborhoods where these poor performing schools reside. Until we build up our families and communities around failing schools, school leadership, effective or otherwise, cannot of in itself overcome the detriments to learning created by living in impoverished conditions.

One of the common sayings in American society is "if it ain't broke, then don't fix it!" I apologize for my brutalization of the American language; however this saying is repeated time and time again by those believing in the status quo. The fundamental question then becomes, "should we be happy with the status quo as it regards the training of schools leaders?" To this question I respond absolutely not! While it may take miracle upon miracle for America to cure the ills of poverty, we cannot and will not stop doing all we can as members of the academic academy to prepare the very best teachers and the very best principals possible. We must become even more resolute in our efforts to equip school leadership with the skills and resources they need to turn failing schools into schools that exude success and excellence for all children.

I serve as dean of a college engaged in the preparation of educators, including school leaders. There is much excitement around the way we are preparing teachers, principals, school counselors and other professionals who work in schools. With specific reference to the training of school leaders, programs are being developed that focus more heavily on the provision of enriched clinical practice opportunities, coupled with a concomitant investigation of the many theories and constructs that frame effective school leadership. In other words, following along the lines of the "theory into practice" paradigm. The Leadership Academy, housed in the Center for Educational Leadership at the University of Tennessee is one model for training effective school leaders that provides exciting opportunities for aspiring principals. Working in partnership with Knox County Schools, these dedicated women and men are already making a difference in the education of Knoxville's youth. The successful replication of this model and others like it is critical to the future of Tennessee and perhaps the entire United States.

BIG ORANGE, BIG IDEAS, AND QUALITY MATTERS

Jimmy G. Cheek
Chancellor, University of Tennessee, Knoxville

What do schools do in society? As a scholar of educational administration I know that they serve as a place for learners and teachers to work together to create a new generation of contributors to the betterment of a community. As Chancellor of The University of Tennessee Knoxville, I continue to marvel at the immense potential schools have in terms of building and improving community. Our institution has an enormous

288

capacity for energy in terms of the excellent students, dedicated faculty and staff, and committed alumni and donors. We are a competitive institution with proud traditions and a keen sense of focus on the future.

In my career, I have come to understand that improving educational delivery systems rests with captivating the energy of those dedicated to change and bridging the gap between the worlds of research and practice. The Center for Educational Leadership is one of the big ideas generated from our institution and educators. It is dedicated to K12 school improvement that interconnects the efforts of school leaders, academic visionaries, and passionate community stakeholders. The Center is a primary example of how big ideas *can and do* bridge the worlds of both practitioners and policy makers, and practitioners and scholars.

What we have seen from the Center's Leadership Academy is a consistent group of Fellows who graduate with a post Master's degree in leadership and use their skills to conduct authentic research relevant to their day-to-day practice as school leaders. The Leadership Academy experience has also invigorated some to push father and enroll in a University of Tennessee doctoral program. Fellows are contributing to their schools in impressive ways and they are making a difference in term of teacher staff development, instructional accountability, and the celebration of school community. Staff morale reports, students achievement test scores, and state accrediting agencies are regularly generating evidence supporting the positive change work that Fellows are doing.

Quality matters, especially in the preparation of school leaders. What I find exciting is that the Center's model for leadership preparation is one of the very few in the United States that allows leadership candidates to experience a fully paid 15-month administrative internship, and enlists the support of individual mentor principals and a leadership coach. Also unique to this program is the enlistment of an interdisciplinary curriculum and practitioner teaching partners. What this means is that each Fellow works with instructors who are world-class scholars of school leadership, current practitioners of school leadership, and leaders practicing in a different discipline other than education. For example, a class for Fellows has been taught by the Center's Director (a former school principal and current researcher) in tandem with an internationally known architect who teaches for The University of Tennessee and simultaneously maintains two architectural firms in Germany. This results in the rare and wonderful opportunity for Fellows to think globally and locally about schools, school structure, and organizational leadership across two continents.

These structural hallmarks have ultimately enabled the Center's Leadership Academy to produces school leaders who are proving that new leaders can and do make a difference in school reform efforts across the state of Tennessee. The University of Tennessee is the home of "Big Orange and Big Ideas." We are a place that sparks innovation and celebrates the courage to facilitate change, lead, and give back to society. The work of the Fellows and Center for Educational Leadership is exactly the kind of instructional innovation and "Big Idea" that we, the university community, support.

REFORM IS A DOT ON THE MAP: GREAT LEADERS ARE WHAT GET US THERE

Kevin Huffman
Commissioner of the Tennessee Department of Education

Tennessee currently sits 46th in the country in math achievement, according to the 2011 NAEP assessment. Most children are below grade level. Fewer than one in three seniors graduates at a "college-ready" level in math, according to our ACT scores. Given these unpleasant truths, it is incumbent upon us to change what we are doing—at the state, district, and school level. This urgency to change results led us to apply successfully to the Race to the Top program. It led us to seek a waiver from No Child Left Behind, so we could build our own accountability framework. It fuels our passion as we work tirelessly to reform the state education system.

But reform alone is meaningless. We know through our daily experience that effective leadership at the district, building and classroom level can make most reforms look smart; and ineffective leadership can destroy virtually any education reform. Without the buy-in of a passionate and effective leader, key innovations—evaluation, curricular changes, longer school days or higher standards—end up changing routines, but little else.

From the moment I started my job as Tennessee's education commissioner, I set out to meet our state's great leaders in education. There are teachers, principals and politicians across this state who want better for our kids, and I see it as my role to empower them and remove barriers that stand between these leaders and true reform.

We recently received a waiver from certain portions of the No Child Left Behind law, and that accountability model, which will guide the work we do for the next several years, hinges on holding district leaders accountable for raising the achievement level of students in all their schools, while simultaneously closing persistent and unacceptable achievement gaps between various groups of students.

And everyone's plan for how to do that is going to look different. We've told districts that they must grow achievement by 3 to 5% every year, but how they get there is largely up to them.

In Dickson County, Superintendent Johnny Chandler and his team have talked to me about a strategy that has led to significant growth in ACT scores over the last 2 years. Dickson County began giving a practice ACT to all freshmen and providing students and parents with a report that analyzes the results and lists specific areas students should work on in order to improve their scores. Students, parents and teachers have all been using this report to work on targeted areas before taking the ACT in 11th grade. At a relatively low cost, ACT scores have gone up significantly.

In Athens City, Superintendent Robert Greene's team implemented a benchmark assessment program, where they administer tests every 10 days across grade levels in order to keep all classes on track with school-wide pacing and progress. His team has noticed increased achievement, as well as some residual impacts like lower staff absenteeism as everyone works to maximize each 2-week period.

In Metro Nashville, Jesse Register and his leadership team have built a first-rate data warehouse in an effort to provide classroom teachers with access to student achievement data cut multiple ways. They also created an Innovation Zone for the most chronically low-performing schools, removing bureaucratic barriers that stood in the way of building effective staffs and running longer school days.

Each of these districts has different needs, different populations, and therefore must employ different strategies in order to succeed. Our reforms in Tennessee, from implementing the Common Core State Standards to our new teacher evaluation system, will succeed only with great leadership in local communities.

NEW LEADERS EQUAL NEW SCHOOLS

James P. McIntyre, Jr.
Superintendent, Knox County Schools

The public school is a quintessentially American institution. For more than 100 years, schools in the United States have strived to provide our young people with two elements crucial to their future, and crucial to the future of our country: knowledge and opportunity. My great hope for our students is that they will grow to be academically successful, economically competitive, and personally fulfilled. Our purpose is to work in partnership with parents and our communities to ensure that all of our students have both a strong foundation of important factual information and the intellectual skills and tools to analyze and apply information, so that they can mean-ingfully access our economy, our democracy, and all the possibilities that their future holds. But I also strongly believe part of the purpose of our schools, is to ignite and inflame a love of learning and intellectual curiosity that will burn brightly with our students throughout their lifetime, so that even when they are no longer in school, their *schooling* will continue.

How can we make schools better?

The perceived ills of the American school are not incurable. While we sometimes retain deeply ingrained cultures in our schools that are diffi-cult to change, change is in fact upon us. Obviously the world has changed greatly since the nineteenth century and the inception of the Common School Movement, but the basic fundamental belief that we are a better, stronger nation when we have a well-educated citizenry remains a bedrock philosophy in this country. Perhaps one of the most important changes in perspective (and keys to our future success) has been the devel-opment of our strong belief that public education is for all children and that expectations should be universally high. This adjustment was both a moral and strategic imperative, but it requires us as educators to be much more effective in differentiating instruction, providing interventions for students who are struggling, and ensuring that we have developed multi-ple pathways for students to achieve success. This greater emphasis on the individual learning needs of students and universally high standards requires our educators to develop and sustain an intensive focus on the content and pedagogy of our work, greater teacher collaboration, and a culture of continuous reflection, feedback and improvement.

New teacher evaluation systems are emerging, in Tennessee and else-where, that facilitate and support effective instruction, reflection on teaching, and strong results for children. These new systems give struc-ture to what we know about best instructional practice, require self-analy-sis, and connect the evaluation conversation to the everyday work of teaching kids. The challenge, of course, is that any good evaluation sys-tem depends on the quality of the evaluator. These new innovative evalu-ation systems require an evaluator who can provide insightful observation of the classroom, a sophisticated understanding of teaching across disci-plines, and the professionalism to have difficult conversations about class-room performance in a way that is motivating rather than demoralizing. If we are going to fulfill the promise of great schools for every child in our society, teacher collaboration, effective use of data to inform instructional decisions, and a culture of continuous improvement will be important ingredients. Each of these elements requires a shift in thinking and a level of organizational discipline and support that are somewhat new to public education. As a result, leadership in our schools has taken on a new level of complexity and importance. In order to facilitate this important change in our schools, but keep the focus squarely on student learning, our school leaders will need to possess a level of knowledge, skill, discipline, and professionalism unprecedented in our field.

Why should we change how school leaders are trained?

These new realities require a new way of thinking about how we identify, train, develop, and support our school leaders. The traditional model of leadership development in schools had many strengths, but also many drawbacks. Among its disadvantages, candidly, was that historically potential school leaders were too often identified because of their gender or athletic coaching success. A second significant drawback was that the learning curve for potential administrators was somewhat steep, but very, very long. In our new reality, school leaders must be identified exclusively by capability and potential, which will mean a more diverse set of candidates across gender, age, race, and subject matter expertise. In our new reality, the timeframe for identifying school leaders and training them has shortened greatly. With the increasing complexity of the job, and a smaller potential pool of candidates that will be truly effective in the modern school principalship, we no longer have the luxury of having an assistant principal learn the job of leadership over a 10 or 15 year period before they are ready to take on the role of executive principal. Given these changes in the educational landscape, we need to make significant changes to our leadership development strategy. More proactive identification of potential leaders early in their career, a more intensive preparation and support experience, and a more robust on-going support structure for school leaders are absolute imperatives in creating and sustaining a viable and effective leadership pipeline to address the needs and demands of public education in the twenty-first century.

Exciting changes and school leadership

We are living in an extraordinary time for public education in Tennessee. In the last few years, we have moved to radically higher academic standards, implemented a new performance evaluation system for educators, significantly restructured teacher tenure, allowed for performance pay systems, and eliminated collective bargaining in public education. These changes, coupled with greater accountability and the need for our instruction to enable our kids to be globally competitive have led us to carefully rethink school leadership development and principal preparation.

As a result, in 2010, the Leadership Academy was formed as a collaborative venture between the Knox County Schools and the University of Tennessee. It is a 15-month, instructionally focused fellowship that equips aspiring principals with the skills and knowledge they need to be effective school leaders in the complex environment of modern public education. This innovative new model seeks to integrate educational theory and leadership practice in an intensive but supportive environment for the aspiring principal candidates. The carefully selected fellows are immersed in the work of school leadership under the tutelage of an experienced and excellent principal 4 days a week, and spend the fifth day in classes and seminars with professors and practitioners exploring the research and concepts behind effective instructional leadership. This unique partnership between the college of education at a flagship research university and a large innovative metropolitan public school system strives to give our aspiring leaders a comprehensive professional growth experience that will quickly and effectively prepare them for the rigors and challenges of the modern school principalship.

The third annual cohort of our Leadership Academy has been selected, and our school system, our community, and most importantly our children are already beginning to enjoy the tremendous benefits of this important investment in effective school leadership.

LIGHTING IN A BOTTLE

Autumn Cyprès
Director, Center for Educational Leadership
at The University of Tennessee, Knoxville

On March 7 of 2012, I was sitting in the main assembly room of the City County Building watching the Knox County School Board conduct business during a regular meeting. Our staff was in attendance to announce the members of the third cohort of the Leadership Academy. The evening's had a few items before the announcement including a performance by the Pond Gap Elementary School Full Service Program Chorus. I was deeply focused on my preparation notes until the voices of 8 year-olds took my breath, and concentration, away. They sang:

> "*I was born to be somebody; Nothing is ever going to stop me. I light up the sky like lightening. I'm going to rise above and show them what I am made of. Because I was born to be somebody, and the world will belong to me.*"

The mix of the lyrics and voices of innocence was undeniably potent. I glanced over to my right to see the 32 Leadership Academy fellows rapt in attention. All of them exemplars of commitment, tenacity, and bridging the gap between the ivory tower of academia and the real world of school leadership. Twelve of our fellows were now graduates doing the hard work of change in schools. And their efforts are bearing fruit in terms of increased test scores, faculty satisfaction, and rich community support.

Our second cohort is feeling the weight of balancing 50 plus hour a week internship with a full time schedule of graduate courses. They are near the end of the 15 month arduous scope and sequence of graduate courses. Members of Cohort Two do not know rest or personal time; they only know studying, working, and reflecting on the advice of mentors. As of this night they also know the new responsibility of mentoring members of Cohort Three. Like their predecessors, the newly selected members of Cohort Three represent the very best and brightest of aspiring school leaders in the state of Tennessee. Like their colleagues, this group remains numb from a 6-week application process that included several intensive interviews and appraisals of their leadership skills and potential. Selection of an Academy Fellow is not a political event. It is a calculated and unbiased process in which practitioners and academics make a Homeric effort to crawl up into the mind of an applicant and determine if that applicant has what it takes to effectively lead a school. The selection team understands it is both an honor and privilege to choose candidates worthy of a full scholarship to one of the most unique leadership preparation models in the country. I couldn't help but think about how the selection process was truly a chance for applicants to show what they are made of. And the Leadership Academy is indeed a bottle of lightening captured right from the sky. The Academy, and it's sister pillars in the Center for Educational Leadership is a wonderful example of what we do best at the home of Big Orange.

The Center for Educational Leadership is a Big Idea that is demonstrating everyday its potential to generate *more* big ideas. The synergy found in the Fellows, the staff development opportunities, and the connections between great leaders and great schools has grown exponentially in 2011-2012 school year. Outside of my office window at the university campus there hangs a large banner proclaiming, "Big Orange, Big Ideas." I found myself the other day hearing the chorus from Pond Gap Elementary singing about lightening across the sky while I looked at banner. I have seen that lightening. It is in eyes of 32 Leadership Academy Fellows listening intently to children singing. It is in the determination of our staff and instructors dedicated to elevating our aspiring leaders to a higher level of excellence.

This is an exciting time to be part of the Center for Educational Leadership. In these pages we have examined the Center's infrastructure and nuts and bolts of delivering such a training program. More importantly, these pages show that the model is working and that the leaders produced are using relevant, authentic research to push forward big ideas that move Tennessee schools from good to great. As our work continues, we remain vigilant in fostering the newly creative and tireless efforts our school leaders contribute to ensure that every student can sing and believe, "*I was born to be somebody, and the world will belong to me....*"

LEADERS OF CHANGE
Donna Wright
Assistant Superintendent, Knox County Schools

The Leadership Academy's hallmark is the deliberate, research-grounded themes embedded throughout the course work and underscored in the year-long internship required of the Fellows. In creating a new structure for developing educational leaders, it was important that we captured powerful emerging directions from those recognized as *leaders of change*— practitioners who evoke passion, are tough performance managers, take risks, have strength of character, believe schools are for learning, and most importantly, instinctively know to value those individuals who professionally contribute to the success of the organization.

What we have come to appreciate from the initial conception of the Leadership Academy, besides identifying and recruiting the very best talent, were to understand that unless there was a radical change in the construction of school leadership preparation, few schools would be able to meet the new challenges of preparing *all* students to meet high standards and expectations. Richard Elmore (2004) advocated creating a new structure for leadership development, stressing that, "improvement, then, is change with direction, sustained over time, that moves entire systems, raising the average level of quality and performance." We are preparing a new generation of educational leaders who will over time, transform schools and school systems, elevating schools into recognized institutions of learning for all students, and as a testament to their professional belief system, identify and mentor future leaders of change.

Reflecting on the first leadership cohort, we found they developed a confident assurance about their new role and the initial reluctance in transitioning from the classroom was to afford them credibility with their new staff family. It has been further reinforced in the midyear reflections of the second cohort, as one Fellow was reassured by the "humanitarian approach to leadership—my mind, heart, and attitude have changed dramatically, in ways I don't understand yet," as another ruminated on "guiding principles that have emerged over time that I am not sure I would have recognized as a belief system a year ago." Richard Elmore noted the challenge of harnessing leadership as "learning how to do new things and, perhaps more importantly, learning to attach positive value to the learning of doing new things." I believe that is an underlying premise of what the Leadership Academy is providing for our new leaders: a landscape to practice and learn new things in a way that challenges their belief systems to think beyond what is accepted practice.

What we have found, and what I believe we will continue to find, is the realization that we are identifying a new generation of *leaders of change*—leaders who will value and be responsive to human beings, both students and teachers, and will have the will and fortitude to move schools forward to higher levels of performance, giving students a greater chance of achieving success.

EPILOGUE

Great Leaders Are Vigilant

John Breckner

This collection of chapters and essays succeeds on many levels. It presents honest discussions of the sticky work of school reform in policy, K-12 systems, and academia. Creating and carrying out the shared visions of those dedicated to improving the lives of students is never easy but it is, without question most rewarding.

The book's success also is found in its example of bridge leadership. That is, the work chronicles the work of people authentically attempting to traverse spaces between the assumptive world of policy, practice, and research. Pam Angelle and Vince Anfara eloquently open up the first part (called The Model) of this discussion by exploring the process, challenges and people involved in creating together a vision for preparing school leaders and energizing practicing administrators that is unique in the field of educational leadership. Their effort is followed up with Jason Huff's reflection as a neophyte faculty member teaching for the academy. The values of particular curriculum efforts and lines of inquiry are explored by these authors along with other instructors in the Leadership Academy including John Bartlett and Donna Wright.

New Leaders in Action, the second part of the book, is the heart of this effort. It unpacks and examines the work of Leadership Academy Fellows

Great Leaders Equal Great Schools:
Alliances and Discourse for Educational Reform, pp. 297–301
Copyright © 2012 by Information Age Publishing

as scholar practitioners and harbingers of school reform. It is here where we witness school leaders struggle with choosing a question to chase in their day-to-day work as well as struggle with what to do with the implications discovered from their findings. There is a grittiness to these efforts; a rawness found in the voice of educators making Homeric efforts to distill difficult concepts into axioms that are easy to digest. Distillation is not the main goal of these efforts, rather the focus here is on the real questions of school reform that capture school leaders' attention.

This part of the book begins with the voice of a true turnaround principal, Beth Blevins. Beth Blevins has the unique distinction of heading the only administrative team that consists entirely of Leadership Academy Fellows. At the time of publication, her school has experienced the largest growth in student assessment scores in her district. She and her team are credited with this significant change. Her chapter, *Critical Leadership Responsibilities for Change,* explains what it really takes to push the dominoes of change in a school. Her results suggested that authentic teacher involvement in the implementation process is crucial to eliciting program change. At first blush one could say this is a statement of the obvious. Not true because the key word here is authentic. Lots of leaders claim they are including teachers in the change process and the litany of literature on change tells us that claims of involvement are not always justified.

Paula Jo Brown follows Beth's insights by looking at the *Implementation and Obstacles of Assessment Practice in the Seventh and Eighth Grade.* Mrs. Brown, is an Assistant Principal at Bearden High School, and she explored obstacles that seventh and eighth-grade math teachers encountered in implementing formative assessment practices at the middle school level. Her work helped her (and her staff) to understand that middle school math teachers will likely encounter obstacles implementing formative assessments in three areas: technical, political, and cultural. Paula's colleague Jonathan East addressed the extensive knowledge base concerning best practices and instructional techniques for the classroom in Chapter 6, *Data Reflection: How Looking Within Helps Middle School Teachers Improve Instruction.* He explains how he learned that after reflecting on best instructional practices, teachers showed an increased level in Bloom's taxonomy, use of summarizing and note taking strategies, and a decrease in use of whole group strategies.

Kimberle Harrison switches gears for the reader by examining literacy in *Yes, We Can! The How and What of Improving Language Arts and Literacy Achievement,* her analysis of site-based professional development activities explains how customized, site-based professional development program improves student achievement at the third and fourth-grade levels. Tiffany Mclean also considered literacy in schools but from the aspect of writing strategies. In her Chapter 10 entitled, *Writing in the Third Grade:*

Teacher Strategies and Student Strategies the Six Traits Writing Model's influence on teacher's strategies for teaching writing is examined along with its effect on improving student writing.

Alisha Hinton's grandmother was the only woman bus driver for Knox County Schools in 1959 and her commitment to community service echoes through Alisha's interest in student leadership teams development. In *Student Leadership Teams: The Key to Sociopersonal Development*, Hinton, an Assistant Principal at A. L. Lotts Elementary School, describes the limited access that elementary-age students have to leadership opportunities in the school setting. She also deftly explores how the lack of organized student leadership groups contributes to the lack of sociopersonal development in students. At the heart of this chapter is a focus on two specific areas: fourth-grade student representatives' perceptions of sociopersonal development and fourth-grade teachers' perceptions of student growth as a result of participation in the student leadership team. The findings confirm what many student government teachers already know: that student representatives report an increase in leadership opportunities and a heightened self-perception as a leader, which plays out ultimately in the classroom. So why are we not advocating for more leadership opportunities in extra curricular activities? This question is the true nugget of implications from this rich effort.

Renee Kelly, the Assistant Principal at West Valley Middle School, looked at successful attendance interventions. Her work stemmed from interest and research in determining if the attendance and achievement of high-risk students increases because of an academic intervention or social program. The voice she writes with is one that resonates with heart and compassion. The experimental design she used to study how interventions work consisted of paired-samples t tests and she discovered that *all interventions* yielded positive results in her school. Like Hinton's chapter, the implication from Kelly's work begs the question as to why there is not more focus given to systemic interventions. Terry Neiporte, Assistant Principal at Halls Middle School joins her colleagues Kelly and Hinton in looking at issues that contribute to classroom success that are not focused on the delivery of instruction. Neiporte is the only author to consider discipline in her research and her struggle to understand how punishment within schools helps or hinders student achievement is mesmerizing.

The summer that is this collection of research stretches on with the efforts of Ryan Siebe who serves currently as the Assistant Principal at Austin East High School. His discussion of *Fostering Instructional Practices* examines the extent to which an administrator might expect implementation of research-based strategies that are shared through professional development at the High School level. Another look at professional development was taken by Shay Siler within the context of Middle School.

Her Chapter 13 explores a taboo subject in the faculty lounge: that educators feel unprepared to teach writing at the middle school level. Siler's purpose was to see if something called the Writer's Workshop (a professional development workshop to help faculty teach writing more effectively) increases student achievement in writing.

To examine the types of information math teachers use to inform instruction and how teacher planning influences instructional methods, Jamie Snyder, Assistant Principal at East Knox County Elementary School, wrote Chapter 14, *Do This, Not That! Inside Data Analysis and the Instructional Decisions of Math Teachers*. To accomplish this objective, Jamie used a case study design and found that math teachers use multiple and varied instructional methods but may be inconsistent connecting planning to actual teaching methods.

This tapestry of action research reaches its zenith with considerations of what it is that lifts teachers to the next level of excellence. Chapter 15, *The Best Five: Effective Professional Development Components Utilized by School Leaders that Really Affect Teacher Practices,* authored by Rob Speas, explores the professional development opportunities for teachers that elicit change in their instructional practices. Rob's findings lead us to the itchy reality that sometimes the answers are not neat or obvious. He invites us to wonder about how professional development truly affects teacher practices.

We leave the work of the Leadership Academy Fellows with some insights from those who work in and around the world of policy and practice as it relates to school leadership. This section is called Leadership Discourses and there is a charm to the symmetry found in reading Senator Lamar Alexander's recounting of the implementation of a career ladder program right before reading the reflections and history lesson offered by Betty Sue Sparks who was one of the very first principals to hold a Level Three Certificate in the state of Tennessee. Moreover, we find an underlying theme in these reflections that rests on shared compassions for improving schools in order to improve the lives of others in our society.

With that said I am left to the steadfast conclusion that we must continue to push the bounds of what is thinkable when we consider what and who owns the arena of research and school leadership. This is critical because the processes of teaching, learning, and leading are on-going. For all of us who come to this work with a sense of urgency beyond institutionalized schooling and traditional research methods, we can take valuable lessons from the authors of this book: to question (Speas, Siler,), reflect (Kelly, Neiporte), participate (McClean), collaborate (Brown), connect (Hinton), transform (Blevins), fight back (Snyder, East), and rebuild (Harrison, Siebe). Whether these meanings translate into a construct that we call bridge leadership, or action research, what must remain is our vigilant commitment to ensure that great leaders equal great schools.

ABOUT THE AUTHORS

Lamar Alexander is currently serving as the 27th Chairman of the Senate Republican Conference. Senator Lamar Alexander is arguably one of the great forces in educational reform in modern United States history. His efforts to improve schools and the quality of educators are well documented in the national arena. He is a graduate of both Vanderbilt University and New York University School of Law. Under President George H.W. Bush, he served as the fifth United States Secretary of Education. From 1979-1987, he was the 45th Governor of Tennessee. Following that service, he was installed as president of the University of Tennessee and served from 1988-1991. He also was a professor at the Harvard University's Kennedy School of Government. Along the way in 1987, Mr. Alexander helped to found Bright Horizons Family Solutions, a company that has now become the largest provider of worksite daycare in the nation. Senator Alexander boasts a legacy as visionary, politician, leader, and reformer.

Vincent Anfara is professor and chair of the Department of Educational Leadership and Policy Studies at The University of Tennessee, Knoxville. He received the PhD in educational administration from the University of New Orleans in 1995. Before entering the professorate, he worked for 23 years in both middle and high schools in Louisiana and New Mexico. His research interests focus on middle school reform, school improvement planning, leadership in middle schools, and issues related to student achievement. He is past chair of the National Middle School Association's (NMSA) Research Advisory Board, executive director and past-president of the American Educational Research Association's (AERA) Middle Level Education Research Special Interest Group, and a member of the National Forum to Accelerate Middle-Grades Reform. He was recently appointed an ERIC Content Expert in middle grades education for 2007-2009 and is a member of AERA's SIG Executive Committee and Program

Committee. He has authored over 80 articles published in journals including *Middle School Journal, Research in Middle Level Education Annual, Education and Urban Society, The Journal of School Leadership, NASSP Bulletin,* and *Educational Researcher.* Vincent is the author/editor of 14 books related to middle grades education and qualitative research. Recent works include *The Encyclopedia of Middle Grades Education* (with Andrews & Mertens, 2005), *The Developmentally Responsive Middle Level Principal: A Leadership Model and Measurement Instrument* (2006), and *Theoretical Frameworks in Qualitative Research* (with Mertz, 2007). He serves on the editorial boards of *Urban Education, NASSP Bulletin, Research in Middle Level Education Online,* and the *International Studies in Educational Administration.*

Pam Angelle is an associate professor in educational leadership and policy studies at The University of Tennessee, Knoxville. Prior to her appointment to the professorate, she was a school improvement coordinator for the Louisiana Department of Education where she assisted PK-12 schools in organizational change and improvement. Dr. Angelle's research interests include school reform, with a focus on distributed leadership and those organizational conditions and contexts which contribute to a collegial school community. She has been designated The University of Tennessee Plenary Session representative to the University Council of Educational Administration, is a College of Education representative to the American Association of Colleges of Teacher Education, and is a reader for the Educational Testing Service's School Leader's Licensure Assessment. Dr. Angelle has presented at numerous annual conference meetings including AERA, AACTE, UCEA, and NSDC. Recently, she has authored articles in *Journal of School Leadership, Research in Middle Level Education,* and *Middle School Journal.*

Beth Blevins is currently the principal of South Doyle Middle School in Knoxville Tennessee. She started her career in education as a talented and gifted teacher for three schools. Shortly after, she moved into a classroom position in a magnet honors academy. Her experience spans from elementary to the middle school levels. She has been a classroom teacher, literacy manager (elementary level), and reading and language arts coach (middle school level) prior to moving into administration. Beth also works as an independent contractor with staff development for educators, developing and facilitating trainings for current educators across the country. She has a bachelor's degree from The University of Tennessee, Knoxville; initial certification from Kennesaw State; an urban specialist certificate from The University of Tennessee, Knoxville, and a master's degree from Lincoln Memorial College. She is a graduate of the Leadership Academy and currently pursuing her in a PhD in educational administration at The University of Tennessee, Knoxville.

John Breckner earned his doctorate in the field of Counselor Education at the University of Tennessee in 2012. He holds a bachelor's of arts degree in psychology from Syracuse University where he graduated Magna Cum Laude. John holds a master's of science degree in counseling with a specialization in school counseling from Canisius College. He has school counseling experience in both the states of New York and Tennessee. Additionally, he has worked as a mental health counselor and program coordinator for the Sexually Inappropriate Behaviors (SIB) clinic at Children's Hospital of Buffalo, New York where he counseled children who were acting out sexually. John has presented at national and international conferences on topics related to the fields of counseling and educational leadership. He has been published in the *Journal of School Counseling* and is a reviewer for the *Journal of School Leadership*. John has also taught master's level classes in counseling theory, introduction to school counseling, and qualitative research design.

Paula Brown is currently the assistant principal at Bearden High School in Knoxville, Tennessee. She earned a bachelor of arts in Psychology and Special Education from East Tennessee State University, a master of science in curriculum and instruction from the University of Tennessee a Lyndhurst Fellowship and Elementary Education certification from the University of Tennessee, and an Education Specialist Degree in school administration and supervision from Lincoln Memorial University. Her past experiences include serving as educator/program assistant at Camelot Care Center (Kingston, Tennessee), director of education at Camelot Care Center, second grade internship at John Sevier Elementary, fourth grade teacher at Cedar Bluff Intermediate, past president of the Knox County Education Association, component manager/coach for Project Grad.

Jimmy Cheek became the seventh chancellor of the University of Tennessee, Knoxville, on February 1, 2009. Through his leadership, the campus is focused on improving the student's educational experience, enhancing faculty research and scholarship as well as outreach and service. A first-generation college student, Dr. Cheek has set in motion several initiatives to broaden UT Knoxville's diversity and student access to the university. As the state's flagship research campus, UT Knoxville is currently ranked as a Top 50 public institution. In early 2010, the campus launched its quest to become one of the Top 25 public research universities in the nation. It helped solidify strategies for growing the research base and graduate programs, improving graduation rates and attracting and retaining top faculty. Dr. Cheek chairs the Board of the International Fertilizer Development Center Advisory Committee, a new global research effort to develop and commercialize clean, environmentally sustainable, cost-effective and renewable fertilizers for the developing world. He serves of the board of directors for the Association of Public and Land Grant Universities (APLU), as chairman of the group's Commission on Food, Environment and Renewable Resources and as a member of the APLU Presidential Advisory Committee on Energy. He serves on the UT-Battelle Board of Governors, the UT Health Sciences Center Board of Directors, the Tennessee Higher Education Commission Master Plan Steering Committee and the UT Athletics Board of Directors. Prior to his UT appointment, Dr. Cheek was a member of the faculty and an administrator at the University of Florida for 34 years, last serving as senior vice president of agricultural and natural resources. While at Florida, he received the President's Medallion and Student Body Resolution 2009-104 for dedicated and loyal service to the university and outstanding service to students, respectively, and the Morton Wolfson Faculty Award for outstanding contributions to the quality of student life. He was named to the Academy of Teaching Excellence in 2008, a Fellow of the American Association for Agricultural Education in 2005, and a Fellow of the North American Colleges and Teachers of Agriculture in 1998. His research has focused on the influence of experiential learning on student achievement and educational accountability. He has authored more than 80 journal articles and reports and is the senior author of a book. Dr. Cheek earned his bachelor's degree with high honors and his doctorate from Texas A&M University. He received his master's degree from Lamar University. A native of Texas, he is married to Ileen, and they have two children and two grandchildren.

Autumn Cyprès was a professor at Kent State University for 10 years before assuming the position of director of the Center For Educational Leadership. Prior to her appointment in academia, Autumn served as an administrator at the elementary, middle, and high school levels in Phoenix, Arizona. Autumn's research has been recognized nationally by various organizations that include The National Association of Elementary School Principals and The University Council For Educational Administration. As a principal and teacher in Phoenix, Arizona, she was honored by The Flynn Foundation and the Mayor's office. She began her career in education as a biology teacher, with a bachelor of science in secondary education from Arizona State University. After earning a master's degree in educational administration from Northern Arizona University, Autumn returned to Arizona State University to earn a doctorate in educational leadership and policy studies in 1996. Autumn is the 50th president of the premier research organization in the field of educational leadership, The University Council for Educational Administration. Her research has been published in international and national tier-one research journals such as *Educational Administration Quarterly* as well as in journals for practitioners such as *Educational Leadership*. Autumn's research has centered on the politics of school leadership and school reform with an area of emphasis on the principalship. Professor Cyprès' international work has centered on building university collaboratives cross culturally to prepare leaders in The Bahamas. Autumn's primary area of interest is centered on building bridges between schools, those who lead schools, and those who prepare aspiring leaders. The core belief that schools can be improved through bridge building is what drives her commitment to The Center for Educational Leadership, the University of Tennessee community, and educational delivery systems. She is happily married to photographer Jean Philippe Cyprès.

Jonathan East is currently the assistant principal at Fulton High School in Knoxville, Tennessee. He also served as an assistant principal at Gresham Middle School. He holds a bachelor's of music education from the University of Georgia (Magna Cum Laude) and a master's of science in educational administration and supervision from Lincoln Memorial University (Summa Cum Laude). He is also a graduate of the Leadership Academy at The University of Tennessee.

Kimberle Harrison is currently an assistant principal at Carns Hill Elementary School in Knoxville, Tennessee. She was a leadership fellow in the first cohort of the Leadership Academy at the Center for Educational Leadership at the University of Tennessee and completed her administrative internship at Lonsdale Elementary School. Prior to her administrative experience, Ms. Harrison was a special education teacher for 24 years at Karns Elementary School. She has her education specialist degree in educational administration and supervision from the University of Tennessee, through the Leadership Academy (2011), masters degree in educational administration and supervision from Lincoln Memorial University (2010) and a bachelors degree in special education from the University of Tennessee (1986). Her 26 years in education has fostered a love for children with learning differences and works collaboratively with other educators and parents to meet the needs of all children.

Alisha Hinton serves as principal at Sequoyah Elementary School. She holds a bachelor's of arts degree in psychology with a minor in elementary education from the University of Tennessee, a master's of science degree in K-8 elementary education from the University of Tennessee, and an education specialist/administration degree from Lincoln Memorial University. She graduated from The Leadership Academy in 2011.

Jason Huff earned a BA in international relations from Stanford University, and he worked as a product manager in the software industry for 3 years before moving into education. He completed a masters in teaching at Seattle University in 2000 and taught high school history and social studies for 5 years in Seattle, Washington. He completed his PhD in 2009 in the leadership, policy, and organizations department at Vanderbilt's Peabody College where he focused his studies on professional development and support strategies for school leaders. His research interests have targeted the role that school leaders play in supporting and sustaining teachers' high quality instruction and students' opportunities to learn. At the core of these interests have been the methods to evaluate leaders' expertise and what benefits they gain from participation in different training programs. Dr. Huff's recent research projects have included work on Department of Education-funded grants to evaluate (a) a rigorous districtwide training program for existing principals, and (b) the impacts of intensive teacher feedback and coaching on principals' actions. His current work has also examined strategies to identify and scale conditions in effective schools to additional buildings within and across districts, and differences between charter and traditional public schools. His work has been published in the *Journal of Educational Administration* and *Leadership and Policy In Schools*.

Kevin Huffman serves as the commissioner of the Tennessee Department of Education. Huffman has spent nearly 2 decades working with public education systems as a teacher, lawyer, nonprofit executive and nonprofit board member. Huffman began his education career as a first and second-grade bilingual teacher in the Houston Independent School District, teaching students in English and Spanish. He was a member of his school's elected shared decision making committee, and trained new teachers as a faculty advisor and school director at Teach For America's summer training institutes. As a lawyer at the Washington D.C. law firm of Hogan & Hartson, Huffman represented school districts, state departments of education and universities, working on policy and litigation matters including challenges to state finance systems, desegregation litigation and special education hearings and trials. Huffman joined the senior management of Teach For America in 2000, serving as the general counsel, the senior vice president of growth strategy and development, and the executive vice president of public affairs during more than a decade with the organization. As head of growth strategy and development, he grew

Teach For America's annual revenue from $11 million to over $110 million and managed the opening of 14 new regional sites. As the head of public affairs, he managed all federal policy and legislative work, including passing authorizing legislation through Congress, managing organizational engagement in the reauthorization of education and national service legislation, and overseeing federal grants including receipt of a $50 million Innovation Fund grant. Huffman also managed research and evaluation, communications, state and district policy, and relations with nonprofit and faith community leaders. Huffman served on the organization's leadership team throughout his tenure, as Teach For America grew into the largest provider of new teachers in the country. In 2009, Huffman won the Washington Post's "America's Next Great Pundit" writing competition, besting nearly 5,000 competitors. He wrote opinion columns for the Post's editorial page, and has written columns, articles and blogs for multiple publications. Huffman graduated from Swarthmore College with a BA in English literature in 1992, and from the New York University School of Law in 1998, where he was a member of the Law Review. Huffman has served on the advisory boards of KIPP-Denver, Explore Schools Inc., College Summit, and the National Science Resources Center.

Renee Kelly is a graduate of the Leadership Academy and currently serves as the principal at West Valley Middle School. She has worked as a seventh-grade teacher in language arts and reading. She holds a bachelor's of science in business administration/marketing from the University of Tennessee and a master's of science in elementary education from the University of Tennessee.

Tiffany McLean is the assistant principal at Ritta Elementary School. She served as a prekindergarten teacher at Fair Garden Preschool. She holds a bachelor's of science degree, bachelor's of science in human ecology/child development (minor in business) from the University of Tennessee and a master's of science degree in early childhood education from the University of Tennessee. She is a graduate of the Leadership Academy. Currently she is pursuing her in a PhD in educational administration at The University of Tennessee, Knoxville.

James P. McIntyre, Jr. has served in the field of education for more 20 years, with experience at both the K-12 and postsecondary levels. He began his tenure as superintendent of the Knox County Schools in July, 2008. In his first year as superintendent, Dr. McIntyre led the school system and the community through a process that produced a focused vision for the future of the Knox County Schools and a 5-year strategic plan designed to achieve Excellence for All Children. Prior to his appointment in Knoxville, Dr. McIntyre served as the chief operating officer for the Boston Public Schools, where he was responsible for the day-to-day operations of the school district. Jim had also served as the budget director for the Boston Public Schools for 7 years. During Dr. McIntyre's tenure, the Boston Public Schools was named one of the top performing urban school systems in the nation. As a teacher at Vincent Grey Alternative High School in East St. Louis, Illinois early in his career, McIntyre taught English, anatomy, and physical education to a diverse group of at-risk students between the ages of 16-21. McIntyre has served on numerous state-level working groups aimed at enhancing public education, and was also selected as a fellow in the prestigious Broad Foundation Superintendent's Academy, an intensive 10-month fellowship in the urban public school superintendency. In 2010, Governor Phil Bredesen invited Dr. McIntyre and three others to join him in presenting Tennessee's Race to the Top proposal to the United States Department of Education. Tennessee was one of only two states in the country to be selected in the first round of this national competition, and was awarded $501 million for school reform and improvement. As a parent of two Knox County Schools students, Dr. McIntyre is incredibly honored that the statewide Parent Teacher Association (PTA) has named him the Tennessee Outstanding Superintendent of the Year for 3 consecutive years (2009, 2010, and 2011). Dr. McIntyre holds a bachelor of arts degree in english from Boston College, a master of science degree in education administration from Canisius College, a master of urban affairs from Boston University, and a PhD in Public Policy from the University of Massachusetts.

Terry Nieporte is an Assistant Principal at Halls Middle School in Knoxville, Tennessee. She has an education specialist degree from the University of Tennessee obtained while a member of the first cohort in the Leadership Academy, an innovative partnership between the University of Tennessee and the Knox County School District for educational leadership. She has worked for Knox County for 18 years as teacher, instructional coach, and assistant principal. Terry is married with five children, four grandchildren, and an assortment of dogs. She and her husband enjoy connecting with family and friends, although sneaking off with grandkids is hard to resist. They spend time reading, hiking, riding bikes, and helping out in their church. Recently they have begun scuba diving and hope to include more scuba diving trips in their travels.

Ryan Siebe has been an educator in Tennessee public schools for 14 years. He has worked in rural, suburban, and urban schools. He has been an administrator at Bearden, Fulton, West, and most recently Austin-East Magnet High school. He has worked as a small learning community consultant for the Standord School Redesign Network. Ryan was a member of the inaugural class or the University of Tennessee /Knox County Schools Leadership Academy.

Shay Mercer Siler earned her bachelor of science in elementary education from the College of Charleston and her masters and EdS in education administration and supervision from the University of Tennessee. She has previously worked as a classroom teacher, curriculum coordinator, and assistant principal in South Carolina and North Carolina. She has cowritten and implemented grants including Comer School Development Reform and Twenty-First Century Community Learning Centers during her tenure in North Carolina. She is currently principal of Carter Elementary School Strawberry Plains, Tennessee, and resides in Knoxville, Tennessee with her husband.

Jamie Snyder is currently the principal at Carrington Elementary School in Knoxville, Tennessee. A member of the inaugural Leadership Academy Cohort, she served as assistant principal at Ritta Elementary School for her administrative residency internship. Her experience in administration began as interim principal at Inskip Elementary School. Her passion for leadership and mentoring began at Inskip Elementary School where she served as a literacy leader for Reading First in Tennessee. Her teaching career began at Mount Olive Elementary School where she taught kindergarten, fourth and first-grades. Additionally, Ms. Snyder serves as an expert reviewer and trainer for projects at the National Council on Teacher Quality and also for the TPRI Early Reading Assessment. Recently she was interviewed about the role of differentiated instruction for the Spring 2011 edition of *Instructor* magazine. Ms. Snyder earned bachelor's and master's degrees from The University of Tennessee, Knoxville and EdS from Lincoln Memorial University. She enjoys reading, jogging and being a mom of two active children.

Rob Speas currently serves as assistant principal Fulton High School. Past leadership posts held by Mr. Speas include assistant principal positions at Fulton High School and Austin-East High School for Knox County Schools in Knoxville, Tennessee. He taught chemistry and physics at Oak Ridge High School and Austin-East High School. He holds an educational specialist from Lincoln Memorial University in Educational Leadership, a master's of education from the University of Tennessee, and a bachelor's of science in chemistry from the University of Tennessee.

Bob Rider has been dean of the College of Education, Health, and Human Sciences, the University of Tennessee, since July of 2004. He previously served as dean of the College of Education at Butler University in Indianapolis. From 2000 to 2001, Dr. Rider was associate dean for research and graduate studies in the College of Education at Florida State University. He joined Florida State as an assistant professor in 1979, served as cochair of the Department of Movement Science and Physical Education, and was director of the Center for the Study of Teaching and Learning. He has presented at various conferences and published numerous articles in the areas of physical fitness and teacher education. From 1988 through 1998, he served as project director of PERFECT HARMONY, an extracurricular fitness and leisure program for individuals with disabilities. The program was named an exemplary status community education program by the Florida Association of Community Education in 1991. Dr. Rider has received several honors and awards, including the "Bell Ringer Award" from the Indiana Department of Education in 2004, the "Special Contributions" Award from the Indiana Association for Health, Physical Education, Recreation and Dance in 2003, and the Peter W. Everett Honor Award in recognition of distinguished service to the profession from the Florida Alliance of Health, Physical Education, Recreation, Dance, and Driver Education, 2000. He received a doctorate in education from the University of North Carolina, Chapel Hill where he also earned a master of arts in teaching degree in health and physical education. He holds a bachelor of science degree in physical education from the State University of New York.

Betty Sue Sparks earned her bachelor's degree and master's degree at the University of Tennessee, spent 10 years as a special education and elementary school teacher. She was principal at Knoxville Adaptive Education Center, Mooreland Heights Elementary School, Cedar Bluff Intermediate School and Farragut Primary School. She also served as an elementary supervisor and spent 8 years as director of human resources for Knox County Schools. After retiring in 2004 she spent 5 years as executive director of the Distinguished Professionals Education Institute, a partnership of the Public School Forum of East Tennessee, Pro2Serve and the Knox County Schools designed to address the growing need for teachers with expertise in math, science, foreign languages and other areas of critical shortage. She also provided mentoring and training services for new principals and new assistant principals by serving part-time as Knox County Schools' facilitator for administrator development. Currently, she works with the University of Tennessee where she shares her experiences with aspiring principals in The Leadership Academy. She offers professional development opportunities for Knox County School administrators through The Educational Leadership Institute and provides "job-embedded support" by inviting area educational leaders to monthly training meetings and by traveling to their schools to work with them on specific projects.

Oliver "Buzz" Thomas, executive director of The Knoxville Public Education Foundation and noted First Amendment authority is an accomplished attorney, author, educator, minister and community leader. As an attorney, Thomas has practiced at every level of state and federal courts including the United States Supreme Court. As an author, he coauthored *Finding Common Ground*, the First Amendment handbook endorsed by the Department of Education and used in many of the nation's public schools. As an educator, Thomas taught First Amendment Law at Georgetown University Law Center and lectured at Harvard and Notre Dame. And as a minister, he served churches in Tennessee and Louisiana. In 2001, he founded the Niswonger Foundation to create opportunities for individual and community growth through education. After 8 years as executive director, he left the Niswonger Foundation to help Knox County develop a similar program, the Knoxville Public Education Foundation. In addition, he writes a column for *USA Today*.

Nicole Wilson is a doctoral candidate in educational leadership and policy studies at the University of Tennessee. She is currently a facilitator of the School Improvement Grant for the Knox County Schools. Ms. Wilson has worked as an elementary teacher, curriculum instructor, and classroom management consultant. Her research focuses on principal support of novice teachers and classroom management. Ms. Wilson has been published in *Educational Leadership Review* and *New England Reading Association Journal*.

Jamie Woodson SCORE's work as president and CEO and has been a leading figure in spearheading Tennessee's education reform efforts. Prior to joining SCORE, she served for over 12 years in the Tennessee General Assembly in both the House and Senate (1999-2011). As chairman of the Senate Education Committee and later as Senate Speaker Pro Tempore, Jamie was a key leader in Tennessee's First to the Top Act, the largest piece of education reform legislation since 1992. In addition, she sponsored the overhaul of Tennessee's K-12 education funding formula and led the effort to reform Tennessee's public charter school laws. Jamie serves on numerous statewide boards including the First to the Top Advisory Council and the Tennessee Business Roundtable. Jamie received a bachelor of arts and doctor of jurisprudence from the University of Tennessee at Knoxville. She was selected as "Torchbearer" which is the highest honor an undergraduate may receive from the University. Jamie attended public schools in Tennessee.

Donna Wright is currently the assistant superintendent of middle and high schools for Williamson County Schools and is an adjunct professor for the Leadership Academy. She received an EdD and master's degree from The University of Tennessee in education administration. Her undergraduate degree, also from The University of Tennessee is in secondary education. She has taught courses for Lincoln Memorial University and Tennessee Tech University. She has also served Knox County Schools as the director of high schools, and was the principal and assistant principal at West High School. She began her career in Knox County as a computer science and mathematics teacher.